Never a Yes Man

The Life and Politics of an
Adopted Liverpudlian

ERIC HEFFER

V

VERSO

London · New York

First published by Verso 1991
© Verso 1991
All rights reserved

Verso
UK: 6 Meard Street, London W1V 3HR
USA: 29 West 35th Street, New York, NY 10001–2291

Verso is the imprint of New Left Books

British Library Cataloguing in Publication Data available

ISBN 0-86091-350-3

Typeset by Leaper & Gard Ltd, Bristol
Printed in Great Britain by Biddles Ltd.

*To my mother-in-law
Janetta Murray (née Conley),
the embodiment of all that is
good in working-class women.*

Contents

Acknowledgements

I would like to thank all those who have helped make this book possible. I had hoped that on retirement from the House of Commons I would have had plenty of leisure time to write my memoirs, perhaps over a period of years. Because of illness this has not proved possible, and I have had to concentrate on writing the book in a matter of a few short months. I have been helped and encouraged by many people, too numerous to mention them all. There are, however, some whom I would like to thank individually: Carole Andrews and her colleagues in the House of Commons Library supplied me, at short notice, with all the material and books I requested – their assistance has been vital. I would also like to thank George Matthews of the Communist Party Archives, Edward and Hilda Upward, Mike Ambrose of the *Morning Star*, those in the Marx Memorial Library, and Liz Nash, for sending me vital documentary material. Once I had embarked on writing the book I received generous encouragement from Ian Aitken, Alan Watkins and Elinor Goodman, all political journalists, who kindly read parts of the manuscript and gave good professional advice. I would like to thank Tony Benn, Dennis Skinner and other House of Commons colleagues for their help and encouragement.

I also wish to thank Colin Robinson of Verso, who, after seeing the manuscript, immediately urged his company to publish it, Jeff Cloves, who assisted in editing and my brother-in-law, Dr David Murray, who helped in reading the proofs.

Last, but by no means least, I thank my wife Doris, whose assistance has been invaluable. She typed the manuscript twice and, under difficult circumstances, gave strength and encouragement. Without her help the book could not have been produced.

Any faults and mistakes in the book are mine alone. I hope, nevertheless, that it is a serious contribution to socialist history.

Foreword

by Tony Benn

Eric Heffer was a lovely man, larger than life and always true to himself and to his beliefs. The many personal tributes paid to him after his death came from people right across the political spectrum, and both his funeral in Liverpool and his memorial service in Westminster were packed with those who had admired his sincerity and courage.

This is one of several books that he completed after he knew that his illness was terminal, and because it tells his own story it is the most revealing. It is also the very best account of the major events and debates that have taken place between socialists for the last half-century or more, which are all the more interesting because they are reflected through Eric's own life and experience. And what a life he led: from his early days in Hertfordshire, where he was born, through his war-time service in the RAF, to Liverpool where most of his industrial and political work has been done, and whose people he served so faithfully.

His personal ideological and religious journeys took him from Christian faith in childhood, through atheism and Communism, on to democratic socialism and liberation theology and a mature adherence to the twin inheritance he cherished that came from Jesus Christ and Karl Marx. Following Eric's pilgrimage of faith and commitment in these pages, it is fascinating to watch the development of his thoughts, each step richly documented with extracts from the texts which influenced him, all seen in their historical perspective and illustrated in a way that excites the imagination without the dry academic language that can so easily become remote and unintelligible for the general reader.

Eric was a genuine intellectual, immensely well read and with a voracious appetite for learning and for books, which he devoured and absorbed in a way that put him head and shoulders above most of his colleagues.

Eric was always a man of the people, immensely proud of his background and his trade as carpenter. Parts of his story, and the vignettes he gives of those with whom he worked, forcibly remind us of that other

classic *The Ragged-Trousered Philanthropists* by Robert Tressell whom
he so much admired. His experiences as a shop steward, and later as a
councillor in his beloved Liverpool, were never forgotten. He remained
true to his first loyalties throughout his life, and paid a personal price for
doing so.

As we progress through this autobiography, we can read Eric's
accounts of his trips abroad, and of the debates on the left in which he
was involved. Most significant of all are his criticisms of the distortion of
socialism which occurred under Stalin in the Soviet Union and other
Eastern European states in the years following 1917, views which owe a
great deal to the influence of Rosa Luxemburg.

Given his own deep attachment to political pluralism, tolerance and
democratic values, it was a tragedy – and an outrage – that he should so
often have been pilloried in the right-wing press as if he wanted to
impose a similar dictatorship on the British people. But Eric was equally
suspicious of the revisionist tendencies which have blotted the record of
social-democratic politics and have led so many Labour leaders to
dissolve their own socialism into a capitalist consensus that owes little to
its founders, offers no hope of social transformation, and could, by
blunting its radicalism, even deny Labour electoral success.

All of this is brought out very clearly in his telling critique of the
record of Labour governments since 1964, when he was first elected to
Parliament. At the Department of Industry in Harold Wilson's government he and I worked as a team to implement our manifesto until he was
sacked at the time of the Common Market Referendum in 1975 for
openly arguing that the Treaty of Rome would inflict great damage on
our democratic rights – as it has done.

The breadth of his own interest in everything that happened during
the quarter century of his service in the House of Commons is wide,
extending from his unswerving support for trade unions under attack,
through the Vietnam, Falklands, Rhodesian and Biafran wars, the Arab–
Israel conflicts, the Prague spring, the overthrow of Allende in Chile
and, finally, the Gulf War, which he strongly opposed.

Eric's work on the National Executive Committee is also fully
recorded. While he was on the NEC, he took an intense interest in the
development of Labour's relations with other countries, in party organization, where he opposed the witch-hunts and was a great conciliator,
and in the policymaking of the party, where he and I put forward a
whole range of joint policy statements to the Executive on party
democracy, on industrial policy and on the need to review our foreign
policy and Nato membership.

His immensely courageous decision to walk off the platform at the

1985 Labour Party Conference, when the party leader launched into a virulent and unfair attack on the Liverpool councillors, was very typical of his sense of loyalty. It cost him his seat on the NEC, which was a cruel blow for someone who had proved himself to be a first-rate Chairman of the Party. Eric was never a man whose influence depended on the position which he held, and this protected him from the corruption of an ambition dependent upon patronage. Neither his resignation from the government, nor his removal from the NEC in any sense weakened his influence.

This influence is revealed in his comments on the debilitating pessimism which afflicted Eric Hobsbawm, Martin Jacques and others, inside and outside the Communist Party, in the seventies and eighties. Eric entered the argument with these forces displaying characteristic energy, and conducted his case without resorting to abuse of those with whom he disagreed, which is unfortunately the present habit of many who engage in ideological controversy. In restating the values of democratic self-management and internationalism, he protected the basic tenets of socialism and made us all realize its enduring nature and appeal.

Since many of the readers of Eric's books, in the decades that lie ahead, will not have known him personally I would like to give my own assessment of him as a man and as a comrade and colleague, so that they can picture him more clearly.

Eric was a big man physically and intellectually; he was kindly in manner but quick to anger, and as quick to apologize when, on reflection, he believed he had been unfair to an individual. Fiercely loyal to his beliefs and courageous, he was sometimes prickly and difficult but never malicious. He was deeply loved by all those who had the privilege of working with him or seeing him at close hand.

Doris, his wife, friend and closest adviser always played a much larger part in shaping his thinking than was generally recognized, although those who knew him best will also know that he quoted her views on most occasions when issues arose which called for fine judgment.

This is the third book that Eric published. The first, *The Class Struggle in Parliament*, records his work in opposing Edward Heath's Industrial Relations Act, his second *Labour's Future: Socialist or SDP Mark 2?* had a profound effect on the political understanding of his generation. *Never a Yes Man* will be essential reading for all future historians of the period, and will be of immense value to everyone who seeks to uphold the very best traditions of the socialist faith to which Eric has adhered so steadfastly himself.

Eric will be remembered because he was a teacher, and teachers leave deeper footprints in the sands of time than those who pass by in their ministerial limousines. Above all he taught us how to live and he taught us how to die. No one can be expected to do more than that.

July 1991

Never a Yes Man

ONE

Country Boy

How happy is he born and taught
That serveth not another's will;
Whose armour is his honest thought,
And simple truth his utmost skill!

SIR HENRY WOTTON
'Character of a Happy Life'

I was not born or brought up in Liverpool, as many believe, but in the county town of Hertford where I was born on 12 January 1922.

My father William was an NCO of some standing in his regiment and, as a result of an army training scheme, after the First World War he became a shoe-repairer and bootmaker. Between the wars he had his own workshop adjoining our cottage. He was not a successful businessman and if poor people asked to pay later, he always agreed. Often he never did get paid. He was a good kind man with a social conscience.

My father had two brothers and two sisters but it seems that my grandmother was a difficult woman to get along with. At thirteen my father ran away from his home in Hoddesdon, Hertfordshire to join the army as a boy soldier. I have a photograph of him as a young man in the blue, red and gold braided dress uniform and pill box hat of the Royal Horse Artillery. He served in India and Malta, cut a handsome figure, and was known to be a good horseman. In 1914 he was on reserve and was sent to France – serving right through the war and being wounded on two or three occasions. My mother told me that each time he was patched up and sent back to the Front. She did not think much of war, especially the way it affected working people. My father said little about his war experiences but he had an array of medals from many battles.

My mother, the daughter of a cook, was in service prior to getting married. She graduated from scullery maid to kitchen maid, and then to cook. She was a truly great cook and because my father was sometimes

3

remiss about paying the rent, she took on private work for the Free-masons, and various regiments. She was neither contemptuous of the aristocracy, nor over-awed by them and used to say to me, 'They are no better or worse than us. That is why I never curtsy to any of them.'

Food was an important part of our lives and although we were poor, Mother made sure we were well fed. We usually had four cooked meals a day. A proper breakfast, a three-course dinner (lunch), a two-course tea (dinner) and then evening supper – invariably cooked. Somehow, though, I never put on weight and always looked skinny. It was said, jokingly, that I looked as if I could do with a good square meal, which made my mother furious.

When she took on catering contracts, she would come home with one or two baskets of leftovers. I had food unheard of in working-class families. I wonder how many of my school pals had jugged hare, hung pheasant, pâté de foie gras and curries? She also kept a stock pot so that we always had wonderful soups during the week. The kitchen was my mother's domain. My cousin Rene, Uncle Sid's daughter, who lived with us for some years and was like a sister, was allowed into the kitchen but we boys were not. In her own way mother was really a feminist in outlook, but equality stopped at the kitchen door. She was a professional and 'every person to their own trade' was undoubtedly her motto.

There were few rows at home. My mother and father hardly ever raised their voices to each other except when father failed to pay the rent. I recall those arguments with horror. I feared they could lead to one or the other leaving. It never came to that but it left a deep scar.

Threats of eviction filled me with anxiety and a fear of debt which I have to this day. I was so concerned that, when Doris and I were first married, I would not agree to any hire purchase unless it was covered by my post office savings account. This led to some arguments between us as Doris took a more balanced view. I only bought a bicycle on the never-never as a boy because I knew my weekly income of 2/6d as butcher's errand boy would guarantee the instalments.

My mother had four brothers and two sisters. The sisters both went into service. One brother, Tom, was killed in the First World War. He was a pacifist and a stretcher-bearer in the medical corps, receiving a posthumous military medal. The other brothers were shopkeepers: a butcher, a greengrocer and a confectioner. I never enquired as to their politics but they were not socialists. One of my cousins in Hoddesdon, a greengrocer, was a true-blue Tory, and although always friendly to me, did not approve of my politics or those of my parents who supported Labour (or the Liberals if there were no Labour candidates). Although my uncles and my father were self-employed, the family was working class to the core. My paternal grandfather was a signalman at Broxbourne junction and was a member of his union. His little house at Hoddesdon was called 'Granta'. He came from Grantchester, near Cambridge, and claimed he was related to the booksellers and publishers, Heffers of Cambridge. I was always somewhat doubtful about this until I received a letter from a·Mr Heffer enclosing a book about the founder of the Heffer bookshop, who was his great grandfather. This William Heffer had begun his working life as a farmworker and, with the financial help of an Anglican vicar, started the business. Amongst the Heffers in his family the names William, George and Sidney were common. My father's christian names were William George and one of his brothers was called Sidney. So it is likely there was some connection between my family and his. Having read the book about William Heffer I am sure my grandfather was right and, as far as I can see, the mass of Heffers originated from the Cambridge area. My great friend, the late Norman Buchan MP, gave me a poem about two poachers shooting a gamekeeper in the eastern counties. One was named Heffer; he turned King's evidence to save himself. I prefer to forget about him, except to say that every family has its black sheep – or heffer in this case.

My father's brother Sidney was a tram driver in Enfield, but the other brother was a civil servant working in London and, much to the disgust of my father and Uncle Sid, became a Freemason. My maternal grandmother was a cook on the judge's circuit, travelling with the judge and cooking all his food to ensure that it was not tampered with by criminal elements. She was a formidable woman, extremely tough and domineering. I did not know my maternal grandfather but he laboured in the brickfields at Ware for part of the year and in McMullens's maltings for the remainder. When my grandparents on both sides of the family died they left neither property nor money.

Hertford, the place where I lived, was essentially a large village with about 12,000 inhabitants. The countryside was only a few minutes' walk away and London was within an hour by rail. My home at 15, Cowbridge, was a semi-detached cottage next to the River Beane, rented from McMullen's, the brewers. The setting was idyllic, with swans on the river and overhanging trees.

Our house looked very pretty from the road, with a nice garden and trees and roses round the doorway, but it was small and very damp. In the bedrooms bedding and clothes turned green with mould. Every winter we all had colds and my mother once had rheumatic fever. My brother Bill died at the age of twenty-one from TB. There were three bedrooms – with one very small one adjoining another – and downstairs there were two living rooms and a small kitchen with a walk-in larder. There was just one cold tap and for bathing a tin bath was brought in from the yard. The water was heated in a coal-fired copper in the kitchen and bailed out with a pan. It took ages and bathing was hardly worth the effort. Afterwards, you had the job of carrying the bath into the yard to empty the water into the grid. Our lavatory was in the yard and despite putting in a lamp during cold weather it always froze. The house was gas-lit and the mantles were fragile and easily broken. The two small bedrooms had neither light nor heat – only candles. I remember we had lots of holy pictures around including one of Christ holding a lamp with Cardinal Newman's hymn 'Lead Kindly Light' on it.

At one stage McMullen's offered to sell my father the house as he was a sitting tenant, but it would cost £200 or so and he could not afford it. Yet, despite everything, we were considered by some to be a cut above others. There are, whether we like or not, fine gradations amongst the poor which are often developed by themselves.

Just after my father died, years later, the house was flooded. There had been heavy snowfalls and the flood followed the thaw. I remember thinking how horrific it would have been had my father's coffin still been in the house. My aunt Em, a spiritualist from London, was staying with us at the time and we all – together with the cat, the dog, and the chickens – retreated upstairs. What I remember most is the roar of the water against the walls and fearing they would give way. I had managed to get all my books upstairs as they were my most precious possessions. My mother received no compensation. All she got were two pieces of Sunlight soap from the local council. In 1947 soap was still rationed.

I had a happy childhood. On my first day at school, at the age of five, my mother accompanied me. From then on I was never taken to, or met from, school. Bengeo School was two miles away and my little legs really were put through their paces. Two other council schools were within a few minutes' walk of our house but Bengeo was a Church of England school so my mother sent me there.

I was amazed at the number of children crying their eyes out after their mothers had left. Some were crying before they left. I was immune – I had looked forward to school and was quite happy to go. The infant school lay behind the junior school. As far as I can remember it was divided into boys and girls and it was not until I went to Longmore Senior School that I sat with girls. The experience convinced me that co-educational schools were perfectly proper and good for both sexes. Because I mixed with girls I had no hang-ups about women later in life and always understood the genuine equality of men and women. The girls were not only as clever as we boys but often cleverer. My mother believed in women's rights. She taught me to do the housework, wash up, make beds and sew; but, predictably, she did not teach me to cook.

We sat at small desks in rows and were taught by rote. It was the same at the junior school. There was one small room for one class and a larger room for two classes. At junior school I learned to play the violin. We paid for our instruments on a weekly basis. I was not a very good violinist and when I practised Dad would complain about cats wailing. Nevertheless, I persisted and although I never became very proficient, I could play some pieces which at least my mother seemed to appreciate.

On the day of the transfer from the infants to the junior school at Bengeo we were asked to bring back a flower to copy in paint. There being no school dinner I had a four-mile walk at lunch time. In the excitement of the move, I forgot to take the flower. For that sin the teacher caned me. After school my mother noticed my hands and demanded to know what had happened. Next day, without a word to me she went and told the mistress not to do it again, complained to the Head and generally made her presence felt. I was never caned again, apart from one occasion at the senior school. I had been ruler fighting with my pal Syd Saggers when the Head caught us and took the appropriate action.

I remember once, when I was off sick from school, mother was looking out of the bedroom window and saw a teacher hitting a child in the school across the river. She was out like a flash and stopped it. She could not bear it and never hit me or my brother. I was only ever hit once by my father and that was for being very rude to my mother. I was given the chance to back off, refused and was smacked across the face – I was so shocked I never did such a thing again. Even when I took 2/6d from the mantelpiece and bought all my mates tops and whips my parents understood that I had done it for my friends. I already had a top and whip myself.

Because I attended a church school I spent a lot of time in church. I became a choirboy at Christ Church which, like my two schools, has since been pulled down, and also went to St Andrew's which was high church and suited me better. Sometimes I went to the Catholic church with my friend Reg Carter. Ritual has always pleased me and colourful vestments were more attractive to me than the sombre dress of the Church of England.

After leaving Bengeo I went to Longmore Senior School which was more or less in the church yard of All Saints Church. I had tried for one of the few scholarships to Hertford Grammar School but failed. I did well, however, at Longmore Senior, coming either first or second in my various classes. The person who was first or second with me was Sylvia

Fountain. I mentioned this after I became an MP, at a public meeting in Hertford in support of a Labour candidate, and at the end Sylvia Fountain introduced herself. I was delighted to find that she was a member of the Labour Party too.

Although our school was in a small town we learned a great deal. Years later I sat for an examination in my union so that I could stand for deputy-general secretary. There was a rather complicated maths paper. I had not done maths of any serious kind since I left school, but I answered all the questions correctly. At school I was taught woodwork and some of the things I made there I have to this day. One is an oak cupboard which has four doors and contains many of my papers and documents. The important thing about the school was that we were taught how to read, how to write and how to *think*. I wish that more youngsters were getting as good an education today. That may appear to be a reactionary statement but what I want for the children of the disadvantaged today is the same type of individual attention as that available in the best public schools.

A teacher who had a profound effect on me was a Welshman from the valleys. He was clearly a socialist and suggested books I might read. Hertford library was very small but I spent every spare moment there and read books that undoubtedly influenced me: *War* and *After War* by Ludwig Renn, an ex-German officer of the 1914–1918 war who became a communist in Germany and ultimately fought in the Spanish Civil War; *All Quiet on the Western Front* by Erich Remarque; books by John Steinbeck, Jack London, Upton Sinclair and Sinclair Lewis. I read and read and read. My mother did not approve but I think my father was quite pleased.

During the summer holidays we used to walk miles, tramping all around the beautiful countryside into the villages and hamlets. We bathed in the River Beane (although I did not learn to swim until I was forty-two), and played for hours on Hartham Common and in the Warren, a thickly wooded area across the river overlooking the common. It was in the Warren that, after seeing the film *Sanders of the River* starring Paul Robeson, we pretended we were actors from the film and trooped along the paths in the wood chanting I-EE-O-KO. I had some good friends, a few of whose names I still recall: Clive Guppy, Syd Saggers, Jimmy O'Smotherley, Fred Currell, Reg Carter. Some of them, too many, did not survive the Second World War. We played football, kick the can, cricket, rounders and I was a useful long-distance runner. Somehow the summer days seemed hotter and longer then and as we went to school we used to press the tar bubbles on the roads, oblivious of the future.

We had a white terrier called Prince. He hated rats which were numerous at Cowbridge. They lived in the banks of the river or under buildings like our garden shed next to the river. On summer evenings Prince would sit for hours just watching and waiting. When he saw a rat in centre stream he would jump in, catch it, throw it up into the air repeatedly and shake it until the poor thing was dead. He would then swim back to some steps, climb up and resume his place. Sometimes there would be three or four rats lined up before the evening's work was over. Poor old Prince unfortunately fell incurably ill and I took him to be destroyed as humanely as possible at a small abattoir nearby. I was broken-hearted. He had accompanied us on our walks on Hartham Common and in the Warren and elsewhere and was regarded as part of the gang.

Hartham Common really was a common in those days. Cows were put out to grass on it and horses allowed to roam free. Each year at Whitsun we had a fair and on Whit Sunday a sports day. I loved that day – not so much for the fair but for the sports. I remember watching the hurdling, running and grass track cycle races. My brother once took part in the cycle race and, before his death, he had won many medals, shields and clocks for road racing. Lord Burley, a great hurdler, once took part in our sports and outshone all the others. I loved the tug-of-war. To see heavy, tough men lined up at each end of a rope using their strength against each other, tugging away, moving step by step until one side gave way, was most impressive.

Hertford is a town of rivers and canals, and I spent many happy hours punting and fishing on the River Beane. Our neighbours across the river, Mr Fred Ransome and his sister Nell, had a punt which I was allowed to use. I'm afraid that my fishing was illegal. I fished with rod and line, but I also had three pronged hooks which were used against pike or jack. The river also had trout which, when cooked by my mother, were superb. We also fished for crayfish. We would put some bait on a chickenwire frame and let it into the muddy areas of the river, wait until the crayfish had climbed aboard and then pull it up to the surface as quickly as possible. Freshwater crayfish are delicious if cooked properly.

My first ever girlfriend was from the girls' Bluecoat School, Christ's Hospital. We met on Hartham Common and I used to walk out with her on occasions. It soon ended. She was from a different class and that was enough. In my day the pupils of Bluecoat School were the daughters of reasonably well-heeled families. Some might have been in straitened circumstances, but they were not *really* poor like my family. On the other hand, there were poorer families than mine. Some, like the Stamps, lived in a two-up, two-down house, and wore second-hand clothes.

Despite that, their children were highly intelligent and sharp and often took the rise out of the likes of me. I seldom had answers to them.

Nearby was Hertford Heath, where the public school Haileybury is situated. I delivered meat to the schoolmasters and their families. Earlier on, I had worked for my cousin, Bernard Nicholls, who owned a fruit and flower shop. He had paid me two shillings a day, plus a bag of spoiled fruit. But then I was offered 2/6d by the butcher plus a joint of meat, sausages and so on; he also promised to teach me how to make sausages and rib and roll a joint. I happily defected and Bernard was furious. He complained to my mother who said he should have paid me more. It was a long uphill ride to Haileybury but a pleasant ride back. It was going to the school to deliver the meat that made me realize just how much we were divided into two nations in Britain.

As an MP, I once attended a Commons debate on public schools. A Tory MP was holding forth and I asked whether he knew that I had gone to a public school. Members gasped and Tory MPs shouted, 'Which one?' I replied, 'Haileybury, I used to deliver meat there on a Saturday morning'. It was then that I realized that Margaret Thatcher, who was Minister for Education, had little sense of humour. She said, despite the laughter all around, that I must have a chip on my shoulder; *her* father had sold tuck in a tuck shop. The press reported what I had said and I received a letter from the headmaster at Haileybury inviting me to speak. When I went there, the entire school was present and there were many questions. I referred in my speech to Attlee and my friend Sir Geoffrey de Freitas having been old Haileyburians. I told the boys that I did not know what their future held, but had they gone to Longmore Senior School in Hertford, they might become well-known MPs. It went down well; much better than my quotes from R.H. Tawney on public schools.

Saturday was market day in Hertford. Many of the stallholders were from London. At one time near the market there had been an area in which most of the houses were timber framed. Now they are all gone and there is a yuppie shopping precinct in their place. The working-class houses across the Folly Bridge at the end of Bull Plain seem to have been taken over by London weekenders and sell for highly inflated prices, squeezing out young local working people who can no longer afford to buy a home in their own town. I well remember cattle being driven through the streets towards the market and the horse-drawn barges. There were lots of horses in the town. The brewers' drays were pulled by shire horses, as were many other carts. Near my home was a blacksmith's and I used to spend many happy hours at his door, watching him shoe the horses. By the blacksmith's was the local barber's shop and next to that a fish and chip shop which sold the best in the town.

There was little industry: there was McMullen's brewery which owned many pubs and whose beer my father-in-law much praised, there was the Addis brush factory and one or two other small enterprises. Nevertheless, there were trade unions and a Hertford and Ware Trades Council was formed.

I was both a cub and a scout, in the Third Hertford Troop attached to Christ Church, and every year we went camping to a seaside resort such as Clacton-on-Sea. It was always a great adventure, but one of the camps led to my downfall. A friend of mine, Tom, who lived in a two-up, two-down in Port Vale Road, had gone with me into the resort one afternoon. We got talking to two young girls and arranged to meet them the next afternoon. When we got back to camp we were told that we were playing cricket against the Boys' Brigade at the same time as we had agreed to meet the girls. We refused and were told unless we played we would be thrown out of the troop. We dug our heels in and out we went. The irony is that when we went to meet the girls they did not turn up. Later I joined the Rover Scouts.

I was also thrown out of the choir. When I joined the Christ Church choir I thought we sang because of our love of the church and its teachings, but I soon discovered that we were also paid. The choirboys felt the payment was too small. They discussed it and said we should ask for more money. I was deputed to lead the delegation and we threatened not to sing at the Easter Services. We won the increase but then the choirmaster said my voice was breaking and I would have to leave. I still attended the church, however, and carried out my other church duties. Throughout my childhood I attended Sunday School. I had a truly traditional childhood: school, church, cubs, and scouts. But I suppose I always had a somewhat rebellious spirit. My mother used to say that when I was born I 'grizzled a lot' and have continued to grizzle to get my way ever since. Maybe she confused grizzling with determination and self-will and, in that, I was exactly like her. She tried to dominate me, as she did my brother. It got to the point where I would go out in the cold without an overcoat if she had told me to put one on.

Yet beneath the traditional surface of my childhood there were other elements at work. Politics was discussed on most days. Our meals were always taken around a large table which was in the living room. It sat eight people and was often full. The daily papers my father took were the *Daily Herald*, the *News Chronicle* and the *Reynolds News* on Sunday. When the *News Chronicle* had photographs and headlines about the International Brigade marching through Madrid in defence of the Republican government it had a tremendous effect on us. My father and brother were very enthusiastic about supporting the Spanish Republicans. I remember on one occasion my father grabbed some copies of *Action* from some young blackshirts (National Union of Fascists) and threw the papers into the river. They attacked him but came off worse as his military training proved its worth. Sometimes my brother would bring in the *Daily Worker* and other communist journals. Bill was not a communist, but he and his friends were undoubtedly influenced by the Communist Party because of the rise of Hitler and the civil war in Spain. Each week, the Co-op insurance man, Mr Hale, called around. He usually stayed for dinner – as the midday meal was called in our house – and then political issues were discussed. He was a member of the Labour Party and became a councillor after the war.

My mother was a member of the Co-op Women's Guild and also a member of the Enfield Highway Co-op Society. Our staple groceries and all our clothes and shoes were bought there and the dividend was most important. She often attended members' meetings and believed passionately in the Co-op movement. In that sense I was born not only into the working class, but into the Labour/Co-op Movement. My brother was a member of the Electrical Trades Union (ETU) and I joined my union, the Amalgamated Society of Woodworkers (ASW), in 1938 at the age of sixteen. I have been a member ever since.

I left school at the age of fourteen. My father tried to get me an apprenticeship as a compositor and then as an electrician. I was put to work as an electrician's mate with two qualified electricians. They were both Londoners and swore a lot. One used 'f.....g' all the time. He would say, get the 'f.....g' hammer, or pliers and so on. I hated it and one day I said, 'I haven't got one of those'. He looked at me in amazement, considered boxing my ears, then thought better of it. In fact, it had its effect. He toned down his language considerably. I found some of the older men with children of their own very kind and helpful and they made certain I was not put upon.

I quite liked that job, cycling out to it each day, but it didn't last long and soon Dad found another job for me. It was a temporary post at Hertingfordbury flour mill, then used for curing and colouring leathers. There were only two of us lads working under the direction of the boss's son. He was just a few years older than us but we called him the 'Old Boy'. All we had to do was paint the leather in various colours. It was terribly boring work and lasted only a few weeks. The wages I got on both jobs were pitiful; hardly more than I was getting working for the butcher on a Saturday.

Then, one day, Fred Green, our next-door neighbour, a painter and decorator, put his head over the garden fence and told my mother that his firm wanted an apprentice carpenter and joiner. That is how I entered my trade. In those days, to have a trade was very important and carpenters and joiners were regarded as part of the labour aristocracy. I only appreciated that later on after I began to read Marxist socialist theory. There was certainly nothing very aristocratic about my pay when I started as an apprentice – 5 shillings a week – and I had to provide my own tools. These had to be collected over the years. My parents helped me but they were not able to equip me all at once.

After two years of working at W.H. Lee, a local firm, I found I was being used as a full craftsman before I was halfway through my time as an apprentice. The working conditions were reminiscent of those described in Robert Tressell's *The Ragged-Trousered Philanthropists*. I objected to the way I was treated and, as a consequence, the firm decided to 'finish me up'. My trade union branch secretary, Dan Carter, intervened and got another firm, Welwyn Builders, to take me on so that I could complete my apprenticeship. I worked in their joinery shop and on the building of Welwyn stores. Had it not been for his help I would probably not have completed my five years. The Carter family had a very big influence on me. Dan Carter and his brother, Wally, were both excellent carpenters and joiners. Wally was a member of the Communist Party and Dan joined later at my suggestion after I had formed a branch in Hertford. Sometimes I would cycle to Welwyn Garden City with Dan but he was always late. I would wait for him on my bike and he would hurtle down Bengeo Hill and turn into Cowbridge at tremendous speed. I would then have to pedal like mad to catch him up. We would get to work about five to six miles away in a very hot and sweaty condition even in deepest winter.

When I was fifteen I became seriously ill. I had peritonitis brought about by a burst appendix. When I was taken to the Hertford General Hospital and was told I needed an operation immediately, I just said, 'I don't care, anything to get rid of this pain'. It was touch and go and my parents were summoned as it was thought I would not survive the night. It was an experience I have never forgotten and three months elapsed before I went back to work. I convalesced at St Leonard's, and there found myself arguing with the matron who ran the home. I thought she was too strict and said so but I enjoyed my stay and the sea air and rest did me a lot of good. (I still have a postcard I sent to my mother on which I wrote that the matron was 'snotty'.) The hospital staff, nurses and doctors, however, were really wonderful. It was, of course, a voluntary hospital and became part of the NHS in 1947. My doctor in Hertford was a Dr Mortis – you can imagine the jokes about him – and

13

those of us on 'the panel', as the system for non-paying patients was called, had to wait in a shed at the bottom of his garden. His private patients waited in a room in his house.

It was about this time that I became involved with the Rover Scouts and kept and raced pigeons. I built a pigeon loft and bought pigeons from members of the Hertford Pigeon Club. Active members of the club were the Vigers boys who were farmers at Bengeo. They were great pigeon fanciers, often winning the first, second and third places in the races. On Thursday or Friday evening we would take our birds to the club premises at the top of Cowbridge. The birds were ringed and the numbers noted. Special clocks were synchronized and checked, the birds placed into pigeon baskets, taken to the railway station and sent on their way to places like Newark, Peterborough, Doncaster, Newcastle or Edinburgh. At the agreed time the pigeons would be released. They would circle in the air, getting higher and higher and then suddenly head for home. The distances could be hundreds of miles, or even thousands when they were sent to France and Spain.

The birds we worried about were those who became 'fielders' and stayed around the cornfields, making their way back at their leisure. Such birds usually ended up with their necks wrung. I could never do that and was not ruthless enough to be a good pigeon fancier. I never won any important prizes. The best I did was to come second with a bird I bought from the Vigers boys. It had gone back to their loft first, but they had been good enough to throw it out and it flew home to Cowbridge.

I gave up pigeons and the scouts when I became political. All the time I was seeking to become involved in things that would take up my energy and give me a real purpose in life. I found that purpose soon with my involvement in the Labour and trade union movement.

Hertford Council was ostensibly 'non-political' – that meant it was made up of so-called Independents who, in the main, were members of the Conservative Club. There were also one or two Independent Radicals, one being Mr Joseph Wren who owned a baker's shop on Old Cross. After the Second World War when I stood as a communist for the council he sent me a most encouraging letter together with a book. Hertford, however, was a real Tory stronghold. They were against introducing 'politics' to the council and that was their main objection to the Labour and Communist Parties after the war. Tories of the old school equate the status quo with being 'non-political'. Those who, like me, introduced party politics into local government were simply bounders.

Slowly but surely I got drawn into organized politics. In 1936, hunger marchers arrived in Hertford on their way to London and a public meeting took place at the Corn Exchange. One of the speakers was Wally Carter and I went along with my father. The *Hertfordshire Mercury* observed: 'Hearts had been moved by the appearance of these men who, however misguided, had chosen the rigours of a long march in order to raise their voices on behalf of a great social evil. Red-hot communists were certainly among them, and "the red flag" was not a welcome sight in Hertford, but the town had been privileged to receive them and the Labour Party, the Co-op and the clergy had been true good Samaritans.'

Their visit to Hertford had a big effect on me. So did my Welsh teacher at school. I shall always be grateful to him and I only wish I had got to know him better. When I first joined the Hertford and Ware branch of the ASW we had an elderly chairman who was a JP. He had side-whiskers and always wore a bowler hat, dark suit and large fob-watch and chain. He was in the Labour Party and often talked about socialism and what Labour stood for and why the unions created the Labour Party. I listened intently to all he had to say. I had also listened, on at least one occasion, to Father Conrad Noel from Thaxted, an Anglo-Catholic socialist priest. He argued that Christ was a revolutionary and that was why the Roman and Jewish establishment of the day crucified him.

Over the years the teachings of priests like Conrad Noel have had a strong influence on me. In his book *Conrad Noel and the Thaxted Movement* Reg Groves writes: 'At Thaxted the natural, the beautiful, music and dancing, and the social gospel had been woven into the old and graceful social life,... Noel and the others believed that the people would turn to it everywhere given the chance – turn not to the church as an institution but to the living, continuous church that stretched back down the centuries to those early days when "the multitudes of them that believed were of one heart and of one soul; neither said any of them that aught of the things which he possessed was his own; but they had all things in common. Neither was there any among them that lacked; for as many as were possessors of lands or houses sold them and brought the prices of the things that were sold and laid them at the apostles' feet; and distribution was made unto every man according as he has need."' I thoroughly agree.

The teachings of the church, the politics of my parents and my Welsh school teacher, and my membership of my trade union, all combined to make me a socialist and a militant one at that. My education continued at work, especially in Welwyn Garden City.

15

TWO

Party Member

No saviour from on high delivers;
No trust have we in prince or peer.
Our own right hand the chains must shiver;
Chains of hatred, of greed and fear,
Ere the thieves will out with their booty
And to all give a happier lot.
Each at this forge must do his duty
And strike the iron while it's hot.

EUGENE POTTER, *The Internationale*

I had played little part in politics in Hertford, but I now became very involved in Welwyn Garden City. It was there that I joined first the Labour Party, and then resigned to join the Communist Party at the age of seventeen.

In order to appreciate why people like myself were attracted to the CP it is necessary to understand the pre-war political situation. Britain had a National government – Tory in practice – led by Neville Chamberlain who was concerned more with appeasing than fighting fascism. There was widespread unemployment; the unions were subject to anti-trade union laws; poverty was endemic. Hitler was in power in Germany, Mussolini in Italy, and in Britain the National Union of Fascists was actively led by Oswald Mosley. Democracy was threatened everywhere. The Civil War raged in Spain with an elected government under attack by General Franco and his religious and fascist supporters.

Labour dragged its feet. Clement Attlee had visited the International Brigade in Spain, but the leadership had driven Sir Stafford Cripps out of the party and people like Nye Bevan and George Strauss had been expelled. We who were young were naturally impatient and wanted action against the fascists. We did not understand the nature of the Soviet Union then; we believed that it was a workers' state, where socialist policies were being fully implemented. Soviet propaganda about the Moscow trials was accepted by us and we were deceived by claims that those charged were the agents of nazis and capitalists.

A joiner I worked with, an elderly Labour man, lent me a copy of the Webbs' *Soviet Communism – a New Civilisation?* I read it from cover to cover. It convinced me that Russia was socialist and that Stalin's constitution was genuinely democratic. The Webbs have a lot to answer for. Soon I was buying *Soviet Weekly* and believing just about everything I read by communist writers. I began to read Left Book Club editions like Strachey's *What Is To Be Done?*, *Why You Should Be A Socialist* and *The Coming Struggle for Power*. Strachey had originally been in Mosley's New Party, but when he recognized Mosley's fascist tendencies, he gravitated towards the CP. He never actually joined but became a fellow traveller and apologist.

Soon I joined the Left Book Club and bought as many of their books as I could afford. I also bought books by Lenin and the *History of the CPSU* by Joseph Stalin. To me, Stalin was the greatest of men. Having read *The Communist Manifesto* by Marx and Engels and other Marxist literature, and because I felt the CP was truly a workers' party, I left the Labour Party and joined it. That was how I met Frank Roy, an Oxford double-first, who gave me a university education without my realizing it. He organized a series of Marxist classes at his home in Welwyn Garden City. About six of us regularly attended. I think I was the only working-class youth who went. We had set books to read and essays to write which we discussed at the next meeting. Frank not only encouraged us to read Marxist books, he had us reading and discussing the bourgeois economists as well. I have since greatly appreciated the value of this study, both in the Commons and when I have given lectures at schools. Frank also heightened my interest in poetry, literature, theatre and music. It was a very catholic, rounded education, a valuable continuation of that received from my Welsh teacher. Meetings, political and trade union, became my life. Books became almost an obsession. They still are.

The CP in Welwyn Garden City had many interesting people in it apart from Frank: there was Lucien Ameral, architect Ken Campbell and his wife, Harold Lydell, a South African Rhodes Scholar, Wally Carter, a joiner, and Tom Thomas who was involved at one time with London's Unity Theatre. The middle-class intellectuals well outnumbered manual workers like ex-miner Joe Henry and his wife. During the war many of the intellectuals, including some like Frank Roy who did not need to work, went into the factories as ordinary workers. Harold Lydell became a prominent shop steward at De Havilland's at Hatfield and in the early part of the war was one of the leaders of an unofficial strike. Some were also members of the Labour Party. I never agreed with such entryist tactics; I believed that one should not be in two parties at the same time.

The CP had meetings in the Civic Hall and at various open-air sites in Welwyn Garden City. I made my first political speech near a bus stop and after that spoke regularly at outdoor meetings. When I joined the CP, the party line was totally anti-fascist and pro-Popular Front. It was no surprise then, when the war broke out, that Harry Pollitt, the General Secretary of the party, should write a pamphlet called 'How to Win the War'. As far as we in the party were concerned the war was just and anti-fascist, and Hitler had to be defeated. On 3 September 1939 in a debate in the Commons, the communist MP William Gallacher urged 'the speedy and effective defeat of the Nazi regime as a sure way of bringing about hope for a lasting peace for the peoples of the world'. In 'How to Win the War', Pollitt wrote, 'To stand aside from the conflict, to contribute only revolutionary sounding phrases while the fascist beasts ride roughshod over Europe, would be a betrayal of everything our forebears have fought to achieve in the course of long years of struggle against capitalism.'

I was so taken up with the party line I remember going home and telling my father I intended to join up. He was not at all enthusiastic; he told me, 'Go when you are called, not before. Anyway, I've done all the fighting that needs to be done in this family.' Nevertheless, he agreed that the war had to be fought and had already become an air raid warden. When the government brought in conscription, all young men were called up for a period of training, only avoidable by joining the Territorial Army. I decided to do national service but the day war was declared my friends in the TA were called up as well.

The CP policy in support of the war did not last. Executive Committee member David Springhall arrived back from Moscow with orders to change the line. He had instructions, ostensibly from the Communist International, but in reality from Stalin. Very quickly the British CP policy changed and almost immediately it issued a statement on the suppression of the French CP, saying that the war was 'now being conducted against the interests of the people of Europe'. On 2 October 1939 the Central Committee met and R. Palme Dutt decreed that it was not a just war, but an imperialist war. He outlined the party's task as: 'to unmask the character of this imperialist war ... and to show that British and French imperialism have become the spearhead of international reaction, against which our main fire must be directed'. A CP membership form issued that month stated: 'The Communist Party declares that the war is a fight between Imperialist powers over profits, colonies and world domination. All warring powers are equally responsible. The Soviet Union is leading the world fight for peace. The immediate issue is the cessation of hostilities and the calling of a peace conference'.

In Marjorie Pollitt's book *A Rebel Life* she noted that Harry Pollitt at the Central Committee meeting in October 1939, said 'I don't envy comrades who can so lightly in the space of a week, and sometimes even in the space of a day, go from one political conviction to another; I don't believe that augurs well for a leadership that can command the confidence of the party, the working class and the majority of the people'. Marjorie herself, at the London District Committee of the CP, had voted against the change of policy on the war. One other person abstained – they were the only two who took a stand.

Why then had the CP line changed? It was not because of an upsurge of feeling for change by its members; they certainly did not accept the Trotskyist position on the war. No, it changed because the Soviet Union under Stalin decided it must. After the signing of the Nazi-Soviet Pact it was in Stalin's interests to say the war was imperialist. He wanted peace with Hitler at almost any price. There were a few members and supporters in Welwyn Garden City, and elsewhere in the country, who did not accept the change and some left the party. But most of us stayed in: as members of a 'democratic centralist' body we accepted decisions handed down from above. We also accepted that if the Soviet leaders said the war was imperialist, then it was. They were the true socialists, the vanguard of the international working class. They, above everyone else, had to be defended and supported. The emphasis of CP education also changed. We began to read and study Lenin more closely and the wider policy of the anti-fascist Popular Front was dropped.

Once the war had begun I started a branch of the CP in Hertford and acted as secretary. I did not have sufficient knowledge and experience at that stage to challenge the party policy, and I accepted it entirely. George Matthews, whom I got to know very well after the war, explained the way we felt when he was quoted by Kevin Morgan in *Against Fascism and War*: 'The original Pollitt line fitted in very well with the whole emphasis that the party and myself in the University Labour Federation had been pursuing, because of the fact that it was clear that the Chamberlain Government certainly was not really keen on the anti-fascist war and it was dragging its feet, and in France the communists were being arrested, and so on and so forth. I mean looking back I think that the original line was right and the change of policy was wrong, but at the time it was accepted.'

During the 1939–41 period there was great confusion in the CP. Were we in favour of war or peace? Lenin's writings told us that the

1914–18 war was an 'imperialist war' and he had urged its transformation into a 'civil war' while the CP instructed us to support the
People's Convention which advocated friendship with the Soviet Union
and a 'people's peace'.

I attended the convention in London in January 1941 where, it was
claimed, 2,234 delegates represented 1,200,000 people. It advocated
policies similar to the CP's and a *Mass Observation* report noted: 'There
was of course, a liberal sprinkling of CP and extreme left-wingers, particularly among helpers, bookstalls, assistants, etc. The vast majority of
rank and file were, however, ordinary trade unionists, etc., of varying
shades of leftish opinion.' That I think was a correct analysis of those
attending. I was certainly there as a genuine trade union delegate – the
Hertford and Ware ASW branch was hardly a bulwark of the CP. We all
worked hard to make the convention a success which, in a sense, it was.
I was thrilled, inspired and, I have to admit it, taken in. Though the
convention was billed as a 'people's parliament' it was carefully stage-
managed. The chairman was a leading trade unionist, Harry Adams, and
the speakers included the communists Palme Dutt and Krishna Menen,
a Church of England priest and two soldiers in uniform. Harry Pollitt
also spoke and was rapturously received. At the end of the convention a
national committee of twenty-six people was set up and from there on it
ran the movement.

The committee claimed that 632,000 pamphlets, and 1,336,000
leaflets and manifestos had been issued and 200 local committees established. Later in the year it intended to have another convention which
would be bigger than the first. This never took place. Before it could be
held the Soviet Union was attacked by Germany and the CP line
changed yet again. It was no longer an 'imperialist' war and reverted to
being a 'just anti-fascist' war.

I remember attending a meeting of the CP branch at Welwyn Garden
City on the very day the line was changed. That night a public meeting
had been organized and Tom Thomas was to be one of the main
speakers. The meeting had been arranged when the war was still
'imperialist' and was to explain CP policy and, no doubt, drum up
support for the People's Convention. The first item on the branch
agenda was the Nazi attack on the Soviet Union. What would our
speakers say at the public meeting? One member said the Soviet war was
a 'just' war but ours was still an 'imperialist' one. Someone else said that
could not be so because Churchill said Britain would send arms to the
Soviet Union and we would fight together against the Nazis; our war
was *also* a just war. The argument raged and then somebody said this
was ridiculous, why didn't we ask King Street (then the CP headquarters

in London). I think it was Tom Thomas who phoned. After some time he came back to the meeting and said he couldn't raise anybody and, whether we liked it or not, we would have to work out our own line for the meeting. I had to leave to get back to Hertford and never knew what they decided. When the line was *officially* changed, however, I was only too happy to accept it without question. Now, of course, we were more or less back to Pollitt's 'How to Win the War'. Once again it was the interests of the Soviet Union that dictated the situation, rather than the interests of the British working class.

I have a vivid memory of the banning of the *Daily Worker* around the time of the People's Convention. I used to organize a weekly Marxist class at a friend's house. One of the speakers was Frank Pitcairn, and another was the famous journalist Claud Cockburn who arrived late because, that day, both the *Daily Worker* and his journal *The Week* had been banned. He gave us a first-hand account of the events. Cockburn had not been happy with the party line on the war but had decided to stay with the CP because of the principled way Harry Pollitt had acted. Unable to accept the switch in policy, he gave up the General Secretary-ship, going back to the shipyards to work while following the party line publicly. There is no doubt that Pollitt had prevented wholesale desertion from the party.

The Hertford branch was never a large one but during the war it received an influx of members who had come to Hertford to escape the blitz. Also, once the Soviet Union had become our ally and the CP supported the war, its membership grew, not so much because of its Marxist ideology, but because of Anglo-Soviet friendship. The struggle of the Soviet people impressed British workers and Uncle Joe Stalin became a real favourite. The attitude of the CP towards the war from September 1939 until June 1941, the Nazi-Soviet Pact, the Soviet war against Finland, the occupation of half of Poland, the annexation of the Baltic states, and anti-Soviet propaganda from most of the British press had alienated the mass of British people from the CP. People like Harold Laski, Lytton Strachey and Victor Gollancz of the Left Book Club had turned against it. The pre-war anti-fascist Popular Front had broken up. But the alliance with the Soviet Union turned the tide for the party. Its membership grew, its journals and pamphlets were widely sold; in fact it became respectable. The party argued that *it* had not changed, but that Churchill had taken over its policy. Yet, when he became prime minister, the war to the CP was still an 'imperialist' one which the party continued to oppose. Churchill, despite his reactionary policies in general, had been against German rearmament and Hitlerism. He also created a coalition government – bringing leading Labour people like

Herbert Morrison and Ernest Bevin into the cabinet and government.

After the Dunkirk retreat and the disaster in Norway it was clear to us communists that the people were behind the war. They responded to Churchill's speeches. They joined the LVD, and the Home Guard. (I also joined before I was called up.) They were both patriotic and anti-fascist. Had the CP policy of supporting the war continued it would have given the left an advantage from the beginning. I remember getting hold of a copy of *The Politics of Victory* by Tom Wintringham (published in 1941) and being very impressed by it. The ex-CPer argued passionately for a 'people's war'. Certainly, many in the CP at the time agreed with him and were influenced by what he said and wrote. In a sense, the 'people's war' concept was implicit in the 'People's Convention'.

During those early days of the war, I continued to read as widely as I could but party members were not exactly encouraged to read anti-Soviet, anti-CP socialist literature. The reviews in the *Daily Worker* and weekly CP journals ignored such books. We read Marx but not Bakunin, Lenin but not Kautsky, Engels but not Hegel. The anti-Marxists were referred to but not studied. Maxim Gorky was acceptable but others were not; although no index *officially* existed I did not read Ignazio Silone, George Orwell, Leon Trotsky, André Gide and so on until after the war and my expulsion from the CP. I read the pre-war poetry of W.H. Auden, Stephen Spender and C. Day Lewis. I read Francis Cornford, A.L. Morton, Andrew Rothstein, T.A. Jackson and many others. It was all important, it developed my education, but I am afraid it was one-sided.

However, one person who did broaden my thinking was a man to whom I delivered a Saturday *Daily Worker*. He had left the party after its about-turn at the beginning of the war and we had lengthy discussions in which he was particularly scathing about the Nazi-Soviet Pact. He argued that it had made the war inevitable. He also strongly opposed the Russian occupation of Finland. I insisted the Soviets were protecting themselves from Nazi aggression. He was a likeable man and, although he remained on the left, he would no longer advocate or accept the party line. Looking back, I am sure those discussions had an effect on my subsequent political thinking.

Although reading and political activity had begun to dominate my life I found time to buy jazz records – which I still have – and I went to the occasional Saturday dance. I learned to dance the waltz, quickstep, slow fox-trot, tango and rumba in our front room with the aid of charts which had the steps marked on them. On Saturdays I tried them out and too many young women suffered the consequences. I also did a little crooning in dance-hall competitions. I was not very good but I once won a prize at a Young Communist League dance.

By now the phoney war was over. London had been blitzed and even Hertford had been bombed. The People's Convention had come and gone and my apprenticeship had ended. I worked briefly on building sites and was unemployed for a short time. At that point the RAF sent for me.

THREE

Serviceman

Parties drilled for the election,
All accoutred to perfection,
March for national inspection,
Parties on parade!
Labour's serried ranks resplendent,
Tories with their aims transcendent,
Liberals, proudly independent,
CP shock brigade.

SAGITTARIUS, *The General Election*

On my call-up my father had only one thing to say: 'Keep away from ladies of easy virtue and keep your money in your pocket'. Bill Rowe of Bedford CP gave me different advice. He told me that there were many members of the CP in the RAF and I was sure to meet up with some. I did and also become friendly with many leftish airmen, some of whom were trade unionists, a few in my own union. One of them, a Scot, was nicknamed 'point of order' because of his constant interruptions at site meetings.

I was kitted out at Cardington – an RAF station not far from Bedford which had housed the R101 airship. The huge airship sheds were still standing. Kitting out was quite a performance. Some of my colleagues appeared to get more than the rest of us and I noticed when this happened that the person behind the table gave a knowing wink. No-one gave me a knowing wink.

We recruits came from all walks of life. This was evident when we went to bed. Some had no pyjamas and slept in their shirts, some slept in their underwear, and some, like myself, had good striped flannel Co-op pyjamas. The posher ones had poplin and one or two actually had silk pyjamas. They had their legs pulled unmercifully but everyone recognized that we were all in the same boat and we had to get on together. We did – very quickly.

We were soon on our way to Blackpool for our square-bashing. It was the first time I had ever been there but it had intrigued me since I was a child because my Aunt Em was always ready to talk about her trip in an aeroplane from Blackpool beach. I found the town vulgar, brash, noisy and wonderful. The first day we were given our inoculations. As we lined up the lad behind me kept saying 'It won't hurt, it's all right you know'. He was obviously trying to reassure himself because when his turn came he passed out.

We did our square-bashing on the promenade in full view of the holidaymakers. We seemed to be doing it for weeks. We also went on route marches. One corporal took us to a field just outside the town, rested us for about an hour, then marched us back, saying 'Don't forget – look tired and exhausted.' We also spent a lot of time at the swimming baths being taught how to swim. Not me. We were encouraged to box, and I volunteered. The matches were held on one of the piers. I was to fight a lad called Sullivan so I went to watch him. He was superb. He stepped into the ring, sprang at his opponent and flattened him. Next day I told the Sergeant Instructor that I had decided to withdraw from the boxing.

We were billetted in various boarding houses. My landlady was a music hall caricature – a real tyrant and mean with everything including the coal. At times it was very cold so one night, when she and her husband went out, we helped ourselves to the coal and made up a fire. She was furious and complained to the RAF. I am pleased to say they took no action. The sheet on my bed split down the middle. It was thin and very old. She was very angry: such a thing had never happened before. I told her the sheet had never been as thin before. Now, when I hear north-country comedians make jokes about landladies I really appreciate them.

When we were training we had to salute officers as we passed them, even if we were marching in a squad. One day an officer was sitting on a railing with the beach about six feet below him. As we passed, our instructor said, 'Eyes right' and saluted. The officer was so startled that, in trying to get his hands out of his pockets, he fell backwards onto the beach.

I had tried to join the RAF as aircrew. My educational qualifications were insufficient for me to be a pilot and when I asked about being an air-gunner I was told I was too tall. Now I realize I was probably lucky, as so many air-gunners were killed. Although in the early days of the war the overwhelming majority of pilots were officers, it was clear that a rigid class system could not continue for ever. Increasingly, sergeants became pilots and they were quite as good as those of higher rank.

There is no doubt that the class system, although weakened during the war, still operated in the services. On RAF stations where there were 'cinemas' (huts with a projectionist), the senior officers sat in the first row, the second and third rows were for junior officers, sergeants, corporals, and so on, and we sat right at the back. Sometimes it was impossible to see. On one station an Australian squadron arrived. The first night a film was shown the men and officers stormed into the hut, taking over the front seats regardless. When our officers arrived, there was little they could do. My friends and I were delighted.

After our training we were allocated to squadrons or units according to our capabilities. At first I was sent to a works department. That annoyed me because it meant I was doing my old job as a joiner, at less pay with exceedingly strange hours. Afterwards I was sent to a maintenance unit, then to a training course, again in Blackpool, and after that I traversed the country, constantly on the move, repairing and reconstructing aircraft. Then, for some reason, I was sent to liaise with the American Eighth Army Air Corps. Later I did other military training and became involved in Combined Operations.

The authorities knew I was a member of the CP. During the 'imperialist war' period a close eye was kept on me in civilian life and my politics would have been known when I was called up. At one of the early camps I went to a discussion group about Rudolf Hess flying to Scotland and trying to make contact with the Duke of Hamilton. I said I was not surprised, as many of the British ruling class preferred Hitler to the Russians and would have liked an all-out war against the Soviet Union. No doubt, I said, the Duke of Hamilton was in that category. What I did not know was that the CO of the Station was a relative of the Duke. I was posted away from there very quickly to a rather obscure base where I found some fellow CP members. I was held back for no apparent reason; one officer told me, 'I suppose it's because you are a communist.'

I always carried some pamphlets on CP theory like Little Lenin Libraries, *Communist Manifesto*s, and so on. I lent them out and got involved in discussions the whole time. Like all CPers in 1942, I argued for the opening of the Second Front, and I remember a weekend leave when I attended a great Second Front demonstration in Trafalgar Square. When I could, if I was in a city or big town, I made contact with the local CP and would often be put in touch with CP members on the station where I was at the time. The web of CP contacts in the RAF was remarkable. At just about every camp you could find other members and our meeting place was the education discussion groups. There was nothing sinister about these; in the discussion groups it was easy to sense what one had in common with other men and have a cup of tea or a pint together afterwards. When I was in Glasgow I was asked to write something about the Soviet Armed Forces and broadcast it over the Station radio. I am sure someone with CP connections was involved in that episode. It was in Glasgow too that I met Willie Gallacher one evening. We talked for hours about the party and the working-class struggle in Scotland. I also met Peter Kerrigan, a member of the CP Central Committee, who lived at Pollockshaws near the camp. I went to see him because I had read that the Communist International was to be disbanded. The press claimed that Stalin wanted to prove to his British and US allies that the Soviet Union was no longer in favour of the world revolution. I was furious. What right had Stalin to decide? The Communist International was not the instrument of the Soviet Union but of world communism. When had the Communist International decided to disband itself? I put these questions to Peter. His replies left me far from satisfied.

I suspect that this was the beginning of my disenchantment with the CP. The Russians said what should be done and everyone jumped. The announcement of the proposed dissolution of the Comintern was made in Moscow on 15 May 1943. On 28 May Stalin stated in an interview with Reuters News Agency that he was fully in support of the dissolution. The Presidium of the Communist International didn't meet until 8 June and reported that thirty of the most important CPs (there had been 76 registered at the 7th Congress in 1935) had unanimously endorsed the proposal. The dissolution was declared as a fact on 10 June. What it proved was that over the years the Comintern had become the instrument of the Soviet Union and the tool of Stalin.

In Glasgow I marched in uniform at the May Day demonstration. It was there that I first saw the legendary Harry McShane who years later became a close and wonderful friend. After I left Glasgow I went to Liverpool to a Maintenance Unit at Fazakerley in the Walton Constituency. At the first opportunity I took a tram to the Liverpool Pier Head. Looking across the River Mersey to Birkenhead there seemed to be hundreds of ships on the river and I was absolutely thrilled. I wondered what the city would bring me whilst I was there. I soon found out.

I met my wife at a meeting which was held above a CP bookshop in Fazakerley. I had gone to the CP Headquarters in Liverpool to make myself known to the secretary and was asked to speak on Marxism at a meeting of the North Liverpool YCL. At the age of twenty-one I thought I knew everything, of course, and without a second thought I agreed. When I arrived, there were about twenty young people present and I learned that one of the speakers at a previous meeting had been the Labour Councillor, John (Jack) Braddock, husband of Bessie. I spoke for about three quarters of an hour and as I waited for questions, someone said, 'Who wants chips?' Hands went up, somebody went out to get them and I was somewhat deflated. In front of me was a young girl with masses of blond curly hair and from the moment I saw her, I liked her.

Later at YCL dances and social events I got to know her better and she invited me to meet her parents. At the age of eleven Doris Murray had won a scholarship to the Queen Mary High School. She did very well and achieved very good matriculation results. However, because she had received a grant from the local authority and the school knew that she would not get another to go to university she was not encouraged to go into the sixth form. Her father was a labourer and could not afford tuition fees. She did, however, win a place at the Liverpool College of Commerce where she excelled in French. She has since studied other languages and become an Associate Member of the Institute of Linguists. She had three brothers: Ken who was a POW and later a salesman in the fruit market in Liverpool, Bob who became an engineer, and David who, after the war, went to university and is now a lecturer in American Studies.

When I first met Doris I thought she must be rather middle-class. Then I discovered she lived in a council house with a father who read the *Daily Worker* and was very left-wing. After I left Liverpool I wrote almost daily to Doris and visited Liverpool as often as I could. It became clear we would marry after the war – provided we survived.

It was during the war that I first met West Indians. Many served in the RAF and they were lively colleagues. We got on well together. Among the Americans there were some racist attitudes to black soldiers but most I met were not racist and some were very progressive. One thing that surprised me was that many American officers read comics. Another was that the US Air Force, despite its apparent casualness, was stricter on discipline than we were. On one occasion I was late getting back to camp with some US airmen and they told me that being a leading Top Sergeant in their forces did not stop them being reduced to the ranks for such indiscipline.

I cannot say I was thrilled by air force life, yet on reflection, I am glad I was part of that great effort to defeat the fascist forces in Europe. I am particularly glad because I had the opportunity to meet not only US airmen, but Poles, Frenchmen and Italians. It helped me to keep and develop my Socialist Internationalism.

One event that really shook me was the arrest of the CP member

David Springhall in 1943 for spying. He had obtained secret information from the Air Ministry and from an army officer and passed it to the Russians. He was sentenced to seven years' imprisonment and was immediately expelled from the CP. Harry Pollitt issued a statement saying that the British CP had been unaware of his activities. Springhall's arrest and subsequent imprisonment were played down by the government and the press because the Soviet Union was now our ally. Nevertheless, I was horrified that a CP member was part of a Soviet spy apparatus. The later uncovering of the Cambridge spies was a revelation to me. Perhaps I was naive in the extreme but I felt you could be a communist, believe in internationalism, and be a patriot as well.

By the time of the General Election of 1945, I was stationed at Banbury and went to the Labour Party headquarters to offer my services. The candidate's name was Brian Roach and he had been a member of the International Brigade. I was delighted to work for him and was asked if I would speak at the eve-of-poll meetings. I said I would but I could only speak in uniform if I was a candidate. 'Don't worry,' they said. 'We'll fix you up.' When I arrived they had found a suit but the trousers were short and the jacket sleeves rode up my arm. Still, I had agreed to speak and speak I did. I began well. The Tories were arguing that Mr Churchill won the war on his own; if that was so, I said, what had we servicemen and women and civilians been doing? We must have a Labour victory; we needed a Labour government; that was the next step towards the building of a socialist Britain.

My speech went down well but after the meeting a party member came up and said he understood I was in the CP, but I had not put the party line. He told me that although it was supporting Labour now, the party wanted a government of national unity which included 'progressive Tories like Churchill and Eden'. I thought he was joking. He asked whether I had read the recent policy statements. When I did read them I profoundly disagreed. It was the second issue that caused me to question CP policy.

The servicemen's vote was delayed, so it was three weeks before we got the election results. They were announced on the RAF Station radio all day and every Labour gain was given a great cheer although Brian Roach narrowly failed to win Banbury. There is no doubt whatsoever that servicemen and women wanted a new society. With the election of the Labour government we thought that this had been achieved. During the war the British people, especially working people, were united in a common purpose to change things. They knew what they wanted and were determined to get it. This time they were not going to be fobbed off with promises of a world fit for heroes. They wanted that world now.

The war had proved that personal gain could and should be sub-ordinated to the general good. If the interests of the people could be put before profits during war, why not in peace?

Unfortunately, some Labour leaders did not want that. When Ian Mikardo persuaded Conference to accept more public ownership Herbert Morrison's comment was, 'You have just lost us the next general election'. Morrison was wrong. Mikardo was right. And once Labour was elected, the programme was in the main carried out. Attlee ensured that ministers put manifesto commitments into effect. That is surely why, in 1951, despite losing the election because of the electoral system, more people voted Labour than ever before or since.

A revolutionary spirit was abroad in 1945. People wanted change. Even in Hertford there was a great deal of poverty. Behind the lace curtains of the cottages there was no electricity, no hot water, dirt floors and outside lavatories. The occupants were often farm workers and their dwellings were tied. They were always afraid of being thrown out of their homes, and without their vegetable gardens they would have gone hungry too. The threat of illness and poverty always hung over these people. For example, one of my cousins was gored by a bull – he suffered from his injuries for the rest of his life. A good free health service was essential to people like him. My mother was terrified of being put into a workhouse when she became old. It was a nightmare for many like her. After the welfare state had been created it gave me great pleasure to tell her she no longer had cause to worry.

People needed council houses to rent. Those who could afford to buy houses did, but millions had no resources, could not raise a mortgage and relied totally on the local authorities to provide them with a decent home. We discussed these matters at great length in the RAF, no matter where we were. We servicemen were going to get a square deal for our people. Work would have to be found in the areas where it was needed.

After the First World War people were tricked into electing govern-ments which made empty promises. Unemployment went up because no real steps were taken to rehabilitate those returning from the forces. Workers rioted in many places and, in Luton, they burned down the town hall. This time we would avoid that sort of thing by electing a Labour government that would put our interests first. It was our govern-ment, warts and all, and we looked to it with great expectation. The war itself raised our expectations. When I went back home I missed hot water and the bath houses of the RAF. The need to begin the change was staring me in the face.

Doris and I got married in Liverpool in December 1945. I wore my demob suit – navy blue with broad pin-stripes. Our wedding breakfast was held in a Liverpool restaurant and, despite food rationing, it was fine. After the reception we went by train to North Wales and spent our honeymoon in a guest house. It was the middle of winter and we were the only guests. Although things were pretty frugal, we were well looked after. The main thing was we were married. I was out of the forces and we were beginning a new life. We were lucky, we had survived the war; to this day I think of my friends and comrades who were killed. I was twenty-four, Doris was nineteen, and our life together lay ahead of us. We moved to my parents' house in Hertford.

FOUR

Dissident

The working class is either revolutionary
or it is nothing.

KARL MARX

It was a great mistake to share my parents' home. My mother was a
good woman but possessive and domineering. It was 'her house' and she
would have no 'interference'. There was a lot of friction and rows over
small things. We were not eligible for council accommodation, we could
not raise a mortgage and we always seemed to just miss any affordable
flats or rooms to let. It was a very frustrating. For Doris, coming from a
council house with all mod cons, our home – with no bathroom, no hot
water and only gaslight – was like a return to the dark ages. However,
Doris did learn a lot about cooking from my mother who encouraged
her to watch what she was doing. My mother used to get Doris to set the
table, make the mustard and mint sauce, and so on, but would not allow
her to do any actual cooking. We both worked. I went back to my trade
and worked on building sites all over the area. Doris, who had been a
junior civil servant at the Tax Office in Liverpool, got a transfer to the
office at Bull Plain, Hertford. There was much laughter in the Liverpool
office when she told them her married name was Heffer and her address
was Cowbridge.

I immediately got back into political activity in my trade union and on
the Hertford and Ware Trades Council; once again, I became secretary
of the CP branch. At the Municipal Elections in 1946 I stood as the
communist candidate for the ward in which I lived. We campaigned very
hard and I almost won. Our programme was forthright. On the election
address I was shown wearing my RAF uniform which, I am sure, helped.
We had a number of public meetings and I attacked local landlords for
not keeping their properties in good repair and for their attitude towards
the tenants. The local brewers were very powerful landlords in the
locality. Their offices were only a stone's throw from my home. Following my interventions I received a letter from Peter McMullen asking if I

would be prepared to meet him at his office. I agreed, wondering whether some kind of pressure was about to be applied. When I got there, he said that he had read the article I had written about landlords in the *Hertfordshire Mercury* and wanted to discuss it. He had been in the forces in Yugoslavia and he described his experiences and his attitude towards Tito and the Yugoslav CP. He was not unfriendly to them. He said he would take seriously what I had said.

I think it was after that meeting that an offer was made to sitting tenants that they could buy their property. For my parents, like most tenants, this was an impossible dream. My father had not been able to continue working for himself and had been working for a boot repairer in Maidenhead Street. He used to take the odd drink or two of whisky but he was never drunk and never wasted his hard-earned money. He never gambled and smoked only Woodbines or Ardath cigarettes so that he could get the gift coupons. Yet after a lifetime of service to his country, in the end all he could show for his pains was sixpence in the post office, his clothes and his shoe-repairing tools.

After the municipal elections I was elected to the newly organized County committee of the CP, becoming its chairman. By now, however, some of us were very critical of the party's current line. Frank Roy in Welwyn Garden City and Dan Carter in the Hertford and Ware branch, as well as many others, feared that the party was becoming too reformist. We felt it was to the right of some of Labour's policies and the views of many Labour Party members. The 'Export or Die' policy was the official line of the CP. Workers going on strike were discouraged and often attacked. The government was defended when it seemed to us that the party should have exposed its policies, particularly as they affected the workers. But our main dispute with the leadership was theoretical and revolved around the attitudes that the party should adopt towards the state and revolution; Lenin's ideas were being abandoned as we began to formulate alternative policies. The flavour of the arguments and debates is conveyed in Edward Upward's *The Rotten Elements*, which I read some years after our discussions in Welwyn and Hertford. It mirrored our experience exactly and I realized that we had not been as isolated as we had thought we were.

I wrote letters to party theoretical journals including *World News and Views*, and following the publication of one of these I was visited by Ted Grant – then of the Revolutionary Communist Party, a Trotskyist organization which published *Socialist Appeal* and sold Trotsky's works. I had never read Trotsky and my first reaction was to turn him away. But, out of courtesy, I invited him in to our front room and listened to what he had to say. He said he knew I was not a Trotskyist but felt I

33

should try to understand his views. He left me some papers and pamphlets including one called 'The Death Agony of Capitalism and the Programme of the 4th International' and one or two of Trotsky's minor works. When I read them I was surprised how much I agreed with what they were saying. Subsequently, after I left the CP, I studied Trotsky more closely. I came to the conclusion that, in their acceptance of vanguardism and democratic centralism, Trotskyists were wrong. Despite many friends and acquaintances who were members, I was never again attracted to the Trotskyist groups.

The arguments which developed in the Hertford and Welwyn Garden City branches centred on the policy the CP leadership was pursuing before and after the general election of 1945. That policy was adopted by CPs throughout the whole of Europe, especially in Eastern Europe. It was dictated by the Soviet Union, although we were not aware of this at the time. The Soviet government was in favour of governments of 'national unity' because these gave the CPs a foot in the offices of power. In Eastern Europe, countries which had been 'liberated' by Soviet troops were also subjected to this revival of the 'popular front'. The CPs there were keen to control the Ministries of the Interior and of Defence but their real influence was achieved through the secret police and the presence of Soviet troops. Although anti-Nazi communist partisan groups existed, the 'socialist revolution' in most East European countries was not the result of genuine popular uprisings. The 'revolution' was made on the points of Soviet bayonets. Many leading communists who had been in partisan groups were later arrested and eliminated on Stalin's orders.

In Austria, France, Italy, Belgium, Holland and Britain the cry also went up for governments of national unity. In France and Italy the coalition demand led to the CPs becoming part of the government whilst damping down the revolutionary fervour of the workers. Stalin accepted the division of Europe into 'spheres of influence' at the Potsdam Conference. As a result, when the Greek CP was fiercely suppressed by the forces of the West and Britain in particular Stalin did not interfere. Even Tito, before his break with Stalin, was pressed not to help the Greeks on any large scale.

In Britain it was absurd for the CP to argue for a government of 'national unity'. The Labour Party was strong enough to win the General Election and form a government of its own. Labour's National Executive Committee (NEC) had turned down the notion of a popular front in the 1930s and there was no reason for it to change this position now. In 1944, the Labour Party Conference decided that Labour had to fight the General Election with a radical programme. People had accepted Churchill as the war leader with Labour backing, but in peace-time they wanted their own government. When it became clear that the proposal for a government of national unity was a non-starter, the CP leadership somewhat reluctantly urged support for Labour.

Attlee and Bevin were opposed to an early election. They thought that Churchill would win because of his wartime leadership. An earlier offer from Churchill for a coalition had been considered, and Attlee and Bevin thought it should be accepted. However, the NEC turned the proposal down. Labour's Conference supported the NEC. On 23 May 1945, Churchill handed his resignation to the King and a caretaker government was formed. Just before VE Day a by-election took place and a Tory majority of 23,000 was swept away.

Churchill tried to play for time by raising the frightening prospect of Labour bringing in a 'Gestapo', but that went down like a lead balloon. Polling day was 5 July 1945. Labour received 11,992,292 votes to the Conservatives' 9,950,809. This victory is even more impressive when you consider that in those days, businessmen were eligible for two votes. Labour gained 212 seats, making a total of 393 Labour MPs. The Tories had 213 seats and the Liberals 12. There were fourteen Independents, seven of whom were from the Universities. D.N. Pritt held his seat as unofficial Labour, the ILP had three seats and the CP two. The Commonwealth had one MP who took the Labour Whip in 1946. Labour's *Northern Voice* heralded the occasion thus: 'The revolution without a single cracked skull. The pioneers' dream realized at last. Nothing to stand in the way of laying the socialist foundation of the new social order'. A Gallup Poll revealed 56% wanted 'sweeping changes such as nationalization'.

The CP now became the most ardent of Labour supporters. For communists in the trade unions this was embarrassing. The leadership said that Britain was in transition to socialism. Bernard Stone wrote in a letter in *World News and Views* in 1947: 'Why join the CP, if their policy is the same as the Labour Party's? Give the Labour Party time and they'll do the job, is a remark heard by canvassers these days.' That letter was symptomatic of the mood amongst many party members. We in Hertford and Welwyn challenged the leadership on the question of the character of the capitalist state, and the way socialism would be achieved. We had drunk long and deep at the Leninist well. In a letter to *World News and Views* I pointed out that whilst British Imperialism on a world scale had been weakened, it had been strengthened internally by integration with the state apparatus. That, I argued, was the root cause of the predatory foreign policy being pursued by Britain: 'Imperialism is not a policy preferred by this or that group of capitalist politicians, but a definite stage of capitalism.' The policy of the CP leadership was 'Left Social-Democratic, i.e. opportunist'. I quoted Lenin: 'Only a proletarian, socialist revolution is able to lead humanity out of the blind alley erected by imperialism and imperialist wars.' This, I said, has little in common with the theory of peaceful transition.

One of the 'big guns' replied, someone we all had the greatest respect for, namely Emile Burns. In a very lofty manner he said that we represented 'the unfortunate effect of reading Lenin like a cookery book, to find recipes for making pies'. Personally, I think cookery books are useful to read when making pies, especially if one is not a professional cook. He went on: 'It would be a good thing if the Hertford and Welwyn Garden City comrades would extend their reading of Lenin to "Left-wing Communism: An Infantile Disorder" where they will find that Lenin, stressing that the task of the class-conscious vanguard is to lead the masses forward, observes that "this immediate task cannot be accomplished without the liquidation of Left doctrinism".' This was designed, of course, to make us look as though we had no real understanding of Lenin, but we later discovered that others were arguing the same case as us. Because of the rule – which we strictly observed – against factions within the party, and because the leadership kept us isolated from each other, we were unaware of this.

Many years later, in *New Left Review* 155 (1986), Raphael Samuel published a letter from Edward and Hilda Upward: 'It is often suggested that the "Khrushchev Exodus" of 1956 was the first sign of serious opposition to the leadership of the CPGB. We feel it should be known that there was opposition in the second half of the forties and that criticism of the leadership was largely suppressed, each little pocket of resistance being kept isolated from the other. For example, we heard decades later when we read Harry McShane's book *No Mean Fighter* that Eric Heffer was in dispute with the leadership at the time. We gather his criticisms were much the same as ours.' They also drew attention to a letter from the Australian to the British CP dated 31 March 1948. The Australian referred to the British party's strike policy: 'Their own documents relate that in the big dock strike in which they came out in opposition to the striking workers, Party speakers were in danger of being lynched by the workers and that the strike ended in the hands of Trotskyists and other rotten elements. The same applies to the Party's opposition to a number of strikes in the coal industry ... [it was guilty of] referring to the British Empire in the past tense, of insufficient struggle on behalf of the independence of the colonies; and worse still, the example of the British comrades led to opportunism and confusion in a number of the colonial Communist parties.' The Upwards recount that the letter 'was held back by the British Party until they published it, in a slightly mutilated form together with their reply, in *World News and Views* in the holiday month of August. We were electrified by that letter because its views were identical with ours.' I was in Liverpool at the time but read the letter and, like the Upwards, sent for copies of the Australian *Communist Review*. We also found there was a small group in the Canadian CP which held similar views to our own.

New Left Review 155 also published a statement made by Hilda Upward to Dulwich Branch Committee on 30 September 1947: '...the essential character of Britain has, unfortunately, remained the same. Therefore, I say that here we are not living in a period of transition to socialism. "The path to Socialism" does not as Pollitt says it does "now open gloriously before us" ... I think that at present we should give electoral support to the government because it is more susceptible to pressure than a Tory government would be. This is really a question of tactics and I am open to conviction on this point. But it is essential to explain the true nature of the government, otherwise the workers' support will enable it to put across measures which no Tory government would attempt to do.'

At the CP Congress in 1946 I moved an amendment from Hertford accusing the leadership of abandoning Lenin's ideas and of being opportunist. Harry Pollitt replied that the workers had to play their part in the solution of the crisis: 'The masses have got to be given their place both in the formulation of the plan and in the carrying out of it ... We cannot talk like that unless we also are prepared to assume our individual responsibilities.' The most astonishing part of his speech to me was when he said: 'I would like to see every member of our Party going full tilt in his factory, in his pit, in his mill or on the farm where he is working, putting forward proposals for the immediate establishment of Joint Production Committees that can tackle the grave production crisis facing the nation.'

Then he turned to us critics from Hertford, Welwyn and elsewhere: 'I tell comrades frankly that if you knew the time the District Committee of the South-East Midlands and the Party Centre has spent on Welwyn Garden City and the Hertford Branches in the last few months, you would rightly call us to account. But you gave your verdict this morning and the new Executive Committee will have as one of its first duties the task of ensuring that these branches are reorganized in order that we have the guarantee that the line of this Congress is going to be carried out by people who believe in it ... The line followed out by the two branches I mentioned has done nothing but destroy two of the most promising branches in one of the most difficult agricultural areas in the

37

country.' Actually Welwyn Garden City branch members were mainly the 'intelligentsia' travelling to and from London every day, or they were workers in local industry. And it was the expulsions which decreased the membership in Hertford – not the argument about policy. Pollitt then referred to 'learning by rote' as had Emile Burns. He said we had used Dimitrov's words wrongly and quoted Marx. 'We must take things as we find them, that is we must utilize revolutionary sentiments in a manner corresponding to the changed circumstances. Here is the essence of the matter, and we must never forget it'. I have heard such speeches from leaders of various political parties against concepts I have advocated and fought for all my life. I suppose if you accept fundamental principles you are bound to be called – as Nigel Lawson once called me – a dinosaur. I remember saying the CP had a choice: it could continue to support the reformism of the Central Committee and Harry Pollitt or it could support the revolutionary socialist policies put forward by Hertford and Welwyn. By doing that I had sealed my personal fate. Frank Roy and others in Welwyn Garden City were expelled but my own expulsion was deferred until I had gone to Liverpool.

George Matthews and his wife Betty were leading figures in the District CP which covered our area. George was from a well-heeled family, and was always referred to as 'farmer'. I assume he either worked on his father's farm or had one himself. He had gone to Oxford as, I believe, had Betty. I never once heard the slightest criticism from them on any aspect of the Party or the Soviet Union. Years later they became leading Eurocommunists. They were typical of Party bureaucrats in all parts of the communist world. Possibly, they were less bureaucratic than some although they were very Stalinist. On a personal level they were charming. George admitted in an interview with Bea Campbell on TV in June 1990 that when editor of the *Daily Worker*, he had cut some of Peter Fryer's copy on the Hungarian uprising in 1956. Peter, then the *Worker*'s correspondent in Hungary, resigned from the paper and the Party as a result. What I learned – subsequently underlined by Labour Party experience – is that if you challenge bureaucratic leaders you can expect, not just criticism, but to be attacked and undermined in every way.

Looking back on our challenge to the CP, we were completely blind to the realities of Stalin and the Soviet Union. We thought that if only Stalin knew what was going on in the British CP, he would be on our side. It was seriously suggested at one point that we should send someone over to tell him about our situation. I am glad no one went – they might never have returned! Good honest Bolsheviks were shot by the NKVD shouting 'Long live Stalin'. Look at what happened to Edith

Bone: the British CP leaders knew about her imprisonment in Hungary but did not lift a finger to get her out of jail and back to Britain.

Despite arguments with the leadership, we worked hard to build the CP and propagandize for socialism. In Hertford on Saturday afternoons we took a speaker's stand, which I had made, to the square by the White Hart Hotel. Many people from the surrounding villages came to shop and attend the market. We attracted hundreds of them to our meetings. I am sure our efforts helped to build support for Labour which, years later, Shirley Williams was to draw on when she was elected as Labour MP in Hertford.

We invited T.A. Jackson to speak at a public meeting once. He had written a number of books on Ireland and Marxist theory, and was regarded as a leading CP theoretician. He stayed overnight and, much to mother's surprise, came down to breakfast in his pyjamas and washed his glasses by licking them. It was a topic of conversation long after. My mother persisted in calling him Professor. He was admittedly long-haired and somewhat scruffily dressed, absent-mindedly leaving his pipe to burn a hole in his pocket. A printer by trade, he had left school at an early age. My father got into conversation with him because he had had some contact with the Social Democratic Federation as a lad – even though he was in the army. In fact, father regularly received *Reynolds News* under the cover of less 'subversive' journals.

During the war thousands of Southern Irish volunteered for the British forces. Those in the RAF that I knew went home on leave to Ireland in civilian clothes (they could not enter Southern Ireland in uniform) but rarely failed to return. Many were killed or wounded and I was most impressed by them. I had read something of James Connolly and the Citizens' Army of the Easter Uprising of 1916, of the class and sectarian divisions of the country, of the IRA, of Carson and the Black and Tans, but Jackson's book *Ireland Her Own* gave me new insights and heightened my interest. I became convinced that a united Ireland was essential. The struggle of the workers in Dublin in 1913 under Larkin's leadership, and the efforts to get workers under the same banner in Belfast, I found inspiring. The sectarian divisions of workers, and the use of the Orange card by the Tories in Northern Ireland under Carson and F.E. Smith, was a further example of the divide-and-rule policy of the British.

Connolly's works, in particular, influenced my thinking as a socialist. It was a disgraceful episode of British history when he, a wounded man, was taken out of prison, tied to a chair and executed. Evidently, he was shot not only because he was a Nationalist, but because he represented all that was best in the working-class movement.

39

ERIC HEFFER

We also invited the Reverend Jack Putterell of Thaxted (the successor to Father Conrad Noel) to speak at the Corn Exchange. He was in really good form and very well received. Some time before the meeting I had come across his VE Thanksgiving Sermon on 13 May Ascensiontide 1945, in which he had said: 'We cannot return to our old ways of life. The old roads lead in the same old direction – in the direction of war. How often during the last twenty years from the pulpit did we not warn that the world was rushing headlong into war.... Any talk of the inevitability of future wars is dragon propaganda, and whoever engages in such talk is guilty of future suffering – such a one is indeed a murderer, not of one, but of millions of the future generations.'

It was quite an event for a Church of England priest to speak in Hertford on the same platform as CP members. But Putterell was not the only member of the clergy with radical politics. Hewlett Johnson, the 'Red Dean' of Canterbury, was one of those who toured Britain promoting the idea that the Soviet Union was 'The Socialist Sixth of the world'. Johnson, who had trained as an engineer, subsequently devoted his life to the cause of working people. That is something to be proud of, but like millions of others, myself included, he was completely taken in by Stalinist propaganda.

Johnson was in Moscow on the day war ended, 8 May 1945, having travelled throughout the USSR and Eastern Europe. On the 12th July he met Stalin in the Kremlin. He spent fifty minutes speaking with him. There is no doubt that Stalin made a real impact: 'Stalin is calm, composed, simple. Not lacking in humour. Direct in speech, untouched by the slightest suspicion of pomposity. There is nothing cruel or dramatic, nor any attempt to look forceful ... Stalin is the embodiment of good-humoured common sense, as much a man of the people today as when he plied the secret party press in Tblisi ... A man, furthermore, who sincerely seeks friendship with Britain and believes in its possibility.'

The Red Dean wrote to Sherwood Eddy in August 1945: 'I am just back from three months in Russia; what I have seen causes me great pleasure, though at the same time and quite naturally, there are features in Russian life which I do not like and some tendencies which I think are dangerous.' He did not make his fears known to the public. I heard him speak several times and it was all praise and no criticism.

One has to pose the question: why did so many of us accept that it was in the Soviet Union that the workers had created socialism? I think one reason is that we passionately *wanted* to believe it. Why else, we argued, should the capitalist governments of the world have ganged together to strangle the Soviet Republic at its birth? Why else had the

40

Soviet trade unions offered help to those on general strike in 1926? We were told that the Soviet Union had no unemployment, a good free health service, cheap rents for housing and so on. We felt, also, that if the British capitalist press was against the Soviet Union it must have been doing something right. The communists internationally were fighting the fascists, and in the war the Russians had lost 20 million people. Their heroism was further proof, it seemed to us, that their system was a good one.

Voices on the left, such as the ILPers, the Trotskyists, and the Labour people who had seen through the Soviet system – those who exposed the Moscow trials, those who explained the oppressive role of the NKVD, those who told us about the gulags, and so on – were not to be believed. They were, we believed, instruments of the capitalist class and were helping to keep us tied to a rotten system. Those of us in the CP found ourselves in an organization of good, decent, honest people who wanted a better world. This was especially true of those in the trade union movement. The shop stewards, branch officers, and area and district committee members – underpaid, in fact mostly unpaid – believed in the emancipation of the working class to which they belonged. When the Webbs, Bernard Shaw, Hewlett Johnson and others praised the Soviet Union and Stalin they did so because they truly believed that at last their cherished ideals were being put into practice. If only we had queried and challenged, as Marx demanded, we would not have been taken in so easily.

Meanwhile, the situation at home had not improved following my father's death in March 1947. My mother would not let us have a sitting room of our own but Doris and I did not feel we could leave her on her own just a few months after my father had died. My old aunt Em did not agree. She told us that we had our own lives to lead, and that if we didn't leave, they could be wrecked. Her advice was the determining factor. Some other young couple asked to take lodgings with my mother. That meant she would not be alone. We decided, with some reluctance, to go to Liverpool.

For the first six months there we stayed with Doris's aunt and uncle, both good Roman Catholics. Uncle Dominic, a shop steward in his factory, was a great supporter of the Labour Party as was his wife, Ruth. They, and their daughter Monica, were kindness itself. It was a terrible wrench to leave Hertford but Liverpool was a new start for us. Going there turned out to be one of the best things I ever did. On arrival I again threw myself into political and trade union activity.

FIVE

In My Liverpool Home

You stand upon the highway of the sea
Where in ships, your children, come and go
In splendour at the full of every flow,
Bound to and from whatever ports may be.

JOHN MASEFIELD

The Royal Liver Insurance Company building with its famous Liver Birds stands at Liverpool Pier Head. Coming in by sea from the Mersey Bar, the mythic birds are what everyone sees first, and remembers.

When I first knew it, Liverpool was a marvellous place. Close to the Pier Head was the overhead railway carrying passengers along the dock road from the Dingle to Seaforth. It was known as the 'dockers' umbrella' because the dockers sheltered beneath it in bad weather while waiting for the tram home or before they unloaded the ships. Across the water you could see Birkenhead and Cammell Laird shipyard. Lorries and trains moved in and out of the docks day and night. The streets teemed with seamen from every part of the world. The Lascars, for instance, walked in single file behind one another, after buying hats and clothes from Paddy's Market. The city was exciting, vibrant and alive. The dock road had its Cocoa Rooms where you could buy a bacon sarnie and a mug of tea. There were the pubs, dozens of them, well frequented by the world and his wife. One of the most famous in the South End was the Baltic Fleet. And the people loved to talk. They all had ideas and philosophies on life and many of them, because of the enforced idleness in the days of unemployment in the 1930s, had read a great deal and were knowledgeable on all manner of subjects.

The city was still divided by religious boundaries. The Catholics lived in and around Scotland Road and were mostly of Irish origin. In the past, their forebears had probably voted Irish Nationalist. Everton, the Dingle and parts of Walton were mainly Protestant. They had their Orange Lodgers with their fife and drum bands. Religious sectarianism had unfortunately kept workers apart and had also kept Liverpool a

Tory city, run by city bosses like Archibald Salvidge and Thomas White. Of course, I was not aware of all that when I first visited Liverpool during the war. I did, however, get to know some communists, socialists and trade unionists and in discussions with them I learned something of the history and background of the city.

For twenty-five to thirty years after the war the main industries of Liverpool continued to be orientated towards the docks. The river dominated everything. The Tate & Lyle Refinery in Love Lane was there because cane sugar came in from the West Indies. Dunlop was there because rubber came into the port from Malaya and Burma. There were cold storage depots which stored Argentinian beef and New Zealand lamb. The ship-repair industry existed to re-fit as well as repair. There were shops and industries, large and small, all connected with shipping. The Mersey Docks & Harbour Board had its fleet of ships for dredging, surveying and much else. The docks were kept going by hundreds of maintenance workers. There was a journal concerned only with shipping, and the *Liverpool Echo* listed the movements of ships on its front page. There was a Corn Exchange as well as a Stock Exchange. The shipping merchants were politically powerful and made sure they were well represented in the city council and Parliament.

Most of the dockers and ship repairers were casual workers. Shipbuilding as such was confined to Birkenhead. Deep-sea passenger liners and cargo boats sailed to all parts of the world. Liverpool seamen were well travelled – there were probably more parrots in Liverpool than in any other city in Britain.

I loved the docks and the dock road. It was an exhilarating area and the men who worked there were mostly good, sound, sensible men. They fought hard for their beliefs but were not stupid. In many respects they were conservative with a small 'c', but once they had made up their minds about something they stuck together.

Despite the war, many cinemas and dance halls were open during the week and on Saturdays. The Grafton Rooms was our favourite. As in all dance halls in Liverpool, alcohol was not sold on the premises. Those who wanted strong drink had to get a pass-out so that after the interval they could get back in. This didn't bother us. In those days we didn't drink alcohol apart from the occasional celebration. I saw very little trouble in Liverpool's dance halls. There may have been problems at the Rialto Ballroom in Upper Parliament Street, but that was probably due to some racist white US troops. I often arrived in Liverpool in the early hours on a Friday and walked from Lime Street Station to Norris Green. I was never attacked or robbed.

Liverpool was badly bombed during the war. This fact was given little publicity so as to avoid boosting German morale. Liverpool suffered ninety air attacks in total. The official figures were given as 1,900 dead and 1,450 seriously injured. The number of people left homeless was 70,000. It was rumoured that Liverpool had been placed under martial law. Many leading citizens believed that a demonstration for peace had been staged – a story still circulating years later. There was anger on Merseyside at the ineptitude of the government and city council in dealing with the problems following the bombing.

During one of the spells of heavy bombing Doris's father found a family from the city centre wandering down Muirhead Avenue: mother, father and three children. They just wanted to escape the bombing and had nowhere to go. Mr Murray took them back to his home (a three-bedroomed Corporation house) where they stayed for some months until they could safely return to their own home. Doris's Dad was a wonderful character: outspoken, quick-tempered but never one to hold a grudge. He had great common sense. When the rumours about martial law abounded during the war, he immediately saw them for what they were – an attempt to undermine the morale of the population. His family was forbidden to listen to Lord Haw-Haw's Nazi propaganda on the wireless and he would have no truck with even petty black-market trading. He also felt that Vera Lynn, the 'Forces Sweetheart' was not a particularly good influence because her sentimentality undermined morale. I think he may have had something there.

Mr Murray worked as a 'beltman' at the Automatic Telephone Company. Doris's eldest brother, Ken, was in the Royal Tank Regiment and took part in the landings immediately following D Day. He was taken prisoner and spent eight months in a French civilian prison. Because of its location, it took some time for the Red Cross to make contact and begin sending food parcels. The prisoners were ravenously hungry, existing on a little watery soup and bread each day. It got so bad that they trapped cats and rats and some even ate dog meat – which Ken said he couldn't face. He was nineteen years old at the time and witnessed the public hanging of two German deserters in the courtyard. On his return it was clear his experiences had had a traumatic effect.

When Mr and Mrs Murray were allocated their council house in Norris Green in the late 1920s they felt as if they were in heaven. Prior to that they had lived in rooms with their two small children. Edwina Currie, MP, originally from Liverpool, has remarked in the Commons recently that people do not want to live in 'grotty' council houses but the truth is that, in those days, council houses were highly prized. The Murrays had so little furniture they were able to put it all on a handcart and push it to their new home. In the 1930s unemployment was very high in Liverpool and, in order to keep the family fed and clothed, Mr Murray taught himself to grow vegetables, using a library book for instruction. There was a marvellous community spirit in their road which remains until today. When someone is seriously ill, the neighbours are ready to help and there is always a street collection for the bereaved, irrespective of religious belief. As ever, 'it's the poor who help the poor'.

These old working-class values are sneered at in some quarters today. In essence they are Christian, as well as socialist. William Temple, one-time Archbishop of Canterbury, said that 'Christianity has not failed. It has not been tried'. I suppose the same could be said for socialism, but the truth is that, in the working-class communities of Liverpool, Christianity and socialism exist side by side. People accept that they are their brothers' and sisters' keepers. They are prepared to sacrifice themselves to help others. They rally to each other. I remember when I was in the RAF, travelling to a new posting on a Liverpool tram. I had all my equipment with me and felt somewhat forlorn. Sitting opposite me was an old 'shawly' in her black shawl. She looked intently at me and then delved underneath her wide apron and brought out an orange – something hardly ever seen in those days. ''Ere y'are, son', she said, 'don't worry, it'll be all right'. I could have cried. It was an act of a kindly soul, the best of Liverpool, and I shall never forget it.

Liverpool's reaction to the Hillsborough football stadium tragedy underlines precisely what I am saying. Some of the media, even the serious press, said the response of the Liverpool people with their flowers and temporary enshrinement of Anfield Football Ground was over the top. That, more than anything, demonstrated their failure to understand the nature of Liverpool people. They share their feelings, without worrying about what others think. They do this not to show off, not because they have their hearts on their sleeves, but because they are, even the non religious ones, a deeply religious people, steeped in the concepts of working together, of helping each other – particularly those in need. I heard the phrase 'special children' used to describe disabled youngsters, in Liverpool, long before I heard it elsewhere.

The people of Liverpool have always been able to escape from the city and quickly reach the open sea or the countryside. In my day, we would take a trip along the overhead railway or go for a 'sail' – not on a sailing boat, but on the ferry to Birkenhead, Secombe or New Brighton. New Brighton was a flourishing holiday resort in those days with a fun fair, an open-air swimming pool with its Miss New Brighton contest, and parks and gardens. People from all over, especially northerners, would go there on holiday. Day trippers from Liverpool also went to Moreton Shore, where youngsters used to go cockling. Southport was often the favourite choice for the annual 12 July Parade of the Orange Lodges, who would set off sober and return not quite so well organized. Those who liked rambling and climbing had a number of choices within reasonable reach – the Wirral Peninsula, or further on to North Wales, the Lake District and the Derbyshire peaks.

Going to Otterspool Promenade on a summer's evening was sheer joy. The promenade was one of the best things the Liverpool City Fathers left to the people between the wars. From Otterspool you could see the ships in the distance, across the Mersey, moving along the Manchester Ship Canal. The docks at Manchester were then busy and, travelling by road through Warrington towards Macclesfield, there were long hold-ups because of the swing bridge being closed for ships on the canal.

One part of Liverpool which always intrigued me was Liverpool 8. It was a mixed area, whites and blacks; Doris had some black relatives who lived there. Immediately after the war there was a riot when some racists attacked the blacks. There was also an anti-Jewish riot there after British Army soldiers had been executed by Jewish extremists in Palestine. A friend of mine, Harold Potts, a painter by trade, who joined the CP and became a full-time union official, got caught in that riot. He defended an old Jewish man at the top of Parliament Street and got a hammering from some Fascists. Princes Avenue and Parliament Street were the areas in which the Liverpool merchants had lived. Their houses were large and elegant and in Parliament Street there was a businessmen's club which was burned down in the Liverpool 8 riots of 1981.

What I really liked in the heart of Liverpool were the second-hand bookshops. They were everywhere. In each of them there would be a table where books on special offer were displayed. I picked up many a treasure from among these. Sometimes I was short of money for the week after buying books I could ill afford. I found that I was often competing with my friend Jerry Dawson of Unity Theatre. Like me, he was a great book collector and we would make each other envious by picking up a rare book that the other had missed.

Liverpool, over the generations, has produced its great actors, comedians, writers, poets, artists and musicians. Amongst the working-class authors there was George Garrett, who used to frequent the Unity Theatre. He wrote *Out of Liverpool, Stories of Sea and Land* and *Unemployed Struggles.* In the 1980s Jerry Dawson, John Nettleton, Alan O'Toole and myself set up Merseyside Writers and republished his books. In addition to *Left Theatre, the History of Merseyside Unity* we also distributed *No Boots on my Feet* by Bob Clark, and *From Britain to Spain and Back* by Jimmy Jump, an ex-International brigadier.

Dominating the skyline of the city are the two cathedrals. The Catholic one is nicknamed 'Paddy's Wigwam' or the 'Mersey Funnel' because of its bold concrete shape. They are appropriately situated at either end of Hope Street. The magnificent Anglican cathedral is the last great traditional cathedral to have been built in Britain. When the Pope came to Liverpool he went there with Bishop David Shephard and was visibly moved. Ironically, its architect was a Roman Catholic, and the architect of the modern Roman Catholic cathedral was an Anglican! The services held in both cathedrals following the Heysel football stadium tragedy in Belgium and also the Hillsborough tragedy in Sheffield later were the most memorable I have ever attended. The city, in the aftermath of Heysel, was not just mourning its own fate, but in deep mourning for the dead in Italy. It was letting the world know that Liverpool cared. The death of even one Italian supporter to us was also the loss of a brother or sister. The young people at the services, with their Liverpool scarves and with Juventus scarves which some had exchanged with Italian supporters, wept unashamedly. So did I.

Liverpool people are football crazy. They know the game, its finer points and everything about it. I have heard it said that the two Liverpool teams are Catholic or Protestant, like Celtic and Rangers in Glasgow. That is not true. Catholics and Protestants in Liverpool support both the teams. In fact, Everton, supposedly the Catholic team, began its life as a Methodist youth team. It could, however, be said that the support of the teams can become a religion. It has been known for people to have their ashes strewn on the Anfield pitch. I was married from a house in Blessington Road, Anfield, close to the Liverpool ground. From there you could hear every shout, every 'ooh' or 'ahh' from the crowd, and when a goal was scored the noise was deafening. Actually, I am an Evertonian. That was by accident and arose out of my working on a construction site with an Everton supporter. He regularly went to the matches and asked me to go with him. That was the beginning of my allegiance.

I worked on and off for years along the line of docks. The dock cafés and canteens were like political seminars every dinner hour. I remember the story of the Russian ice-breaker, the *Lenin*, in the dry dock at the Dingle. The ship needed some new plates on its side. The boilermakers had a strict, agreed ratio of helpers to craftsman, which arose during the depression years to ensure union members had a chance of work. The job on the *Lenin* was taking longer than the Russian captain liked and he complained to the repair firm that the job was overmanned. He got short shrift: 'We can do nothing about that, there are too many communists here'. I met with the accusation of being a communist when on one occasion it was pouring with rain (the overhead railway had by then been pulled down, as the cost of maintenance was said to be too high) and I was waiting for a bus. There was a big queue and the conductor called 'Two on top'. I was first on and found there were six or seven seats. I called down to the conductor, who ignored me. I rang the bell to stop the bus. The conductor rushed up and took his cash-bag off, saying, 'You have it, you run the bus, bloody communist'.

The docks were busy. Every week the Guinness boat from Dublin would come in. You could tell the time by it. I remember the day Nye Bevan died. I was passing a ship when a docker shouted down to me: 'Bad day, Eric, it's like your brother dying'. An atmosphere of gloom covered the docks. Those were the days when there were huge meetings of dockers and others. I once spoke at a meeting of 50,000. Once the docks closed down and the trade to the city stopped it was devastating to all of us in Liverpool. Every time I went down the dock road I could have cried.

Liverpool's wealth in the past was derived from the sea – part of it from the slave trade. In 1755 there were eighty-nine licensed slave traders in Liverpool, which at that time was in the process of growing into a port. It had the advantage of being close to the manufacturing areas which produced the trade goods that could be exchanged for slaves. Liverpool merchants proved to be shrewd in their dealings. In no time goods from Sheffield, Birmingham and Manchester were arriving. By the end of the eighteenth century Liverpool was the most important slave centre in England. It has been calculated that during the years 1783 to 1793, ships from Liverpool transported one third of a million negroes from Guinea to the Americas. All those with any money had a share in the trade. The slaving ships from the Mersey were financed by grocers, butchers, drapers and chandlers as well as bankers, businessmen and attorneys. Within a short period the slave trade became a main prop of Britain's and Liverpool's economy.

In recent years, the Tall Ships came to Liverpool. They were seen by thousands and were a beautiful sight. I wrote in the *Liverpool Echo* that, whilst they looked lovely, it was on such ships that slaves were carried and that the conditions on board were inhuman and horrific. The profits made were at the expense of hundreds of thousands of lives. It took some time before this barbarous slave trade began to be understood by the people of Britain and, particularly, of Liverpool. In the offices of the Liverpool merchants, all that was seen were rows of figures on a page, and not what the figures meant in human misery and degradation. The famous actor, George Cooke, in a performance at the Theatre Royal was once drunk. The crowd booed him. He was furious and shouted, 'I have not come here to be insulted by a set of wretches every brick of whose infernal town is cemented with an African's blood'. Because of that outburst Liverpool had a second look at itself. However, when Wilberforce campaigned for the abolition of slavery, the merchants of Liverpool opposed him.

Because of the fight put up by Wilberforce and his friends, the Commons passed an Abolition Bill in 1805. The Lords held it up but eventually the Royal Assent was given in 1807. The Liverpool merchants and businessmen received the news with dismay. It meant a fall in the standard of living of vast sections of local people. The new law which stated that the slave trade was 'utterly abolished, prohibited and declared to be unlawful' came into effect on 1 January 1808. The *Kitty Amalia*, the last legal slaver, left Liverpool in July 1807.

Despite all the years that had passed since the end of slavery and the knowledge we now have of the 'middle passage' with its unmitigated horror, some people wrote in response to my piece in the *Liverpool Echo* claiming that I was wrong: African slaves were better off in America and the West Indies than they were in their own countries. However, there is also a tradition of anti-slavery in Liverpool; in the past, many seamen who protested at the brutality of the slave trade were imprisoned. It must be understood that the working people of Liverpool were, in their own way, also victims of the slave trade system. They did not have a vote and even when the vote was extended it was still only for those with property. The great wealth of the Liverpool merchants never found its way into the pockets of the workers, who had to fight hard for what they got.

The docks of Liverpool developed into a great system between 1760 and 1835. The town council administered the dock estate, and dock dues during the nineteenth century were a regular and essential part of the Corporation's revenue, rising from £23,380 in 1800 to almost £200,000 in 1835.

In 1840 the Cunard company inaugurated a regular fortnightly service to New York. Over 90,000 Irish entered Liverpool in the first three months of 1846 as a result of the terrible potato famine. Almost 300,000 followed them in 1847. Because of these hunger-driven, penniless people, there were 20,000 townsmen sworn in as special constables and 2,000 regular troops were camped at Everton. A majority of the Irish went on to America, but thousands stayed in Liverpool. That added to the already serious overcrowding and misery in the poor working-class areas of the town. They were not the only immigrants. Today there are almost as many of Welsh origin in the city as there are Irish. Because of the various immigrants and trade from all parts of the world Liverpool had, until the 1970s, almost as many consulates as London.

In 1835 an elected council took over from the closed corporation which had previously run the city. The new council took over the functions of the Watch, Lighting and Cleansing Boards and immediately reorganized the policing of the borough. A building surveyor was appointed to deal with unhealthy and unsafe buildings. Dangerous houses were demolished and building regulations were introduced. A health committee was established to regulate sanitary conditions. A pioneering effort was the inauguration of public wash-houses in 1842. The last public wash-house was not closed until 1985. The number of schools increased. St George's Hall was built. Dr Duncan, who had written a pamphlet about the conditions of the poor in Liverpool, and the need for a proper sewerage system, was made Liverpool's first medical officer in 1846. In 1847 an inquiry into insanitary dwellings was instituted and 14,085 inhabited cellars were measured and registered. During that year 5,000 cellars were condemned and cleared of their inhabitants. For the first time people were ensured a good supply of clean water. In the poorer quarters of the town whole courts had only a single stand-pipe. That led to squabbles between neighbours. Because the houses and the people could not be cleaned properly disease was rampant. Eventually, the council itself took over the water supply and built reservoirs at Rivington, north of Bolton. Then in 1879 the magnificent Lake Vyrney project was carried through. Today it has been turned over to private enterprise. In 1852 the Liverpool Public Library was founded – one of the earliest of such institutions in the country. Close to it was built the public museum, and the Picton reading room was also established. Parks were developed, Wavertree playground was given by an anonymous donor, and educational facilities were developed on a large scale. Today, all these wonderful creations are being neglected and privatized as greed is put before public need.

The Rev. Francis Kilvert noted in his diary on 21 January 1872: 'Liverpool left upon my mind an impression of ragged Irish barefoot women and children. Enormous wealth and squalid poverty, wildernesses of offices and palatial country houses and warehouses, bustling, pushy vulgar men, pretty women and lovely children.' In 1880, Queen Victoria granted Liverpool a charter which stated that in future Liverpool would be known as a city.

The other side to Liverpool's history belongs to the ordinary people: the struggle of the unions for decent wages and conditions, against unemployment, for good housing and for a decent education. It was this struggle which drove the City Fathers to make the changes described above. Brian White wrote in *The Corporation of Liverpool 1835–1914*: 'The special conditions of Liverpool – the national and religious divisions among the people, the demoralizing effects of casual employment – all made the growth of democracy difficult – as can easily be conceived. Yet democratic forces were able, if only for a short time, to exert a decisive influence on municipal affairs; and it was at this particular time that the corporation, judged by any standard, functioned most efficiently. These facts, rightly understood, should give encouragement to the defenders of local democracy today.' And they need it. The Tory government, under Mrs Thatcher, did more to undermine local democracy than any other government in this century. In Liverpool, Neil Kinnock lent them a hand.

SIX

Agitator

No country can be looked upon as satisfactory that
does not afford a proper livelihood for every decently-
behaved citizen. I know that all is not well, but very far
from well, indeed; and therefore, I have been what
many persons like to term 'an Agitator', and I am at
this time an Agitator, and intend to remain one.

TOM MANN, ILP Candidate, Aberdeen North, 1896

On arrival in Liverpool I called in at the CP offices in Norton Street to speak to the Area Secretary, Sid Foster, a member of my trade union. He was extremely suspicious. I was under a cloud in the Party and there were those at district and national level who wanted me expelled. We dissidents were categorized by some in the Party as Trotskyists, petty bourgeois, anti-Party, anti-working class and sectarian. Foster wanted to know why I had come to Liverpool. It was obvious he thought I was involved in a plot to spread anti-Party ideas amongst the comrades. I told him the reason was simple. My wife was a Liverpudlian, also in the CP, and had not been happy away from the city. More to the point, we could not find anywhere to live in the Hertford area. Foster was unconvinced – it was not a friendly meeting and did not augur well for the future.

Doris's aunt and uncle lived in Huyton, which was a three-quarters of an hour tram ride from the city centre. I had transferred to the Huyton branch of the Amalgamated Society of Woodworkers (ASW) which used to meet over the Co-op Stores opposite a pub called The Eagle and Child, known locally as 'The Bird and the Babby'. I became a regular attender and very active in the branch. Doris and I also transferred to the Huyton branch of the CP.

Because he was both a communist and in the ASW, I became a close friend of George Dykstra, one of the finest people I have known in my life. He was a shop steward on a housing site in Huyton, a straight-talking but complex character. Despite his seemingly rough exterior, he loved classical music and had a wonderful collection of records. Doris and I would sometimes be invited to his place for Sunday tea followed by a record recital. He was tall and gaunt, with a jutting firm chin. He would give money to workers with problems, as a supposed loan, but often never saw it again. He was a gentle, even saintly figure, yet in our struggles as trade unionists he could be like steel. He did not take easily to compromises, but at the same time he could be remarkably tolerant. During a ship-repair strike we were out chalking slogans when a man came and told us to remove them. I was about to tell him to 'buzz off' but George agreed we should leave. The man turned out to be a plain clothes police officer.

George and I worked for years together on various sites in the shipyard and on ship repair with never a harsh word between us. He had a slight heart condition and could not lift his hands over his head for too long. Any work of that kind I did. He was a fine, hard-working crafts-man and employers got more than their money's worth from him. We enjoyed many a good laugh together. On the ships, especially on the re-conversion jobs, there would be large pieces of veneered ply (mahogany, oak and other hardwoods) left over, which were usually destroyed. George took a dim view of that. He used to wear a large overcoat to work and before going home, he would cut the spare ply into an oblong shape, drill two holes at one end, thread string through the holes, and suspend the wood down his back under his overcoat. After getting through the dock gates we would get the jam-packed tram for Huyton. As it went along workers would get off, leaving empty seats, but George would remain standing. The tram conductor, puzzled, would call repeatedly, 'There's plenty of seats'. George would reply, 'I can't sit down, I've got a bad back'. With the wood he made furniture. They were lovely pieces. He never sold them but gave them to friends. To this day we have a table made by him which we greatly treasure.

George was contemptuous of those workers who used the union as a form of protection but put little into it. There were a few who would get onto a job and not do a good day's work. One such group we used to call 'the overcoat gang'. They rarely took off their top coats, even in summer. He also did not approve of men getting drunk at dinner time and coming back to work. He considered them – as I did – a menace to themselves and to their mates.

Once, when we were out of work, a foreman said he wanted two joiners to build a spiral staircase. George offered our services imme-diately, claiming that we were expert at that sort of work. As we left the site I said: 'I've never done a spiral staircase in my life, have you?' 'No', he said, 'I was relying on you.' We spent the rest of that day at his home poring over the appropriate books on staircases. I believe the staircase is there to this day. On another occasion, we got a job in a joinery shop and were asked if we could make a church pulpit. I said: 'Yes, but what denomination?' 'Does it matter?' asked the foreman. George said: 'Oh yes, of course it does.' 'Well, it's C of E.' 'In that case,' we said, 'that's all right.'

George was interested in hill and fell walking. One weekend the two of us tramped up Helvellyn and along Striding Edge. He kept up his hill walking over the years and on one occasion saved a man's life on a mountain. He always said, despite his heart condition, he would live his life to the full. He did that all right and died whilst on a walking expedition.

Because we often worked on the ships we signed on at 'B' Clearing House, the Labour Exchange along the line of docks. There we met like-minded workers and in the Cocoa Rooms and pubs kept our ties with the dockers, seamen and other port workers. After the war Liverpool ship-repair workers were still expected to go on the 'stand', that is, they took their tools with them to the firms and hoped to be picked for work. It was a humiliating experience and the union ended it simply by saying that from a certain date it would cease. From then on all joiners had to be employed through the union office or the Labour Exchange. George played a big part in that much-needed reform.

My first employer in the Liverpool area was Unit Construction. When I went on the site looking for work, the foreman wanted to know whether I had a fully paid-up union card. Without one I could not start. It was the first time in my life I had been asked such a question. I realized that Liverpool was not Hertford and that Merseyside workers were powerfully organized. Whilst on the Unit job I saw just how influential the unions were in Liverpool. The plasterers had an argument about working conditions and their organizer arrived on the site. After listening to the shop steward he immediately called a meeting of his members. The matter was resolved in minutes.

I then moved with George to Bootle, where we worked for Harland and Wolff on the *S.S. Britannic*. It was 1947 and the reconversion of passenger liners from troop carriers was in progress. We were working on the first-class accommodation. Every day was a joy for me. Using good timber for elaborate work and mixing with hundreds of highly skilled workers was a new experience and I enjoyed every minute of it. The senior shop steward of the whole yard was Michael Head, an Irishman from Dublin, and a member of my ASW branch in Huyton whom I got to know well.

During the war the employers had agreed to pay the ship-repair workers 6d an hour bonus. Now that the war was over they decided, without proper negotiations, to end the extra pay. The men were up in arms and a series of mass meetings were held. At one of them I moved a resolution for immediate strike action. It was seconded by many people. A serious discussion took place and the matter was then put to a show of hands. At least 90% of the workers voted to strike.

Approximately 20,000 of us came out on strike and I found myself a member of the Strike Committee. Michael was elected chairman. We used the Bootle Labour Club as our headquarters and met daily. Committees were formed to raise money, to organize picketing, propaganda and much else. Here was the working class in action, organized, sensible, knowing what its purpose and objectives were. I had been in industrial disputes in Welwyn Garden City but here, for the first time, I was witnessing workers united and fully determined to win.

During the strike I was sent to speak in London at a ship-repair workers' rally. The boilermaker, Ted Hill (later Lord Hill), chaired the meeting. Each week we had a great mass rally of the strikers in Liverpool. I was often on the platform. Sometimes, the legendary Leo McGree, District Secretary of my union and chairman of the Confederation of Shipbuilding and Engineering Unions, would speak. Leo was loved by the Liverpool workers. He was forthright, honest and, above all, humorous. I had heard about him during the war from Liverpool RAF men.

Like all officials in the ASW, Leo had to stand for re-election every year, but each year he was returned overwhelmingly. In the Huyton branch it was always Michael Head who moved Leo's nomination. I once asked Michael why he did this. Not that I objected, but I could see the great differences between the two men: Leo was in the CP and Michael was moderate Labour, Leo was not religious, Michael never missed going to Mass. Michael's answer was simple: despite McGree's politics he was the best official we could ever have. I heartily agreed with him.

On Wednesday afternoons at Bootle Labour Club the strikers used to stage regular concerts for pensioners. On the first Wednesday of the strike the old age pensioners turned up as usual for their meeting only to find the strikers in possession of their hall. They were bitterly disappointed even though they supported the strikers. Michael Head stepped in: 'There's only one thing to be done. We must provide entertainment.' He immediately found a striker who played the piano, another who was a comedian, others who could recite verse or sing. He had a lovely Irish tenor voice himself. He found jugglers, conjurers and more beside. The pensioners loved it. For the first time I saw the talent of Merseysiders in the entertainment field. Humour, in particular, is part of the Scouse scene. To have a good laugh is as important as breathing.

The strike lasted six weeks. The picket lines were only token because the workers came out 100 per cent. In the end the employers gave way and the 6d an hour bonus continued to be paid. It was a great victory.

Arising out of the strike, the Port Workers Committee was formed and I joined it. The Committee endeavoured to co-ordinate the activities of *all* Port workers – not just for strikes but for any appropriate action. I learned a great deal and developed a deep affection for Liverpool workers. They were decent, honest men and women and their sense of solidarity had to be experienced to be understood.

It was during the ship repairers' strike that I first became well known on Merseyside. This had repercussions for me in the CP. In addition to the Huyton branch a ship-repair branch of the CP was formed and I became a member. I was very active and clearly had some influence. The Party line was against strikes and for all-out production. My opposition to the leadership continued as before although I was too much involved in the actual class struggle to make this central to my politics.

In December 1947 the thirteen leaders of a strike amongst seamen were charged with conspiracy, intimidation, false imprisonment and assault. Eight were sent to prison for periods of three to twelve months. Among them were Bill Hart (a member of the CP who signed the November statement ending the strike), Barney Flynn, Patrick Hagan and Lawrence and Arthur Murphy. Whilst the Seaman's Committee of the CP took up their case, accusing the NUS leaders of lack of interest, the CP leadership definitely dragged its feet. For a period Bill Hart was in Walton Prison, Liverpool and I argued that we should be organizing demonstrations at the prison to show solidarity and support. My views on this did not endear me to the leadership of the CP.

I used to speak at other unions' meetings, boosting the sale of the *Daily Worker*, and one evening at the AUEW I was approached by Hugh Traynor. He said he had heard of my argument with the CP leaders and had some sympathy with my point of view, and asked whether he could see any documents relating to the arguments. I said I had some papers at home and he came to see them. I never gave the incident another thought.

In fact Traynor had filed a report on me to the CP's District Official, Sid Foster. Foster summoned me to the Party office and accused me of organizing factions. I angrily denied this but he then produced Traynor's report. I said it proved nothing and explained how I had been set up. It was clear that my story was unacceptable to Foster.

Shortly after this I received a telegram saying that the ship-repair branch would be meeting to discuss my expulsion. Until then, I had known nothing of the branch meeting, but immediately I hurried along to it. The membership had no choice in the matter, for the expulsion was directed from on high. The charges were read out and I was at least allowed to speak, but to no avail. The ship-repair members were not happy about the situation, and some said so. Jack Cohen was one critic, as was George Dykstra. I went home and cried. For ten years I had been in the Party, had given it my all, and now I was no longer part of it. Leo McGree drafted a statement for me admitting that I had been wrong and regretting my political position. I thanked him but I could not agree to sign it. Leo understood and always remained friendly. So did Jack Coward, a seaman, who had been pointed out to Doris when she was a child as the man whose hair turned white overnight from his experiences in the Spanish Civil War. Members were told not to have anything to do with me as I was anti-working class. George Dykstra was so upset that he gave up his job and left to work on the building of the Sellafield nuclear plant for a year or so. When he returned to Liverpool he said 'To hell with them' and resumed his friendship with me. We worked together on a number of jobs. Recently I received a letter from Hugh Traynor's wife saying that Hugh was now dead but had always spoken highly of me – perhaps I judged him too harshly at the time.

The period following my expulsion was very difficult. When Doris and I went to a *Daily Worker* dance at St George's Hall, only a few people spoke to us, although Harry Fairbrother, a Party member, walked right across the floor in full view of everyone and shook our hands. Some time after my expulsion Doris was summoned by Sid Foster and told that associating with someone who was anti-working class and remaining in the Party were not compatible. She suggested that as I was the steward at Bromborough Power Station perhaps he would like to go over there and explain that to the workers on the site. She had no intention of leaving me or leaving the Party. She wrote to Harry Pollitt, who sent a careful reply, friendly in tone, but in effect suggesting that I could get back in if I would agree that I had been wrong. At the end of that year the CP refused to register Doris for membership. She was not officially expelled but she was no longer a CP member either. By this time she could not have cared less.

After about six months, although I was not entirely happy about Labour Party policies, I decided to join as an individual member in the Arundel ward of the Toxteth constituency. We had moved to that area after living in Huyton for six months or so and had managed to get two unfurnished rooms, sharing kitchen and bath, in the house of Mr and Mrs Goldstein at 24, Newstead Road. The Goldsteins were good, understanding people. He was a presser in a tailor's shop and worked all the hours that God sent. During the six or seven years we lived there, we never had a cross word.

There were good people in the Arundel ward too. The secretary was a dock worker, Stan Johnson, who, together with his wife, was the mainstay of the ward. It was in that ward that I made the acquaintance of the legendary I.P. Hughes, a Welshman, who used to give lectures at the Welsh Society on socialism and philosophy.

It was during this period that the great dockers' strike took place in Liverpool. It was sparked off by a seamen's dispute in Canada. The Canadian Seamen's Union (CSU) was progressive, with deep roots in the Canadian working class. When a CSU ship tied up at Liverpool the dockers refused to unload it and 'blacked' the cargo in solidarity. The dock employers suspended the men with the threat of the sack. By the end of that day every docker in Liverpool, Bootle and Birkenhead was on strike. They gained not a penny by coming out. It was a strike in defence of fellow workers and principle. They remained out as long as the CSU's strike went on. I have never in my life seen such solidarity. We in the Trades Council threw our full support and resources behind the CSU. We took Canadian seamen into our homes, raised cash and watched the ship the whole time so that scabs could not be brought in to sail her. It was a shameful episode in Canadian labour history that, in the end, the CSU was wrecked by the anti-communist machinations of its leaders.

Around this time I came into contact with Les Cannon. He was from Wigan and had a similar background to my own. In 1949, he was elected to the Executive Committee of the ETU. The following year he moved to Liverpool and got a job working for the English Electric Company. He was soon involved in organizing a strike for higher wages for women workers at the factory. It was then that I got to know him, speaking on platforms for the strikers together. Cannon had not been friendly to me previously because of his loyalty to the Communist Party. He certainly thought the CP was right to expel me in 1948.

The women got their higher wages, but Cannon also got the sack. The union leadership failed to back him in his demand for reinstatement at the firm. Naturally he was bitter. He got a job at the Liverpool Power Station. It was clear that Cannon did not get on with the Liverpool ETU CP members. He could be a very arrogant man. He complained to the Lancashire and Cheshire District CP about some members who used four-letter words. That surprised me, because whenever I met him, he certainly had some in his vocabulary.

Years later, after Cannon had travelled a considerable distance to the right, he wrote to the *Guardian* saying that Michael Foot and I were wrong to oppose Harold Wilson and calling for our expulsion from the PLP. I replied, pointing out that Les had wanted me out of the CP when I was opposing the CP leadership, and now he wanted me out of the Labour Party for opposing the Labour leadership. I did not get on with Les Cannon or his travelling companion Frank Chapple. Although they had left the CP and fought against it in the union, they still carried their Stalinist organizational baggage with them and used it most effectively in the right wing of the movement.

Joiners in Liverpool worked in many industries. We worked on ship repair, in the shipyard at Birkenhead (Cammell Laird), on building and civil engineering sites, on maintenance, in joiners' shops, shop fitting or furniture making. After leaving ship repair, I went to Bromborough to work on the construction of the power station there. It was a huge site and after a while I was elected senior steward of all the trades and unions there – a very powerful position. We decided to make it an all union site. If non-union workers arrived we gave them a period of time in which to join. If they refused, we asked the main contractor, Brands, to transfer them. Our efforts were successful and we got 100 per cent membership (including the various site sub-contractors and even the teaboys) and maintained it throughout the job. Fifty trade union agreements were in operation there, and I had to master them all, the refractory agreement: the building health and safety regulations, the agreements of various industries and trades affecting their members on the site and so on. I became an expert in agreements. We had a number of strikes about issues like canteen facilities, bonuses, washing and toilet facilities, time off for shop stewards to perform their duties, and a few inter-union trade issues. These latter I did my best to discourage, as I felt workers should stick together, not antagonize each other. We also had a night shift so, if things went wrong, I was called out from bed at all hours. Once was when a foreman hit one of his men and the rest stopped work. I went to the site and got both men suspended on full pay until a settlement was reached. In the end, the foreman was transferred to the Middle East. Later I met him on a train and he thanked me, saying it was the best thing that ever happened to him, and that he was now very well off.

The firm provided me with a hut which served as my office and also a meeting place for the stewards. The original site manager, Mr Hunt, was considered too soft on the unions and the firm replaced him with an ex-officer who thought he was still in the war bossing his troops around. Before Mr Hunt left, the men presented him with a watch and he tipped me off that the firm wanted me out too. One of the first things the new man did was to find an excuse to sack me. It was disastrous. About 2,500 workers stopped work. I was soon reinstated. In those days I had the full support of Leo McGree and the regional National Federation of Building Trade Operatives (NFTBO) Secretary, Stanley May, who sent me a letter thanking me for the work I had done in building the union membership. I did not always get such support from the national leadership of my own union. At one stage, they threatened to withdraw my shop steward's credentials. I told them that the workers had elected me and that only they could remove me.

During one of our major strikes I discovered that the experience and attitude of American trade unionists was very different from ours. Our men cleaned out the cement mixers and pipes when on strike so that the concrete did not harden and ruin the machinery, and the crane drivers dropped their jibs for safety. We had two American crane drivers, and a few other American workers, who had married Liverpool girls. They argued forcibly about why they should leave the jibs up and why we should not clear out the mixers; in a fight, they insisted, you should do *anything* to win. It was a real private enterprise view. I told them that one day we hoped the workers themselves would own the means of production. It was wrong therefore to destroy those means. In one dispute, someone cut the main power supply to the site. As senior shop steward and chairman of the strike committee I thought I could well find myself charged and put into prison. Luckily it did not come to that.

There was a great sense of unity on that site. On two occasions steel erectors fell and were killed. Immediately, work finished for the rest of the day. On pay day, every man on the site and every woman in the office gave a full day's pay for the family of the bereaved. Most of the workers on the site joined the Birkenhead Power Station Benevolent Scheme. Members received sick pay during infirmity and lump sum payment on accident or death. Membership was open to everybody employed for the erection of the power station and benefits were paid each Friday on a weekly basis. From top to bottom, the whole thing was organized and controlled by the workers. It was working class democracy in action. Such things have always convinced me that workers' control of industry can be a reality.

Work at the Power Station had its funny side. On one occasion a full-time official of the T&GWU addressed the members and referred to the local civil engineering magnate Sir Alfred McAlpine. In relation to some problem which had arisen on the site he asked: 'What would Sir Alfred have said?' The reply came back sharp and clear: 'Keep the big mixer going'. The same official on another occasion said: 'Brothers, you have cut my feet from under me, you have tied my hands behind me and you are sending me in blindfold'. The answer came: 'Brother, you're not a union organizer, you're a bloody contortionist'. Liverpool workers are sharp and humorous.

A senior foreman of a section of navvies, a big man who tended to bully his men, got a bit out of hand one day. I went to see him to calm him down. He drew himself up to his full height: 'Do you know who I am? I am Sergeant – of the Commandos'. I took one step back, looked at him and said: 'Now I know who won the war. But I thought quite a few on this job played their part'. He was furious, took a step towards me and lifted his hands which were like hams. I thought, if he hits me that's my lot – I'll never recover. He did not. The lads said I went as white as a flour bag.

One of the men I became very friendly with at that time was 'Mac' McCarthy, a foreman joiner, and a staunch member of the ASW. He had been a POW in Japanese hands and, as a result of his experiences there, died whilst employed on the site. I also got to know Hugh Dalton, the senior steward on the nearby Capenhurst site. Hughie was a member of my union and of the Labour Party. Later, when I became an MP, he was chairman of Walton CLP. He had been a councillor, an alderman and – until he was disqualified and surcharged with forty-seven other Liverpool councillors – he chaired the city council between 1983 and 1986 with dignity and political panache.

The next huge construction site I worked on was the Esso site at Ellesmere Port. After I became senior NFBTO steward there, Wimpey built a brick office for me, a room for a secretary and a meeting room for the stewards. It was clear that there were going to be efforts to buy me off. One day the site manager suggested I ask the stewards to come to a dinner, accompanied by their wives and girlfriends, with top management at a hotel in Chester. Wimpey would lay on a coach or cars and the evening would be at their expense. Whilst I realized that most of the stewards would refuse, I feared that some might think it a good idea. I did not want them to be divided on the issue. There were enough union craft divisions already. I thought it over and at the next stewards' meeting suggested we accept Wimpey's invitation only on condition that *all* the men and their wives be invited. This the stewards could not refuse and I told the management of our decision. That was the end of it.

Another day, when it was raining heavily, a couple of stewards struggled across the site and asked me to go over to a meeting in their section. I looked out of the window and felt very reluctant; the office was dry and snug. It then dawned on me that I was getting cushioned and remote, so I went over in the rain. After thinking seriously about this, I told the management that I would use the office when required but I wanted to go back on the job as part of a 'gang'. I realised how bureaucracies develop. I was one remove from the men, the District Office was two removes, the Regional Office three and the National Officials almost totally remote. The point was brought home to me many years later when, in 1986, a friend of mine, Liz Nash, sent me a poem she had translated from the German by Kurt Tucholsky:*

To a Party Boss

Once we were both the same.
Both: Proles in the German empire.
Both in the same sweaty overalls:
The same work-shop – the same wage –
The same master – the same drudgery –
Both the same miserable bed-sit ...
    Comrade, do you still remember?
But you, Comrade, were quicker than I.
Stirring yourself – you were masterly at it.
We had to suffer, without complaint,
But you – you could speak out.
You knew the books and the pamphlets,
You knew best how to wield a pen.
Comrades in arms – we really believed in you!
    Comrade, do you still remember?
Today that's all in the past.
We can only get to you through the intercom.
You smoke thick cigars after dinner,
You laugh at street agitators and fools.
Know nothing any more of old comrades,
You're invited everywhere.
You shrug your shoulders over good brandy
And represent German Social Democracy
You've made your peace with the world.
Don't you sometimes hear in the dark night
A quiet voice, reproaching:
    'Comrade, aren't you ashamed?'

I think it was after I went back on the site that management decided to get rid of me, and engineered a strike. I could see it coming and urged the stewards to tread carefully. But the firm pushed the men hard. At a

*Kurt Tucholsky had been a member of the USPD a group which had broken away from the SPD in the First World War because the latter supported the war. Subsequently, he left all political parties, was expelled from Germany by the Nazis in 1933, and committed suicide in Sweden in 1935.

great mass meeting, they ignored the stewards and, by an overwhelming vote, decided to strike. The stewards and myself were then sacked. We were out for something like three months, and the firm refused to budge. In the end, I had to urge the men to march back to work as a united body and, at dinner time, elect new stewards group by group to re-build the organization. The firm did not re-employ me or many of the other stewards. It was a traumatic experience and my views about the ruthlessness of employers hardened.

After Labour lost the general election in 1951, attacks on the unions escalated and the press increasingly vilified 'irresponsible' workers. Every strike, especially if it was unofficial, was given widespread, hostile coverage. After my victimization on the Esso site I had some difficulty getting work. Once employers knew who I was they would suddenly find good reasons why I should not be employed. I was on a blacklist. I took any work that the District Office could find – often jobs with small employers which meant almost total isolation. One such job was at the Royal Oak pub in County Road, Walton, for Platts. An apprentice and I did the whole of the oak panelling there. It was good work for which I had to use tools I would not normally use, yet I received only the basic rate.

At Woolworth's in West Derby Road there was an Irish joiner called Tommy Looney who was a real character. At one time he had studied for the priesthood and was a good writer. He had been on the Esso site and was a great one for getting the maximum compensation for 'industrial accidents'. He once bought a rock cake from the canteen and, when he chipped his tooth, claimed it was the cake and that he had been disfigured for life, suffered excruciating pain and so on. He made such a fuss that the firm agreed an ex-gratia payment. On another occasion he hung his old overcoat up in one of the site huts and it got scorched by a stovepipe. He wrote a letter saying that the coat was priceless and could not be replaced. Again, the firm paid up. After the settlement the manager said they would like to have the old coat. Tom told me his wife had cut it up for rags. I passed this story to the manager who, a few days later, said 'Looney's wife? He's not married!' To cap it all, a few weeks later Tom appeared in his old coat, patched up.

For a period I worked on a new factory site at Warrington with about half local and half Liverpool men. We worked well together and although at times the firm tried to divide us they never succeeded. The Liverpool contingent travelled to work in a coach provided by the firm but for a short time Doris was unwell and I used to go in late. The firm told me that I would have to go if I couldn't be on time. All the men threatened to strike and the firm backed down.

After a time I got back into ship repair at Cammell Laird's shipyard at Birkenhead. I had been out of work for a couple of weeks and got a job with a sub-contractor. I was anxious not to miss this opportunity and couldn't sleep properly for fear of being late. In the end, I overslept and rushed out of the house, without a wash or breakfast, with my heavy toolbox on my shoulder. I just managed to get onto a passing bus, changed to the underground for Birkenhead, and slipped through the shipyard gates just as they began to close. You never forget things like that.

At Laird, I was elected a bonus steward on the ship being constructed and then senior ASW steward for the whole yard. I negotiated a good bonus agreement but found we were not getting full payment because of hold-ups by other trades. I told the joiners that when a hold-up occurred, they must take a note of the time, get the foreman to agree it and, at the end of each month before payment of the bonus, I would collate the time lost, and ensure that it was not included in the overall calculations. As a result, the bonus was very good. The firm was furious and decided to get rid of me. To get me out of the yard, close on 1,000 workers from all trades were laid off. After a period most were taken back but the ASW District Office refused to allow joiners to work on the ship whilst I was still sacked. The dispute dragged on and on. I told Leo McGree that the ban would have to be lifted – it was not fair to men with families to be out of work for so long. It was lifted, with me left outside the shipyard gates.

Those days of industrial struggle on Merseyside are times I shall always remember for the solidarity and decency of the workers. They never allowed sometimes deep political and religious differences to come before unity in the struggle for better wages, conditions and overall working-class interests. I remember the occasion when a Roman Catholic priest tried to lead dockers back to work. They listened to him politely, but as he went through the dock gate urging them to follow him, they just stood and waved to him, saying, 'Bye, Bye, Father'. That was a sight to remember.

SEVEN

The Political Stage

Forsooth, brothers, fellowship is heaven, and lack of
fellowship is death: and the deeds that ye do upon the
earth, it is for fellowship's sake that ye do them, and
the life that is in it, that shall live on and on for ever,
and each one of you part of it, while many a man's life
upon the earth from the earth shall wane.
Therefore, I bid you not dwell in hell but in heaven,
or while ye must, upon earth, which is part of heaven,
and forsooth no foul part.

WILLIAM MORRIS, 'A Dream of John Ball'

My expulsion from the CP was one of the best things that ever happened
to me. Once over the initial hurt, I began to read more widely than ever
before. I had collected books, so far as my limited means would allow,
from the age of sixteen: politics, literature, economics, poetry,
philosophy, religion. I began to buy books from second-hand bookshops, remainders from Blacklers and Lewis's basements and Boots
library section. I had already read a great deal of history: about the
Peasants Revolt, the English civil war, the Chartists, the pre-socialist
radicals. I was particularly interested in the rationalist ideas of Charles
Bradlaugh, who refused to take the religious oath on entering Parliament and was barred. (I myself had not gone to church since I was about
sixteen, upsetting my mother in the process.) I accepted dialectical
materialism, thereby rejecting idealist philosophical ideas. In economics
I had studied *The Wealth of Nations* by Adam Smith, the ideas of
Ricardo, and even Marshall.

I had previously ignored, or brushed aside, those modern writers
opposed to the Soviet Union; such authors, I thought, were helping the
capitalist class against the international working class led by the leaders
of the Soviet Union. In hindsight, it seems to me that I rejected my
Christian faith only to accept a communist one. But after I left the CP,
my critical faculties were sharpened and new concepts of what socialism

65

really was were formulated and developed. A turning point had been reached, as it had at the time of my rejection of Christianity. I began to feel liberated. Orwell became a favourite as did Ignazio Silone. I studied books by the anarchists Bakunin, Kropotkin, Berkman and Woodcock; I also read socialist left-wingers like Fenner Brockway, H.N. Brailsford and mavericks like Bertrand Russell.

Russell had been literally a closed book to me. He had been too critical of the Soviet Union and was beyond the pale for any good CP member. But now, when I read him, I discovered that he had opposed the First World War and had been involved in the 'No Conscription League' with Fenner Brockway. At first he had enthused about the Soviet Union, but after his visit in 1920, he had returned very dis-illusioned. In *The Theory and Practice of Bolshevism* he pointed out that the 'dictatorship of the proletariat' had turned into the dictatorship of bureaucrats, spies and secret police, just as Rosa Luxemburg had warned. Russell had joined the ILP and argued in favour of Guild Socialism. He was much influenced by G.D.H. Cole's *Self-Government in Industry*. His book, *Roads to Freedom*, expressed his Guild Socialist ideas. He argued that under state socialism the state would not 'wither away', but would continue after the revolution and be used against the people to maintain power. In his book on German social democracy, he rejected the economic concepts of Marx, but pushed Marx, the revo-lutionary, to the fore. I did not accept everything that Russell wrote. But it was exciting to read him and he helped to free me from CP dogma.

I also learned at this time what the Moscow trials were really about. I argued with my friend Frank Roy about the Soviet Union and Stalin. He was still a believer. Then I began to think seriously about the nature of the Soviet Union. Trotsky had advanced the theory that the Soviet Union was basically a (deformed) workers' state with a bureaucracy which would have to be removed by a political revolution to create a workers' democracy once more, as it had existed in 1917.

I came to recognize that whatever the Soviet Union was called, what-ever its nature, it was not socialist and it was not democratic. Marx and Engels had stated, in the *Communist Manifesto*, that the emancipation of the working class must be the act of the workers themselves and that the struggle for socialism and democracy was basically the same struggle. I began to study the ideas and concepts of Rosa Luxemburg and found that she represented all that was best in the socialist movement. She stood foursquare with the workers' revolution in the Soviet Union, but had criticized the Bolsheviks' methods. It was she who had warned that the 'dictatorship of the proletariat' as understood by Lenin could and would become the 'dictatorship of the party', then the 'dictatorship of the central committee of the party' and eventually the 'dictatorship of one person inside the central committee'. Rosa Luxemburg, more than anyone, helped me to understand fully what had happened in the Soviet Union.

Luxemburg helped create the Spartacus League, the forerunner of the German Communist Party. But she would I am sure have broken with the CP eventually, had she not been murdered by right-wing soldiers. She believed in socialism from below, not the socialism from above which the CP advocated. The CP theoreticians could never deny that Luxemburg was a great revolutionary socialist, but they suppressed her works. They scorned her arguments and caricatured her belief in the spontaneous struggle of a free working class. Luxemburg was an opponent of those revolutionary elitists who believed the workers could not do things for themselves, but needed a disciplined party which would impose on them what was good for them. 'Without the conscious will and the conscious action of the majority of the proletariat there can be no socialism,' she wrote. '[We] will never assume governmental authority except through the clear, unambiguous will of the vast majority of the German working class ... Mistakes committed by a genuinely revolutionary labour movement are much more fruitful and worthwhile historically than the ability of the very best Central Committee.' Her book on the Russian Revolution, her pamphlets on general strikes, her opposition to Bernstein, the great German social-democratic revisionist, and her writings on the national problem had profound influence on me.

I also came across the work of Eugene Debs, the American railway workers' leader. He too argued for socialism from below: 'Too long have the workers of the world waited for a Moses to lead them out of bondage. He has not come, he never will come. I would not lead you out if I could; for if you could be led out, you could be led back again. I would have you make up your own minds that there is nothing you cannot do yourselves ... everything depends on the working class itself. The simple question is, can the workers for themselves, by education, organization, co-operation and self-imposed discipline, take control of the productive forces and manage industry in the interests of the people and for the people and for the benefit of society? That is all there is to it.'

Luxemburg and Debs argued against elitism but maintained the need for a vanguard in the struggle, which is a different matter. Debs put it this way in an anti-war speech in 1917 for which he was jailed: 'It is the minority who have made the history of the world. It is the few who have had the courage to take their places at the front, who have been true enough to themselves to speak up truth that was in them; who have

67

dared oppose the established order of things, who have espoused the cause of the suffering, struggling poor, who have upheld without regard to personal consequences the cause of freedom and righteousness.'

Luxemburg, Connolly and Debs became my mentors. The society for which they fought I wanted to fight for too. They were the modern examples of Christ, of John Ball, of Wat Tyler, of Lilburne, of the Tolpuddle Martyrs and William Morris. I re-joined the Labour Party, despite my misgivings, to fight for such beliefs. Many years later, I came across a pamphlet by Hal Draper, an American socialist, entitled *The Two Souls of Socialism*, in which he wrote: 'How does a people or a class become fit to rule in their own name? Only by fighting to do so. Only by waging their struggle against oppression – oppression by those who tell them they are unfit to govern. Only by fighting for democratic power do they educate themselves and raise themselves up to the level of being able to wield that power. There has never been any other way ...'

I continued to be a member of the Trades Council, as the delegate from the Huyton branch of the ASW, after being expelled from the CP. I soon found myself defending those who had rejected me. Some on the Trades Council, including Bill Sefton, Howell James (Secretary of the Liverpool Co-op Party), Brian Crooks and Stan Maddocks (who were Bevanites), argued that CP members were holding up the advance of the left in Liverpool and should be banned from attending Trades Council meetings. Predictably, the centre and right joined in this demand. They included Jack and Bessie Braddock, Harry Livermore, and their friends. Naturally, the CPers opposed the move, as did some fellow travellers. Others on the left opposed it as I did, on the grounds that the movement should be a broad church. The debate was long and often bitter. I pointed out that as I had been expelled I had nothing to thank the CP leaders for, but I felt it wrong that union delegates who were CP members should be witch-hunted. Union branches had the right to elect who they wanted, not who the executive committee of the Trades Council decreed. We were heavily defeated but my branch supported me and I remained as delegate of the Trades Council until well after I was elected to Parliament in 1964. I was on the executive committee from 1950 to 1964 and was chairman in 1959 and in 1964. I became a delegate from Liverpool to the Lancashire Federation of Trades Councils, and was elected to its executive committee. I also became an executive committee member of the North West Regional Labour Party, defeating Jack Braddock for the position. I was also the Liverpool delegate to the annual conference of Trades Councils for a number of years. There is no doubt that being on the Trades Council helped make my name in politics.

The Liverpool Trades Council can claim to be one of the oldest in the country – older than Manchester's. The first – then under another name – was formed in 1848. In 1887, William Matkin, the Carpenters and Joiners' delegate and local secretary of the Labour Electoral Association, got the Trades Council together with the LEA to fight the School Board elections. This was a real breakthrough and, in effect, the beginning of Labour politics in the city.

When I first became a delegate to the Trades Council in 1947, it was the workers' parliament of the Liverpool area. There were approximately 200,000 trade union and Labour Party members affiliated, with something like 750 to 800 delegates. Each meeting was packed to the doors. In those days, we met in Transport Hall at the T&GWU headquarters in the city. The entire organization was run by a staff of only two, the secretary, Ralph Miller, and a shorthand-typist. I remember smiling to myself when a young delegate complained that we had too many bureaucrats at the Trades Council.

The debates at the Trades Council were excellent. On one occasion, Stephen Swingler, MP, came to meeting and said that the level of debate there was higher than that in the Commons. Over the years we debated various issues facing the Labour movement: the Korean war, nuclear disarmament, the policies of the Labour group, the rating system, local and national strikes, German rearmament, and just about everything else. The Trades Council gave delegates a good political training. I saw men and women who arrived almost inarticulate but who within a few years made contributions of outstanding quality. One of these was a skilled print worker, Tony Mulhearn, who was expelled from the Labour Party after the 1985 Party Conference because he was a Militant supporter.

The executive committee included the Braddocks who, over the years, moved slowly to the right. Nevertheless, they both had excellent records in the movement. Bessie was very popular and just after the war she dramatically took the side of the dockers in their fight against wartime legislation, which continued to prohibit strikes. She was the daughter of Mary Bamber, a well-known socialist and trade unionist. Jack Braddock was from the potteries and had come to Liverpool in 1915. He had worked as a wagon repairer and had been unemployed for six years after the First World War. He became a Co-op insurance agent and married Bessie in 1922. Both Jack and Bessie were CP members who left the Party in 1924 and became Labour councillors. Bessie was MP for Liverpool Exchange from 1945 to 70.

The Braddocks were the leading figures of the left in the Liverpool Labour Party for many years. The other big names in the Trades

Council at the time I joined it were Frank Cain of the General & Municipal Workers Union, and John Hamilton, the father of the John Hamilton who was leader of the council during the 1983–87 period. Hamilton Snr was treasurer of the Trades Council from 1927 until 1958. He was a stonemason, a member of the Plebs League and a lecturer for the National Council of Labour Colleges. In 1930 he was sitting councillor for the St Domingo Ward. In his election address he quoted Eugene Debs: 'You do not need the capitalist. He could not exist an instant without you. You would just begin to live without him. You do everything and he has everything ...' It was, however, a bad year for Labour. A Protestant candidate defeated John Hamilton by exploiting religious sectarianism.

For me, re-joining the Labour Party meant involvement again in a genuine workers' party. The membership of the Toxteth Constituency was almost all working class, with dockers, building workers, seamen, boilermakers and labourers forming the overwhelming majority. There were a few white-collar workers, but only one or two intellectuals.

After we moved to Newstead Road, the Labour Party had decided not to put up a candidate in the Arundel Ward. I was furious and said I would have stood as Independent Labour rather than let it go unchallenged. Labour never again missed putting up a candidate and although we did not come near to winning for many years, my friend Dr Cyril Taylor, later a member of the Royal Commission on Health, eventually won the seat for Labour.

Up until 1950, however, we did have a Labour MP for Toxteth, Joe Gibbons, known in the party as 'Barefoot Joe'. I realised why when I heard him speak at a meeting and he went on at some length about his childhood days when children roamed the streets barefoot. Joe, unfortunately, was beaten in 1950 by Reginald Bevins, an ex-Labour councillor who became a Tory. Bevins held the seat until 1964, when Dick Crawshaw became the MP. Labour held only three seats in Liverpool in the 1950s and early 1960s. They were Exchange, Edge Hill and Scotland. Walton, Kirkdale and Toxteth were lost to the Tories. West Derby had never been Labour, despite a big council estate at Norris Green.

Labour had never had control of the city council. Despite the fact that the Liverpool working class was a strong militant movement, the Tories were dominant. However, these were Tories of a different stripe than those of today. They had civic pride and a sense of duty. They built council houses, cleared slums, maintained beautiful parks and art galleries and built new libraries and swimming pools. They ran children's homes, owned and controlled the water supply, built new reservoirs in

NEVER A YES MAN

North Wales, kept the roads in good order, had municipally owned markets, a municipal golf course, and generally carried out their civic duties in a conscientious way. Of course they also looked after their business friends and defended the capitalist system. But compared with Thatcherites who followed they were decency itself.

The reason for Liverpool being a Tory city at that time is to be found in its history. There was a large Protestant Orange Lodge presence. Workers, politically, often divided between Protestant and Roman Catholic, which tended to split the Labour vote. Scotland, one of the city's constituencies, had, for many years, been Irish Nationalist with T.P. O'Connor, locally known as Tay-Pay, as its MP. When the Irish Nationalists in Liverpool moved to support Labour, following O'Connor, the seat was then won and held by David Logan, a well-known Roman Catholic. Scotland was held by the two men for almost 100 years. Such religious sectarianism took years to break down but today it has more or less disappeared. When the Pope came to Liverpool he visited both cathedrals, Anglican and Roman Catholic, and toured the city, receiving a good reception from all sides. Ian Paisley MP tried to organize opposition to his visit and there was some amusement when he appeared in a side street haranguing his supporters as the Pope went by. It is said that the Pope made the sign of the Cross, blessing those in the side street, including Paisley.

After Nye Bevan and Harold Wilson (who represented nearby Huyton) had resigned from the Labour government in 1951, the right-wing in Liverpool began an onslaught against the left. The Trades Council and the constituencies began to split. Each meeting became a dog-fight. Many of the right now supported Bessie Braddock who, it was rumoured, had moved to the right after being snubbed by Bevan, and some of the previous left followed her out of loyalty to old friends.

The Bevanite left in the city at that time was led by Bill Sefton and Howell James. I was somewhat sceptical of Bevan. I thought he was surrounded by too many fellow travellers. I was not anti-communist but non-communist. At that time the Revolutionary Communist Party (RCP) ceased to exist and most of its members, under the national leadership of Ted Grant, found their way into the Labour Party. In Liverpool that included Jimmy Deane and his relatives, most of whom lived in the Walton constituency. Laura Kirton, a member of the Executive Committee of the Trades Council and Secretary of Walton CLP, did not publicly support the Deane group but she was close to them and gave them a great deal of assistance over the years. I got to know Laura very well and admired her organizing ability and political clout. I did not always agree with her, especially when she seemed to be pushing the line advocated by Ted Grant who at one time was selected to stand as parliamentary candidate for Walton only to have the NEC overturn his selection. But I never thought, at any time, that Laura or Ted should be expelled. I got to know Brian Deane, Paddy (Pat) Wall, George McCartney, Terry Harrison and many other Grant supporters as well. They worked hard for the party but always fought for their own positions as well. Militant thus began in Liverpool.

Because of the move to the right in the Labour Party I became increasingly unhappy. I found, however, that amongst the rank and file, and in the trade unions, there were thousands of good socialists who were also fed up. Bevan, in resigning over health charges and German rearmament, had given expression to that feeling and kept thousands in the party. Ralph Miliband, in his book *Parliamentary Socialism*, rightly said: 'Bevan did not create Bevanism; as a refusal on the part of a substantial minority of Labour's rank and file to endorse the leadership's drift of policy and as an affirmation of the need for different policies, it had existed in the Labour Party and in the trade unions long before Bevan gave it his name and his gifts, and it endured and grew in strength after he ceased to give expression to it.'

In 1945 and 1950 there were serious arguments in the party, but things were not pushed too far because, despite disappointment on foreign policy in particular, on the home front some real progress had been made: the NHS had been created, the welfare state established. Public ownership of the mines, gas, electricity and railways had been achieved and houses were being built on a fairly large scale. The unions had become stronger and most anti-trade union legislation had been swept away. There were industrial struggles, workers had to fight hard, but they found greater sympathy from Labour ministers than they had ever experienced in the past. In the 1945, 1950 and 1951 general elections, Labour's vote increased.

In 1951, one of the issues that involved the whole Labour movement in Liverpool was the dockers' strike which began as a result of the decision of the national dockers' delegate conference to accept an offer of twenty-one shillings a day. The Merseyside Dockers wanted twenty-five shillings. At first, the Liverpool dockers had only marginal support from London dockers. Then three Liverpool and four London dockers were arrested in an East End pub. They were charged with conspiracy and organizing an illegal strike. Two very well-known dock leaders were involved, Bill Johnson and Harry Constable. As soon as the arrests were announced, sympathy strikes began. What had started as a wages dispute turned into a struggle for the abolition of Order 1305, which was used by the government to enforce compulsory arbitration on strikers.

When the seven dockers' leaders appeared in court at the Old Bailey in April, marches and sympathy strikes took place. Thousands upon thousands of dockers participated throughout the nine days of the trial. On one occasion mounted police charged the dockers who, it was reported, sang the line 'Britons never, never, never shall be slaves' from 'Rule Britannia'. On 19 April, the seven dockers were discharged. They had won a great victory and Order 1305 was dropped in August.

Nevertheless, the gains made by Labour in 1945–50 were being put at risk by a right-wing Labour government. *Tribune*, which had increasingly become an apologist for the Labour leaders, now changed tack and opposed the leadership policies. Meanwhile I was selling copies of *Socialist Outlook*. The organization it was associated with, Socialist Fellowship, included left-wing Labour Party members, CP fellow travellers, left-wing Labour MPs and Trotskyists. In the early days of *Socialist Outlook*, Bessie Braddock wrote for the paper, as did Konni Zilliacus, Fenner Brockway, S.O. Davies, Frank Beswick, John Parker, Ellis Smith and leading trade union people like Jim Figgins, John Stanley, Ernie Roberts and Bob Willis. The Socialist Fellowship had developed as the result of the activities of Ellis Smith MP, whom I knew as Chairman of the Lancashire Federation of Trades Councils.

The Socialist Fellowship's first conference was held in London in 1949. There were a hundred delegates from twenty-nine towns committed to 'an association of Labour Party members pledged to work for ... socialization, workers' control, ending the gross inequalities of income, a Socialist Europe and freedom for the colonies'. By May 1950, the Socialist Fellowship on Merseyside had 120 members from most constituencies. I attended a number of meetings, both in Liverpool and London. In June 1950, the Korean war broke out. This split the Socialist Fellowship. Ellis Smith and Fenner Brockway supported the government's position on Korea and, as the Socialist Fellowship's NEC was opposed to it, they both resigned from the NEC. Tom Braddock MP became president and the Socialist Fellowship devoted its energies to opposing the Korean war. There was growing opposition to the Korean war both in the Labour Party and the TUC. G.D.H. Cole spoke out against it, and the Socialist Fellowship called a successful anti-war rally. The demand grew for a special conference of the Labour Party. Meanwhile the SF's policy document, *From Labour to Socialism*, was selling strongly. The Labour Party decided to act: 'The NEC has had under review for some time the activities of the Socialist Fellowship and has come to the conclusion that they are advocating a programme and policy which fundamentally varies from that laid down by the Annual Conference of the Labour Party and therefore decides that membership

73

of that organisation is incompatible with membership of the Labour Party.' Some of us in Liverpool were surprised at this sudden conversion to the acceptance of Annual Conference decisions, but the Socialist Fellowship did not defy the NEC and disbanded – to my dismay.

Socialist Outlook continued as a paper but was now completely in the hands of Gerry Healey's Trotskyist faction. Elers Smith, who had started the group, was by no means a Trotskyist. The real problem for the paper, however, was that once Bevan resigned, *Tribune* became the mouthpiece for him and the majority of the left. In 1954, *Socialist Outlook* was proscribed and Healey and his friends began to write for, and also to sell, *Tribune.* Michael Foot once said to me that he thought Gerry Healey was a charming man. I told him I thought he was something of a thug.

The Keep Left group in the Commons called a meeting in March 1951 from which the Bevanite Group was formed. The Keep Left members were Richard Acland, Barbara Castle, Dick Crossman, Harold Davies, Michael Foot, Leslie Hale and Ian Mikardo. Also present were Nye Bevan, Hugh Delargy, Tom Driberg, John Freeman, Will Griffiths, Jennie Lee, Tom Mackey and Harold Wilson. Over a period the group expanded its membership, but relatively slowly. The right of the party soon condemned the Bevanites as 'a party within a party' and this was reflected in the Trades Council and CLPs in Liverpool and on Merseyside. Bevan was supposed to have spoken at the Liverpool Stadium in December 1952 but permission was denied by its Directors. Harold Wilson wrote in *Tribune,* 'an enemy has done this'. Bessie Braddock declined to comment. An alternative rally was held in Birkenhead in February 1953. I attended it with Doris. It was packed to the doors and was a great boost to the local left.

When *Socialist Outlook* was proscribed, the Bevanites rightly defended it. Resolutions from 119 CLPs opposed the ban; only one supported it. Michael Foot, in *Tribune,* denounced the ban and the 'new tin-pot Torquemadas' who were putting forward the witch-hunt. At a public meeting in Holborn Hall, London, Foot and Kingsley Martin, editor of the *New Statesman,* supported by the editor of *Peace News* and *Co-op News,* spoke against the ban. Michael Foot said that those who had received letters with demands for loyalty oaths from Transport House should refuse to sign them: 'We cannot allow this to go on, and free controversy and free newspapers to be stamped out of existence ...' I only wish he had continued to take that view years later when the *Militant* editorial board was expelled from the Labour Party.

1954 was the year of the great dock strike. The National Association of Stevedores and Dockers (the Blue Union) called for a strike against compulsory overtime and there was tremendous support from the T&GWU dock members (the White Union). The compulsory overtime issue had certain similarities to the dispute over Order 1305 and again it was the rank and file who pushed their leaders. *Tribune*, whose industrial correspondent was Ian Aitken, an old friend of mine, backed the Blue Union. Circulation boomed.

The TUC expelled the Blue Union under pressure from Arthur Deakin of the T&GWU. The Labour Party NEC threatened the *Tribune* editorial board. *Tribune* replied with a 6,000 word statement moving the debate from the dockers question to the principles of free speech in the party. It was issued as a pamphlet, 'The Case for Freedom – An Answer to Morgan Phillips and the NEC', which had a great sale on the docks. The battle inside the party hotted up. Writs were flying around in Liverpool and threats were made against left wingers – especially Bevanites. Generally the atmosphere was poisonous, and Bessie Braddock became a real witch-hunter.

In March 1955, an attempt was made to expel Nye Bevan from both the PLP and the Labour Party. A resolution against German rearmament had been carried at the Party Conference and sixty-two Labour MPs, including Bevan, decided to abstain on the opposition amendment in the Commons because it did not support party policy. By a nine to four vote the shadow cabinet recommended that the whip be withdrawn from Bevan and that he be reported to the NEC. A special PLP meeting was held which decided – after two votes – to withdraw the whip. Bevan threatened a breach of Parliamentary privilege case if the NEC tried to influence the future conduct of an MP. My ASW branch decided that I should move an emergency resolution at the Trades Council against his possible expulsion. It was carried overwhelmingly and with much enthusiasm. This was happening all over the country and I am sure that the party leadership was influenced by the support shown for Nye and the Bevanites. After a sub-committee of the NEC had been set up, a compromise was reached and, by fifteen votes to ten, the NEC condemned Bevan but decided not to expel him. Predictably, the *Sunday Times* said in an editorial (and this contains a lesson for us now): 'The hidden, distant danger is this, that from the division of Labour a new left-wing crypto Communist Party might arise, and in the long run might become the alternative government, the nature of our system being to squeeze out the middle party'. The press in 1955 shared a similar attitude towards the internal divisions of the Labour Party as they did during the struggles in the party of 1981–86.

Loudly and clearly, Bevan declared that he was not going to form a new party. I supported Bevan but I was never part of the Bevanite tendency. I was not enamoured with the concept of socialism from above – Bevanite or otherwise. The struggles on the construction sites and in the shipyards were the actions of the workers themselves. Shop stewards were not bureaucrats. They were elected. They could be recalled at any time and never *instructed* workers to stop work, go slow or take other industrial action. Shop stewards could recommend proposals, but after that full discussions took place and votes were taken. The stewards were often voted down.

My life in Liverpool wasn't all Trades Council meetings. I was also very much involved in the Merseyside Unity Theatre. I believed, like Arnold Wesker, the socialist playwright, that 'Socialism isn't talking all the time, it's living, it's singing, it's dancing, it's being interested in what goes on around you, it's being concerned about people and the world'. As Bertolt Brecht wrote:

> You actors of our time
> The times of change
> And the time of the great taking over
> Of all nature to master it
> Not forgetting human nature ...
>
> Give us the world of men as it is
> Made by men and changeable ...
>
> Acting and working
> Learning and teaching
> Intervene from your stage
> In the struggles of our time ...
>
> Make the experience of struggle
> The property of all
> And transform justice
> Into a passion.

The tiny Merseyside Unity Theatre was in Mount Pleasant and we often used to refer to its 'pocket-handkerchief' stage. I worked on the stage carpentry in one of the back rooms. A member of the Executive Committee of the ETU, Jim Feather, organized the lighting. We were all volunteers. On one occasion, I built some steps for a play and then discovered that I could not get them through the doorways onto the pocket handkerchief. It was mishaps like these that made our endeavour all the more fun. After I became chairman, young actors and actresses would lobby me for particular roles. I was only too happy to tell them that that side of the theatre had absolutely nothing to do with me.

The group not only put on plays and revues, it also provided a choir and sketches for public meetings and rallies. One of the sketches was the 'Money Trick' from *The Ragged-Trousered Philanthropists*. I remember Unity performing this at a May Day rally of the Young Christian Workers, at which I spoke with Archbishop Warlock, the Roman Catholic Archbishop of Liverpool. One of those involved in the Theatre was Nora Rushton, who worked for Lever Brothers at Birkenhead. Because of her political activities – she was in the CP – she lost her job and her family was threatened with eviction from their tied house. The Sunlight Village, where the family lived, was owned by the company. Nice houses were provided for the employees but I thought it wrong that they should be living under such a system of control, and I spoke at a public meeting against this kind of persecution.

The Secretary of the Unity Theatre was Jerry Dawson, who also produced many plays and revues. Some of the actors and actresses were quite brilliant and today I see them in TV films and soap operas. From my point of view, although many of those in the Unity were in the CP, they were not sectarian, and they proved this by electing me chairman. The theatre put on plays from Shakespeare to Sean O'Casey, from Restoration to modern works. It also staged plays in the city's parks in the summer. We had poetry readings, lectures (I once gave a lecture on Howard Fast, the American author of *Freedom Road, Citizen Tom Paine, The Last Frontier* and *History of the Jews*), musical evenings, and so on. The theatre was a real cultural centre for trade unionists, workers and intellectuals. Talks were given on subjects like unemployment and housing, and rambling expeditions were organized. I feel that my involvement in Unity was a serious contribution to the working-class movement. Unity was entertainment, but it was also education.

Meantime, Doris and I had saved enough for a deposit on a house in Avondale Road, off Smithdown Road. It was certainly an improvement on living in rooms and there was now space to build more bookshelves for my ever growing collection.

EIGHT

In Revolt

We often discover what will do, by finding out what
will not do; and probably he who never made a mistake
never made a discovery.
SAMUEL SMILES, *Self Help*

A number of Labour Party members in Liverpool, and others influenced
by the CP, were becoming increasingly disenchanted by both parties and
decided to establish the Socialist Educational Group. They included
myself, I.P. Hughes Richard Bale, Neil Beresford, Norman Forshaw,
Jimmy White, Gerry Atherton and a few others. I.P. Hughes, had a
tremendous record. As a conscientious objector in the First World War
he had refused to put on the King's uniform, had been sent to France,
threatened with a firing squad and, finally, spent a long time in British
jails. He was a fine, honest man who had been in the ILP before joining
the CP. In Liverpool he had been responsible for helping to get illegal
political refugees in and out of the country. He never ever wrote
anything down; he had a habit of committing names, addresses, telephone numbers, and so on, to memory, because of his underground
experiences. Hughes had either left the CP of his own accord or was
expelled, I am not sure which. He rejoined the ILP and later became
involved with the Trotskyists. After that, he was active in the Labour
Party. It was 'I.P.' who brought the legendary Marxist and cricket writer
C.L.R. James to meet me at my home in Avondale Road.

From our discussions in the Socialist Education Group it was clear
that all who came to our meetings were equally fed up with the social-
democratic trends in the Labour Party and the Stalinist attitudes and
policies of the CP. We felt that we should be working for a new and
genuine democratic revolutionary socialist party. A number of events led
us to this conclusion: the tightening of right-wing control in the Labour
Party, the publication of the reformist 'British Road to Socialism' by the
CP, and the conflict between Stalin and the Yugoslav CP led by Tito. In
Britain, the CP had issued a pamphlet written by William Rust praising

the Yugoslavs, saying that Yugoslavia was the nearest to a genuine soviet system. Once the Cominform attacked Tito, however, the pamphlet was withdrawn. The Yugoslavs had fought under CP leadership to free themselves from Hitler's domination but they had not relied on Soviet bayonets. After the war they were deeply shocked to find that the Soviet leadership treated them as a colonial possession. We followed the press reports carefully and also read the Cominform reports in the journal *For a People's Peace and a People's Democracy.* The Soviet denunciation which claimed that Tito and his followers were agents of imperialism and fascist in outlook was so ridiculous that we unhesitatingly rejected it.

In 1953, a rising of workers in East Berlin against the GDR government took place. It is graphically described in *The Third Way* by Heinz Brandt, a man who had been imprisoned by the Nazis but had remained in the CP. After the war, Brandt had become a party official in East Berlin and, because of his criticism of party policy, was once again imprisoned. He noted that some of his jailers were those who had held him under the Nazis. The East Berlin workers who rose up in 1953 had my complete sympathy. Their production norms had been increased without any rise in pay or consultation, so they went on strike. Their action triggered a full-scale revolt against the bureaucratic state system which had bled the GDR almost dry of industrial equipment and made it difficult to develop a modern industry. The East Germans who had survived the Hitler period and who had supported either the KPD (the German CP) or the SPD (the social democratic party) were anxious that the movement should be united. That view was encouraged by the Soviet occupation forces in East Germany. In the West it was the opposite.

In 1946 the KPD and SPD united to form the Socialist Unity Party (SED). However, by 1949, the SED was being transformed into a centralist 'Leninist' party identical to the Soviet CP. As in the Soviet Union, the dictatorship of the party soon became a reality. In 1951, the SED expelled 150,000 members – mostly SPD but also some KPD – who objected to this transformation. After the 1953 uprising the Minister for State Security, Wilhelm Zaisser, and Rudolf Hernstadt (editor-in-chief of *Neues Deutschland*) were pronounced to be too soft and expelled from the party. I had many an argument with CP members about all this at work. At one time, a couple of CP joiners almost came to blows with me. I argued that if we had been construction workers in East Berlin at the time we would have reacted in precisely the same way as the German militants. We would not have stood for being given more work without consultations and extra pay.

The Socialist Educational Group meanwhile had heard that Harry McShane and others in Glasgow had left the CP, so we invited Harry down to meet our group. Those who had left the CP in Glasgow included Eddie Donaldson, Les Foster, Alex Bernstein, Bill Gunn, Bill McCulloch, Hugh Savage and Matt McGinn (who later became well known as a folk-singer and writer). After our meeting with Harry, we agreed to get the various disaffected groups together at a conference in Liverpool. This took place in July 1954. Harry took the chair and I spoke to a lengthy resolution which had been prepared by the Liverpool and Glasgow groups. Even before the Conference in May 1954, the two groups had already produced a newspaper called *Revolt*, the title of which was later changed to *Socialist Revolt*. The paper was given the somewhat grand subtitle, 'The Organ of the Socialist Educational Group, Merseyside and the Clyde Socialist Action Group, Glasgow'. The price for its four pages was 2d.

The Liverpool conference set up the Federation of Marxist Groups which then became the Socialist Workers' Federation (SWF). I decided to join it and, in doing so, gave up my individual Labour Party membership. The Federation became involved in a number of campaigns and in Glasgow co-operated with the ILP in a campaign against conscription. The Clyde branch of the SWF organized a series of John McLean lectures in the Central Halls, Glasgow, during 1955, commencing with Harry McShane as speaker. Harry wrote regularly for *Revolt* and had a considerable impact on its readers.

One SWF activity was reminiscent of my CP days in Hertford. I made a speaker's stand and we used to take it down to the Pier Head on Sunday evenings. I was the main speaker – we attracted some listeners but not many. There was competition from the Catholic Truth Society, the Rationalist Society, and a host of others. We sold *Socialist Revolt* at the Pier Head, but it never had a large sale and it was always a struggle to bring it out. We had to raise cash for every edition. Harry and I did a lot of writing but we were helped by Walter Kendall, I.P. Hughes and some members who had never written before. There were virtually no middle-class people in the SWF. Our membership – it could not have been above 500 at its height – was genuinely working class. Discussion in the group, both at local and national level, was of a very high order. Harry was active on the Glasgow Trades Council and never missed a meeting. He fell foul of some CPers but others in the CP and, in general, the members of the Trades Council, held him in the highest esteem. One of the London groups was led by Tom Cowan and Jack Britz (he later became a national officer of the ETU under the Cannon/Chapple leadership). They were 'Oehlerites', a group based in the USA, who were extremely sectarian.

Walter Kendall's group became part of the SWF but its members remained in the Labour Party. In that sense it was 'entryist' and I was not too happy about this. The Kendall group issued duplicated pamphlets – in particular, those written by Rosa Luxemburg. Walter has remained a friend of mine to this day and wrote a very good book, *The Revolutionary Movement in Britain 1900–21*.

Arising out of internal SWF discussions, contact was made with the ILP. However, the ILP did not want anything to do with us, because it objected to a remark that had been made at the Liverpool conference when somebody had referred to it as 'basically reformist' and 'a corpse'. Wilfred Wigham, the General Secretary of the ILP, made the point: 'We can stand abuse, we have had our share of it, but we will only enter into any closer federation with other organizations as a live revolutionary socialist party or not at all.' The old language of abuse and name-calling dies hard in the socialist movement, and Harry and I were unhappy about what had been said.

The SWF made some interesting contacts abroad. One was André Marty, the veteran French CP leader who had been expelled from the party. *Revolt* published extracts from his book, *The Marty Affair*. In Italy, we made contact with a group in Milan called Azione Comunista. Its leading figures were Giulio (Gino) Seniga and Luciano Raimondo whom Doris and I first met at Alpe D'Huez in the French Alps. We were on holiday there and they drove us at breakneck speed to see André Marty, at the village of Cattlar on the French side of the Pyrenees. I shall never forget that hair-raising drive as long as I live. We talked politics all the way down. Gino and Luciano had both been members of the Italian CP and had fought as partisans against Nazi occupation. Gino had been Secretary to Luigi Longo, a prominent CP leader and ultimately General Secretary of the Italian CP. He was something of a mystery. He had left the CP, taking a lot of money with him which he used for the movement. He was a poor man and lived very modestly, but he was worried for some time about his personal safety and was constantly on the move. I was told he carried a gun.

Through Gino we met such people as Pietro Nenni, Bettino Craxi, Gaetano Arfe, Giorgio Galli, and Ignazio Silone at his home in Rome, where he presented Doris with a copy of his latest book. I attended the 1964 PSI Congress in Milan, with Walter Kendall. There I heard Nenni speak for about three hours. At that congress a split occurred because the PSI and the right-wing Social Democrats (PSDI) were uniting. Basso and other left socialists objected, split from the PSI and formed the Party of Socialist Unity (PSIUP). Given what was happening amongst those of us of the left in Britain, I urged them to be cautious. Lelio Basso was a highly intelligent man and, as far as I could see, a very good socialist.

However, the rank and file delegates were only given access to the platform late in the evening. Their democracy was not as good as ours and I felt ours could stand improvement. Because of the contacts with Gaetano Arfe (editor of *Avanti*) and other journalists, I contributed regularly to the Italian socialist press for a number of years.

Anita, Giulio Seniga's wife, wrote a book about her experiences in the Soviet Union, which I tried unsuccessfully to get published in Britain. Anita's father, a foundry worker, was an Italian communist who had been arrested and imprisoned for years under Mussolini. Through the CP Anita's mother was offered hospitality in the Soviet Union and, believing it to be a workers' paradise, she went, taking Anita with her. For a period she worked in a factory and avoided arrest during the purges by keeping her own counsel and working so hard that she was regarded as a Stakhanovite. Later she became Togliatti's cook and, as he was never arrested, she survived. Anita was in the Komsomol and went to the International Lenin School. When she got back to Italy after the war, she left the CP. What she said about life in the Soviet Union under Stalin made my hair stand on end.

Anita's mother was a charming woman and we once stayed with her for a week in her small flat in Rome. She took us to see *Aida*. It was a marvellous performance with real elephants brought onto the stage. We wanted to buy tickets for the best seats, but she insisted that it would be best at the back in some of the cheaper seats, and she was right. It was an unforgettable evening.

Since meeting Gino, Doris and I have travelled all over Italy. We were in Capri when Togliatti died and we saw the genuine grief on people's faces at our hotel. Craxi, whom we met in Milan when he was the PSI Secretary in that city, has been prime minister as well as leader of the party. I thought him dynamic but too much on the right. It was through Gino that I first became acquainted with Antonio Gramsci's works and ideas. Gino often talked of Gramsci and gave me the paperback editions – about a dozen volumes – of his works. Today the reformists argue that Gramsci was basically one of them. A close study of his work proved to me that this was not the case.

The SWF received plenty of advice from other socialist groups. At one stage we attempted to call a conference of all the various left groups to put our views on the need for a new party of the left. We got absolutely nowhere because the other groups were more keen on recruiting members into their own ranks than discussing the main issue.

In 1953, the Healeyites, as far as I recall, were known as the 'Group' or the 'Club'. In 1959, they produced *News Letter* and created the Socialist Labour League (SLL – later the Workers' Revolutionary Party).

They were then entryists in the Labour Party. The Revolutionary Socialist League of 1953 became Militant in 1964. In 1949 Tony Cliff's group left Socialist Fellowship and in 1962 formed the International Socialists (IS) which published *Socialist Review* and for which I wrote from time to time, as well as writing regularly for *Tribune.*

In 1956, Nikita Khrushchev made his so-called secret speech. It was not published in the Soviet Union, but found its way into the Western press and had a profound effect, not only on British CP members, but on the left in general. Khrushchev revealed that Stalin's regime had murdered 'many thousands of honest and innocent communists'. Those murdered included 70 per cent of the members of the Central Committee elected at the seventeenth Congress of the Party and 1,018 out of the 1,966 delegates at that Congress. He had organized 'the mass deportations from their native places of whole nations, together with all the Communists and Komsomols, without exception'. These crimes were considered to be the result of the 'cult of the personality'. One Soviet journal stated: 'Stalin believed in his own infallibility, began to abuse the Party's trust, and to violate the Leninist principles and norms'. That explanation did not satisfy a great many people in the world communist and socialist movements. What was clear, however, was that Khrushchev had rendered a great service. The movements in Eastern Europe and the Soviet Union, which demanded greater freedom or 'socialism with a human face', emerged at that time.

In the Soviet Union, the anti-Stalin report was read by thousands. It gave great hope that at last things would change. R. Orlova said at a meeting of the Writers' Union: 'The days we are now living through remind me of the days right after October – there is the same mass meeting type of democracy. Everybody wants to speak, those who have long held their tongues – and those who have long spoken nothing but lies.'

Khrushchev's speech intensified the debate in the British CP. Many of my old friends and acquaintances in Liverpool became critics. As the debate went on – and after the Party's Special Congress – they left in droves. That included my doctor and friend, Cyril Taylor, and his brother-in-law, Jerry Dawson. The 'intellectuals' left first, but working-class young people like John Connor and Jimmy Rand followed. In 1956 the membership of the CP in Britain was 33,000, by 1959 nearly 8,000 had left.

On 23 October 1956, political police in Hungary fired on demonstrators and the uprising began. Revolutionary workers' councils took control in many localities. Imre Nagy promised reform. He ended one-party rule by forming a coalition government. The National Trades

Union Council issued a call for workers' councils to introduce workers' management in factories, workshops, mines, offices and so on. However, Soviet tanks smashed the revolution. Janos Kadar set up a new puppet government and on 4 November issued an 'Appeal to the Hungarian People' in the course of which he revealed: 'The Hungarian Revolutionary Workers-Peasants' government, in the interests of our people, working class, and country, requested the command of the Soviet Army to help our nation in smashing the sinister forces of reaction and restoring order and calm in the country.'

The answer to Kadar came in a broadcast by Free Radio Rajk: 'We have very little to say to our Soviet masters. They have convinced not only the whole world, but all communists, that they do not care for communism, that they simply prostituted communism.... to Russian imperialism. We also speak of the traitors.... the Janos Kadars who play the role of colonial governors.... We send them the message that we consider them all traitors to communism.... the sentence has already been pronounced. We Hungarian communists will see to it that the sentence is carried out ...'

We in the SWF were on the side of Nagy, the people and workers of Hungary. It was bitterly disappointing that Khrushchev, the man who had begun the process of destroying Stalinism, was responsible for sending the tanks into Hungary and for kidnapping and executing Imre Nagy, the leader of the CP and head of the Hungarian government.

The Hungarian revolution had had a traumatic effect on the CP. People like Norman Buchan, John Saville, E.P. Thompson, and thousands of others left the party. The atmosphere, debates and agony of the CP in 1956 are described in Doris Lessing's *The Golden Notebook*, a novel based on her own experiences in the party. She describes a visit by her friend 'Molly' to party headquarters to find out what happened to two brothers who had gone to Czechoslovakia and disappeared. She is given very unsatisfactory answers. She asks about the Jews in the Soviet Union but the big chief dismisses her concerns. Molly is so angry that she responds as thousands of party members and supporters were doing then: 'Look, you people have got to understand something pretty soon or you'll have no one left in your party – you've got to learn to tell the truth and stop all this hole-and-corner conspiring and telling lies about things'. Party members increasingly realized that they had been told lies for years, and it was too much to bear. Hyman Levy, a leading Jewish intellectual, after going to the Soviet Union and finding out the truth, came back to Britain, stomped into meetings, told the truth and like many others, left the party.

As the Hungarian revolution took place, the British invaded Egypt to 'protect' the Suez Canal, and to defeat the 'devil' President Nasser. Hugh Gaitskell initially supported government action (as did Michael Foot over the Falklands). As the situation developed, however, Labour came out against the invasion and held a series of 'Law Not War' rallies. Nye Bevan spoke in Trafalgar Square; I spoke at Liverpool University on the same platform as Bessie Braddock. Right-wing students charged the platform with Union Jacks and threw fireworks, threatening to break up a rally organized by the Trades Council on St George's Plateau, where Bessie and I also spoke. Once they saw the dockers and construction workers present with their trade union banners, however, they thought better of it.

The *New Statesman* of 18 November 1956 published a letter which had been refused by the *Daily Worker*. It was signed by fifteen prominent people, including Doris Lessing and Christopher Hill, who stated they were Marxists: 'We feel that the uncritical support given by the EC of the CP to the Soviet action is the undesirable culmination of years of failure to think out political problems for themselves. We had hoped that the revelations made at the Twentieth Congress of the CP of the Soviet Union would have made our leadership and press realize that Marxist ideas will only be acceptable in the British Labour Movement if they arise from the truth about the world we live in.'

I made contact with E.P. Thompson, who was helping to produce the *New Reasoner*, and he came to our house for a discussion. We bought and read the *New Reasoner* and the *Universities and Left Review*. Much of the material they produced we found exciting and relevant but, to most of those involved, we were 'old-fashioned' and too 'workerist' in our attitudes. I have to admit, my personal experience has made me distrust many of the 'intelligentsia'. The charge of being worker-orientated I do not repudiate or apologize for. I am proud of it. The workers produce the wealth of society but they have never received the full fruits of their labour.

The SWF collapsed in 1957 after nearly four years in existence. It had not made a great impact but it had raised the question of whether or not we should work for a new revolutionary socialist party. This is still an important question and has come to the fore again with the rightward swing of the Kinnock leadership of the Labour Party. There really is a dilemma. It is all very well to have political purity but to stand outside meetings selling your journal, instead of being inside, speaking and putting your political point of view, is totally negative. I have been criticized over the years for changing my views on certain issues, sometimes changing them back again under different circumstances, but I have no regrets about the SWF. It was a useful experience and I made good friends in Britain, Europe and elsewhere but, even today, I am not anxious for socialists to be rushing out of the party that the working class created and forming their own separate groups.

NINE

On the March

It is therefore absolutely indispensable for the efficient
training of the working class along correct lines that
action at the ballot box should accompany action in the
workshop.

JAMES CONNOLLY, *Socialism Made Easy*

After the demise of the SWF I applied to re-join the Labour Party. I had
remained an affiliated member by continuing to pay the political levy
and also retained my seat on the EC of the Trades Council. I suppose I
could have been challenged on this but I had not broken any rule. I had
some difficulty, though, and it took two meetings of the Toxteth CLP
before they allowed me to re-join. In the end I was accepted by a large
majority, and I resumed my activity as an individual member. It was not
long before I was elected Chairman of the CLP.

In January 1958 CND was formed. The chairman was Canon Collins
of St Paul's Cathedral. Its first meeting, called and chaired by Kingsley
Martin, editor of the *New Statesman*, was attended by Bertrand Russell,
J.B. Priestley, Ritchie Calder and Jacquetta Hawkes. At a second
meeting it was agreed that CND would support the Easter march from
Trafalgar Square to Aldermaston organized by the Direct Action
Committee against Nuclear Weapons. It was anticipated that a few
hundred people would turn up. In fact, on the day it was more like four
thousand – among them supporters from Liverpool. In 1959 a march
from Aldermaston to Trafalgar Square was promoted by CND. The
organizing genius behind this was Peggy Duff. During that weekend the
numbers on the march were never below five thousand. I could not get
to it but many of my political friends from Liverpool were there. The
Trades Council and most Liverpool CLPs gave full support. I spoke on
many CND platforms in the North West and in Liverpool in particular.
More and more Labour people were drawn in. Many Labour MPs
supported the campaign and Michael Foot was on its Executive
Committee. Frank Cousins, the new General Secretary of the T&GWU,
personally supported unilateral nuclear disarmament, and the campaign

to get the Labour Party to support CND officially was stepped up. During the march, USDAW declared its support and so did the Co-op Party.

In July 1960 the T&GWU officially decided to support CND policy. It was clear that the Labour Party conference that autumn would be very important. CND, however, was divided. The Committee of One Hundred, led by Bertrand Russell, had been formed and had involved itself in direct action. This was unwelcome to many in CND, who wanted to concentrate on winning Labour to the anti-nuclear policy. As Kingsley Martin put it: 'I know of no way of obtaining a non-nuclear Britain except by converting the Labour Party. Unless they work through the Labour movement, nuclear disarmers are simply marching about to satisfy their own consciences and expressing their sense of sin and horror of nuclear war.' I could understand the fears of those concerned but I felt, and still feel, there was room in CND both for direct action and for working to win over Labour.

I was a delegate to Conference from the Toxteth CLP and mandated to support CND policy. I was also vice chairman of the Trades Council. The chairman was Walter Alldritt, who years later became MP for the Scotland division after the death of Bessie Braddock. Walter, as chairman, was automatically the delegate to Conference but decided not to go and, without consulting the Executive Committee, passed his credentials and papers to Jack Braddock, leader of the Labour group on the city council. We on the EC were very angry about this and I called a meeting. We appointed our own delegate and notified the NEC of the Labour Party accordingly. Walter refused to take any notice of our decision but we decided to send our delegate to Conference anyway: I made representations to the Standing Orders Committee on our arrival, arguing that the delegate we had appointed should be accepted. It replied that Braddock's credentials were in order. This was outrageous and undemocratic and I said as much before leaving the Committee. Bessie Braddock was outside and shouted at the top of her voice about Trotskyists and Communists. I am afraid our exchanges became some-what heated. Delegates who were present looked on in astonishment. Later, during the CND debate, Bill Sefton and I intentionally sat behind Jack Braddock to see what he did. When the time came to vote he realized we were there. He voted for the mandate and then cancelled it out by also voting against. We were outraged.

Despite Jack's action the vote for unilateral nuclear disarmament was won. Gaitskell, then made his 'Fight, fight and fight again, to save the party we love' speech. He intended to get the policy reversed the next year and, in the meantime, would stump up and down the country

My grandmother (standing) in the gardens at St Albans.

Mum and Dad on their wedding day.

My first school photograph. I am fourth from right in the second row from the front.

A family holiday in Margate. I am sitting on the sand in front of Mum and Dad.

On leave in Liverpool, age 22.　　　　　　　　Doris, age 17.

Challenging Gaitskell's right to speak in Liverpool, 1960.

Rowing on the River Arno near Florence.

On the march with CND from Warrington to Liverpool, 1960.

Myself, the Braddocks (second from left and far right) and the Gaitskells leaving St George's Hall, Liverpool, 1959.

Harold Wilson, Bessie Braddock and myself in Liverpool.

Campaigning for the bill I introduced to end 'lump' labour on the building sites, 1973.

The Department of Industry team. From the left: Gregor Mackenzie, myself, Tony Benn, Lord Beswick and Michael Meacher, 1974.

On a campaign bus with Pat Phoenix, *Coronation Street*'s Elsie Tanner, in 1980.

Supporting Solidarity at the 1983 Labour Party Conference.

Holding the European Cup with Lord Mayor Hugh Dalton at Speke airport after Liverpool FC's victorious return.

Doris and myself leaving the 1985 Labour Party Conference after I had walked off the platform. Elinor Goodman is just behind us, keeping a customary close eye on the story.

Addressing a *New Socialist* conference in 1982.

speaking and organizing against Conference policy. It was a very deep split. To Dick Taverne, who as MP for Lincoln was later to leave the party, Gaitskell's was the 'most magnificent speech of the decade'. The right wing, in the meantime, formed the Campaign for Democratic Socialism (CDS). Taverne was its treasurer. In *The Future of the Left*, he wrote: 'In the 1940s and 1950s the right-wing union leaders almost automatically supported the Parliamentary leadership with their block votes, much to the consternation of constituency activists. It was hardly democratic, but it made the constitution work because it meant that in practice there was no separation between responsibility and power.'

There is no doubt that, until Cousins and other new trade union leaders were elected, the old guard of trade union leaders had acted in a thoroughly anti-democratic way. Without reference to their delegations, a group of them used to meet in private and decided how to cast their block votes. Frank Cousins broke that mould. He consulted his member-ship and argued democratically for his viewpoint. He was not always successful on every issue but he was like a breath of fresh air.

CDS launched a manifesto. As Taverne put it, 'Spurred on by Tony Crosland, and efficiently organized by Bill Rodgers, it put like-minded supporters in the constituencies in touch with one another and supplied them with arguments and resolutions.... We also sought to organize support for the selection of social democrats as Parliamentary can-didates, again with a considerable measure of success.' What Taverne and his friends wanted was for the party to abandon its socialist basis. Gaitskell was, in essence, their spokesman. After Conference, he came to Liverpool to speak at St George's Hall. The previous evening, when he had spoken in Manchester, a local MP, Will Griffiths, got out of his seat, strode to the platform and interrupted him in a hostile maner. The incident was widely covered in the press. The Liverpool meeting had been called by the Regional Committee and Bessie Braddock was on the platform. As soon as the chairman rose to open the meeting I challenged the right of the region to have a public meeting in Liverpool without consulting the EC or the membership of the Trades Council. The meeting erupted. People shouted out 'Listen to our Liverpool Chairman' and Bessie began to get excited. I realize now that my intervention could be regarded as preventing freedom of speech, but Gaitskell was the leader of the party and he had come to the city to speak against its own policy.

My protest and the attitude of the meeting got plenty of publicity. For the second time in two days Gaitskell had got a rough ride from party members. He had a similar experience in Glasgow when he spoke at the May Day demonstration. All that was very fine, but he and his friends were organizing, while the left was not. We in Liverpool felt that Michael Foot and other supporters of CND, both inside and outside the Labour Party, should have been conducting a great campaign for Conference policy. In his book, *Faith under Fire*, Canon Collins observed, 'if [Labour] had taken the Gaitskell speech at Scarborough more seriously and had worked as hard to ensure a second victory at the 1961 Blackpool conference as the CDS worked to obtain the opposite ... the situation today might be very different'. In 1961, at Labour's Conference, the anti-nuclear decision was overturned. Gaitskell had done his job well.

During this period in Liverpool I became friendly with Peter Sedgwick. He and his wife, Edith, lived off Upper Parliament Street. He seemed slightly out of this world. At the height of the Cuba crisis in 1962, when the USA threatened military action if Russian missiles were not removed from Cuba, Peter said, 'We must have a "Hands off Cuba" demo'. I suggested that this would take time to organize and that it was important to get a good turn-out. He said we didn't have time, the demonstration must take place tomorrow. And it did. About ten people mustered and we ended up walking single file along Lime Street, each carrying a home-made poster displaying the slogan 'Hands off Cuba'. I suppose it was better than nothing.

On the night of the 1959 general election, Peter and Edie came to our house in Avondale Road to watch the results on television. Peter sat in one of our big armchairs and every time there was a Tory gain he would leap from the chair crying 'Oh my God!' and curse Gaitskell's leadership. Peter had left the CP over Hungary and had become active in the International Socialists (IS).

Peter wrote regularly for *Socialist Review* where an argument was raging as to whether or not a new revolutionary party should be formed. Geoff West argued for, and was opposed by P. Mansell. Mansell thought the ILP was wrong to leave the Labour Party in 1932, and that the RCP was wrong to take on an independent existence during the war: 'It is fatally easy for small Marxist groups to keep on seeing and hailing new and false revolutionary dawns.... What must at all costs be avoided is isolation from the mass of workers and the development of their political consciousness.' Peter and I had many arguments on the same theme.

In 1961, Peter became involved in a discussion in *Tribune*'s letter page about Russia's bomb. Earlier, he had supported the Committee of One Hundred but had reservations about its tendency to seek and encourage martyrs in direct action. He thought the Committee should follow the example of Paddy Neary in Liverpool in the 1960s seamen's strike: 'He humbly apologized to the judge for his subversive activities against the bosses – following which he promptly resumed those activities in the National Seamen's Reform Movement.' Peter's advice was that of the anarchist paper *Freedom*, 'Sit down – without illusions.' The correspondence in *Tribune* had arisen when Gerry Healey came out in defence of the Soviet Union having the bomb. Peter however, went straight to the heart of the matter. He attacked the CP and the YCL for participating in CND demonstrations. He pointed out that the *Daily Worker* had accused the first Aldermaston marchers of 'dividing the movement' and added: 'Any unilateralist who tries arguing with CPers over the Russian bomb will soon find that they are quite capable of eloquent exposures of the Western deterrent theory, while arguing that Russia must have the bomb to defend herself against the capitalists.'

Gerry Healey reiterated his support: 'In considering the H-bomb, Marxists make a distinction between the socialist economic basis of the Soviet Union and the capitalist economy of Britain and the United States. We are for disarming the capitalists through the struggle for socialism, but until this is done and a real possibility of international socialism arises, then the Soviet Union cannot give up its H-bomb'. The argument about the 'workers' bomb' was intense inside the Labour Party. Ted Grant's group (today's Militants) supported the idea but the final letter in the *Tribune* series was written by John Daniels and Ken Coates of the Bertrand Russell Peace Foundation: 'whether or not the Soviet H-bombs are healthy or degenerate workers' bombs we think them more likely to lead us into primitive communism than any other sort'.

Peter was critical of all the left-wing minority groups except the IS, whose faults he seemed to be oblivious to. He became a lecturer in politics at the University of York and a member of the editorial board of *International Socialism*. Years later I heard he had split up with Edie and had committed suicide. After I became an MP we had somehow lost touch, but when I knew him he was a great character and a man of real substance.

I was now on the EC of the North West Regional Labour Party (I had defeated Jack Braddock) and in 1962 Gaitskell attended its conference. At lunchtime Gaitskell sought me out and spoke about the party and the next general election. He knew that I had helped wreck his meeting in Liverpool and that I supported CND. He was clearly mending broken fences but I have to admit I was impressed, because he seemed such an honest man. He was against Clause IV and openly said so. He was against CND policy and said so. He was against the Common Market and, at the Annual Conference, also said so. That was preferable to the backdoor methods used to change policy so often seen in the Labour Party, particularly since 1983.

I had chaired the big party rally in Liverpool on the eve of the general election in 1959. Gaitskell had been the main speaker together with the Liverpool and other Merseyside candidates. They all kept to their allotted time, except for David Logan. David had only to move a vote of thanks but was making a real meal of it. I had to get Gaitskell out punctually so that he could be seen live on TV. I had about a minute left, so I turned off his microphone, told the audience the position, and we got out just in time. When we got to the Adelphi, the grandest hotel in Liverpool, someone shouted that it was too posh for a Labour leader. I pointed out that it was nationalized and that it belonged to British Rail.

On the day after the general election I met Harold Wilson by accident in a street in Liverpool. We talked about the election results. He blamed Gaitskell and there was clearly no love lost between the two. Shortly afterwards, I left for the US on a two-month English Speaking Union scholarship to study the US trade union movement but I was very much aware that the attempt by Hugh Gaitskell to carry out wholesale revisionism was a matter of the greatest importance. It was clear that he was not going to dodge a fight; we were in for a rough period in the party. This situation would, of course, be reflected in Liverpool. The meetings of the Trades Council would continue to be as poisonous as ever.

Gaitskell intended to get rid of Clause IV of the Labour Party Constitution. His argument was underlined by Tony Crosland who wrote in *Encounter* in early 1960: 'The Labour Party should have one over-riding aim over the next three years: to adapt itself, without in any way surrendering basic principles, to the realities of social change, and to present itself to the electorate in a mid-twentieth-century guise ... the extremist phraseology of the party's formal aims bears no relation to the moderate practical content of its short-term programme'. Clause IV reads: 'To secure for the workers by hand or by brain and the most equitable distribution thereof that may be possible, upon the basis of the common ownership of the means of production, distribution and exchange, and the best obtainable system of popular administration and control of each industry or service.' Clause IV does not tie the party to any particular form of common ownership; it does, however, mean that common ownership is central to Labour's principles.

Crosland had argued in 1956 in *The Future of Socialism* that ownership of industry was now irrelevant to socialist objectives. The question was not one of ownership but of control. The maintenance of full employment and the abolition of poverty had nothing to do with the question of nationalization; indeed, full employment had been maintained by the Tories. As well as Crosland, Gaitskell and Jenkins put great emphasis on social equality. Labour should be the best defenders of liberal political values. Freedom was the main priority and individual freedom had to be extended. Harold Wilson took up the theme in 1964 in *The Relevance of British Socialism*: 'We believe that no man is truly free who is in economic thraldom, who is the slave of unemployment, or economic insecurity, or the crippling cost of medical treatment, who lacks opportunities in both material and the priceless immaterial scope to a fuller life and the fullest realization of his talents and abilities.'

No one on the left could object to these sentiments. Liberty and individual freedom are an essential component of socialism. However, in counterposing this to common ownership, the Gaitskellites were attempting to effect a transformation of the Labour Party into a moderate Conservative Party. This was not to be. The revisionists had to retreat because the trade unions would not agree to the change. Despite most of them being orientated to the right, their leaders did not go for the anti-Clause IV proposal. Union conference after union conference, and also the 1960 TUC conference, came out in favour of it. Gaitskell was persuaded to drop the amendment he had prepared and Harold Wilson drew up a compromise formula. The left had won a significant victory. We in Liverpool were delighted. That did not mean that we were tied to the old nationalization formula put forward and carried out by Herbert Morrison who was Minister of Transport in the Labour government of 1929–1931. The formula was too bureaucratic and in no way involved the workers in control or management of their industries.

Just after the 1959 election I was one of five trade unionists who visited America for three months on an English Speaking Union scholarship. I had some difficulty obtaining a visa for the USA because I had been a member of the Communist Party. The US Consul in Liverpool insisted that 'some solid citizens' vouch for me. Vic Feather, Deputy General Secretary of the TUC, wrote on my behalf, as did the Principal of the Birkenhead Church of England Theological College where I sometimes gave lectures on trade-union issues. The USA authorities were not just anti-Communist but generally against the left and I concluded I was not really a welcome guest; but, finally, I got my visa.

The trip to the USA was important for me. Whilst there I travelled widely and met representatives of the IWW and many American trade unions including members of the Brotherhood of Carpenters and Joiners and the Longshoremen's Union. I heard John F. Kennedy speak in Pittsburgh and met Harry Bridges and author Eric Hoffer in San Francisco. Those in Liverpool who thought I might be influenced by right-wing ideas in America need not have worried. I came back with a better understanding of the American unions, which generally I found to be less democratic than in Britain, and with an acute sense of the difficulties faced by a working class in a country with only a very limited socialist tradition. I arrived home on Christmas Eve. Doris said she thought I was a changed man, as though I had been to finishing school. I'm sure she exaggerated but America was a valuable experience which certainly increased my self-confidence.

After my return from America, Laura Kirton, secretary of the Walton CLP, pressed me to stand for the council. I have to say I was not keen. The struggle outside on the sites and in the shipyards attracted me more. I was at home negotiating, getting justice for workers at work, addressing meetings and rallies and generally being involved in the wider mass struggle. But Laura and others persisted and eventually I agreed. In those days, as in Liverpool now, there was an almighty struggle between the right and left for the seats. The fiddling that went on in more or less moribund wards in right-wing-dominated constituencies had to be seen to be believed. The numbers of relations and friends who suddenly became party members before selection meetings were legion; it happened particularly in the central areas of the city where membership was low and Labour's vote high. The EC of the Trades Council had a right to attend selection meetings to ensure fair play. I spent too many evenings having to go to such meetings. It was an experience I could have done without.

I was shortlisted for the Pirrie ward, one of the 'safe' Labour seats in the Walton constituency where I had at times helped in council by-elections, although I usually worked either in the Arundel ward or in other parts of the Toxteth constituency. The Dingle area of Toxteth had a strong Orange contingent. Nevertheless, one year in the Princes Park ward, Labour won for the first time. The new councillor was Harry Rimmer, who today is the leader of the Liverpool Labour Group. In those days, believe it or not, he was on the left; it is amazing how people swing from one position to another. In politics, to say that consistency is not the general rule is an understatement.

Prior to the council elections I had a job with the city as a main-tenance worker. For some time I worked at St George's Hall and became the senior shop steward for the ASW. During this time, I was closely involved with the legendary Liverpool working class leader Leo McGree. There were many occasions when I found myself shoulder to shoulder with him. Once, on a May Day march in 1948, there was a move by local Labour leaders to stop the CP joining the procession. Leo was furious; it had never happened before in Liverpool and he wouldn't let it happen then. By sheer willpower and guts he forced the police and the Trades Council officials to agree that we should all march together.

Leo was Chairman of the Mersey District of the Confederation of Shipbuilding and Engineering Unions, also its temporary secretary. In 1951 a national wage increase had been agreed but the Merseyside employers interpreted the agreement in their own way without consulting the confederation locally. At a special meeting the Confederation decided unanimously to operate a strict ban on overtime under the local overtime agreement, until the employers accepted their claim. The press responded furiously, especially the *Daily Express*, saying that McGree was a communist, and that he had sent telegrams to other ports urging the workers to take action. It was all invention. Leo called a press conference to repudiate these stories but only the *Liverpool Echo* reported this.

The EC of the ASW – in those days very right wing – accepted the press version of the events and, at the instigation of the ASW Fulham Branch, decided to take action. They removed Leo from the various positions he held. The charges against Leo were never properly stated and his request for letters and material concerning the issue was ignored. He then appealed to the General Council of the ASW but it upheld the EC by five votes to four. At this stage he went to court. We raised money to help pay his legal costs. Many thought it was wrong to take even right-wing trade union officials to capitalist courts. I could see their point, although I disagreed. The case was heard by Mr Justice Danckwerts who came down in favour of Leo: 'It is difficult to see how it can be in accordance with natural justice to penalize the plaintiff for carrying out the directions to call a mass meeting on the question of banning overtime when he was one of fifty-one members present and unable to vote....' When asked by press reporters outside the court what he thought of British capitalist justice, Leo said, 'In my view, Comrade Danckwerts gave the correct decision'.

In 1962 and again in 1963 there were marches and lobbies of MPs in London against the rising level of unemployment. I was involved, with Leo, in the organization of both of these events and 700 Merseyside workers took the train to London from Liverpool on, appropriately, 5 November 1962. We marched to Parliament demanding work for the 40,000 jobless in the area. Following our highly successful march, a call came from Tyneside urging a mass lobby of Parliament in March 1963: 'Our aim is to make this the biggest demonstration of Trade Unionists seen in Britain since the thirties and we hope to make it the last needed on unemployment.' Liverpool Trades Council was the first to respond. The whole of the Merseyside Labour Movement became involved – the

Confederation, the NFBTO, the CLPs and the CP as well as other groups.

Tens of thousands went from Merseyside and Leo and I addressed the marchers from a wall in a street not far from the Commons. We urged that trouble be avoided – the marchers were restless because of the way they were being treated by the authorities. However, some of the police were provocative, as so often happens, and a few of the lads responded angrily. The marchers lined up to enter the Commons to lobby their MPs but, because of the attitude of the police, and the long wait, in the heavy rain, they got very fed up. At one stage, the police closed the doors to the Commons and a group of demonstrators rushed to the entrance. One climbed above the doorway and hoisted the Red Flag. Then the mounted police charged and, as could be expected, scuffles took place. There were arrests and some Labour MPs demanded an improvement in lobbying facilities. Others, unfortunately, were hostile. One of the lobby-ists was arrested and accused of being in possession of a milk bottle. This, it was said by the mounted police, was an offensive weapon. The man defended himself in court (rather unconvincingly) by saying, 'I was taking the horses a drink'. There is no doubt the lobby was extremely effective. It spotlighted the issue of unemployment and helped mobilize the vote for Labour in 1964.

Leo left office in January 1966 and died just over a year later. It was a great shock to us all. We marched behind his coffin from the Co-op Chapel of Rest in Breck Road (now in the Walton constituency) to the crematorium. The EC of our union did not send a representative but I marched as the ASW-sponsored MP and as a friend and admirer, at the side of John Gollan, the General Secretary of the CP. We were directly behind Leo's wife Hetty and their children. Thousands of workers left the building sites and the shipyards to be there. They either joined the procession or lined the streets, bowing their heads as Gollan quoted: 'It is heartless to deny the sadness caused by death, and the tears that drop in the open grave are tears that sully no courage nor have to manhood anything of shame. Yet, since death must come to all to whom life has come, while it would be cruelty not to sorrow, it would be cowardice to break into despairing and useless repining. Death has no terrors for the enlightened. It may bring regrets at the thought of leaving those we hold dearest on earth, but the consciousness of a well-spent life is all sufficient in the last sad hour of humanity.' Those words affected me deeply.

That evening, I expected the *Liverpool Echo* to carry a big report of the funeral. I saw hardly a word. Yet Leo McGree was a legend on Merseyside. I thought he was wrong in his continued support of the Soviet Union after the 1956 revolution in Hungary but he was a great working-class fighter, courageous, humorous, and intelligent. For example, on the Birkenhead Power Station site the senior stewards went, with Leo, to negotiate with the site manager. For some reason the manager had an Irish shillelagh on his desk. Immediately Leo looked at it and said 'I see you've got your negotiating machinery with you.' That broke the ice, everyone laughed and we came out with a good deal. It was a privilege to have known him and to have been a friend.

After I had been selected for the Pirrie ward I had to leave the Liverpool Corporation job and I managed to get a job with the Mersey Docks and Harbour Board. On the day of the local election in 1960 it rained all day. That was always a bad sign for Labour and we lost a number of seats in the city. I won in the Pirrie ward by a mere fifteen votes.

TEN

Joining the Council

> And he himself must speak though [the mask] saying
> thus ... 'If you think I come hither as a lion, it were a
> pity of my life: no, I am no such thing; I am a man as
> other men are.' And there, indeed, let him name his
> name, and tell them plainly he is Snug the joiner.
>
> WILLIAM SHAKESPEARE, *A Midsummer Night's Dream*

I was elected to the Liverpool City Council in 1960. Most of Pirrie ward
– part of the Walton constituency – was made up of council housing and
was working class to the core. My fellow ward councillors were Hugh
Dalton and Michael Black. Hugh, also a joiner, had been a councillor for
many years, was a member of the ASW, a shop steward on large
contracts and well respected. Michael, an electrician, was in the ETU.
Both were then on the left and it was unlikely that anyone not on the left
would have been selected.

Every trip to my ward meant I had to catch two buses. Nevertheless I
paid regular visits to deal with electors' problems. I also held fortnightly
surgeries with Hugh and Michael and by the 1963 election I had built up
my majority to over 2,500. That helped considerably when I fought the
general election for Walton in October 1964. The greatest problems the
people faced were in housing, employment, and education. At Pirrie
Labour Club, where we used to hold our surgeries, hundreds of people a
month came to see the three of us.

The city council had individual seats for members, with microphones
for each councillor and alderman. I made good use of mine. At the time,
Doris said that I took to being a councillor like a duck to water. I read
and studied the papers very carefully and found myself challenging the
Tories on issue after issue. I also made sure that I regularly had
resolutions down for debate. Right-wing Labour councillors were not
too happy about that, but there was little they could do. Most of the
ward issues I raised were related to wider questions. Sometimes I would
put down resolutions pertaining to national political issues. I was

following the past example of the Braddocks when they were on the left of the party. On one occasion, Bessie had taken a megaphone into the council chamber to ensure that she would be heard.

The leader of the Tory-controlled council was Max Entwistle, a solicitor, always impeccably dressed and, compared to some Tories in the Commons today, a gentleman in the best sense of the word. During the four and a half years before the general election, I was employed by the Mersey Docks and Harbour Board. I was able to get time off work, without pay, to attend the meetings and do my council work. With regard to councillors' expenses, these were much less than I could earn at my trade, but in those days we were on the council on the basis of service to the community and to promote our socialist ideas. We regarded it as a privilege to represent the working people who had elected us.

My mother died just after I had been elected to the council. She was staying with us on holiday and suffered a massive heart attack. She was seventy-nine years of age. Her death upset both Doris and me greatly for she had been a big influence on our lives. Since we had been in Liverpool she had become a great friend of Doris's and the difficult days in Hertford had been well and truly forgotten. She came to stay with us twice a year after we left Hertford, for a month or so each time. The Mersey Docks and Harbour Board gave me a few days' leave to go to Hertford to sort out her affairs.

In those days, the *Liverpool Echo* and the *Liverpool Daily Post* published detailed reports of council meetings. After a full council meeting, the *Echo* carried a complete page of reports. All the main debates were featured with coverage of the main speeches. This helped me to become better known before the general election; Doris used to say that to win Walton, you needed to be as well known in the area as Bessie Braddock.

In July 1960, Liverpool seamen were involved in two strikes. Approximately 200 seamen on the catering staff of the *Carinthia* stopped work in protest at four of their number being logged for minor insolence. The next day the crews of the *Reina del Mar*, the *Apapa* and the *Empress of England* joined the strike. The men formed an unofficial strike committee and sent delegates to Southampton, Hull, Cardiff, Manchester, London and Glasgow. In less than a week there were about 2,000 Liverpool seamen on strike. As a result of the dispute an unofficial national committee of thirty-two delegates from all major ports was set up. This was the first time such a committee had met and it was a harbinger for the future. The stoppage was shortlived, but the rank and file had shown their strength. They were fed up with the way they were treated – by employers and trade-union leaders alike.

Out of the meeting a National Seamen's Reform Movement (NSRM) was created. It wanted improved wages and overtime payments, shipboard representatives, improved facilities for the crew and proper working rates for the deck, engine and catering departments. It also demanded reform of the union. The headquarters of the movement was established at 1, Canning Place, Liverpool. Its chairman was Paddy Neary, its secretary/treasurer Ken Kean, and the national organizers were Barney Flyn and Vic Lilley. The NUS leaders were furious. The General Secretary, Tom Yates, said that the NSRM would not be tolerated: 'I accuse red leaders of threatening the whole structure of command', he fumed. In truth, neither Barney Flynn nor Jim Slater (a newcomer to the Reform Movement) were at any time members of the CP. The NSRM issued a further policy statement amplifying their demands and insisting on no victimization by the shipowners or disciplinary action by the NUS. The seamen again came out on strike. The NSRM had recommended that the men return, but *only* if negotiations went forward satisfactorily. They did not and ships were tied up throughout the country. The situation became serious and a number of the reformers were jailed under the Merchant Shipping Act. Injunctions were taken out against three of the Liverpool men and their names removed from the Merchant Navy Establishment Register. Paddy Neary was later sent to prison at Brixton and became a national hero.

The NUS officials tried to get seamen to return to work and to persuade branch meetings of the NUS to demand a re-opening of negotiations on the issue of a forty-four hour week, the four-pound wage rise and so on. That got nowhere and the Liverpool Trades Council intervened eventually by appointing mediators to sort out the dispute. The mediators were Simon Mahon, the MP for Bootle, Simon Fraser as secretary, and myself as vice-president. I was somewhat unhappy to find myself in the role of mediator but, talking to seamen in Liverpool, it was clearly vital to get a negotiated settlement which would maintain unity and stop victimization.

Our first move was to go to the TUC Conference on the Isle of Man. We travelled by boat and stayed at the conference hotel so that the General Council members and NUS leaders could not avoid us. We met Tom Yates and Jim Scott, the assistant general secretary of the NUS. I found Yates an impossible man to deal with and was not surprised at the mood of the seamen. However, we got a firm understanding from Jim Scott that he would come to Liverpool and address a mass meeting of the seamen under the auspices of the Trades Council. Yates immediately repudiated the proposal. Despite this, the meeting took place at the

Philharmonic Hall. It was a hectic and at times rowdy meeting. At one stage, most of the seamen got up and were about to walk out. It took considerable persuasion on my part, as chairman, to get them to sit down again and allow the meeting to continue. In his speech, Scott made a number of conciliatory suggestions which the men accepted. Unfortunately, the NUS leadership remained committed to the conditions laid down by Yates.

Nevertheless, we persisted and in September at Maritime House, we met six national officials of the NUS together with Bill Hart (who was an ex-seaman and had been jailed in 1947) and two NSRM leaders, Peter Barlow and Ken Kean (who took the place of Paddy Neary who was still in jail). The proposals which emerged were the best we could get in the circumstances: a public declaration of a return to work; permission for branch meetings to be held; official union support against victimization; the recovery of wages owing from before the strike; and a revision of the Merchant Shipping Act. It was agreed to put these proposals before the EC of the NUS, the NSRM and also the employers (who had not been involved in the talks with the mediators).

Simon Mahon and I felt the situation was about to become even more serious and that, unless there was a united return to work, the strike would collapse. That would be disastrous for the rank and file and, in some ports, there was already a drift back to work. I therefore suggested to Simon that we phone the BBC and say that settlement of the strike was now a formality. Simon was not sure. Weren't we taking a chance? I argued that unless we made some kind of statement, it was possible that the NUS leaders would use the opportunity to ensure that the NSRM was totally destroyed. In the end a statement from myself was reported on the BBC's six o'clock news and the NUS officials were denied the room for manoeuvre which would have allowed them to back away from the agreement.

Soon the seamen were all back at work. There remained, however, real local difficulties in some places. Superficially, it seemed as if the seamen had not achieved very much. Time, however, proved the opposite. The real gain was that the basis had been laid for an alternative NUS leadership. There were some in the NSRM who argued for a breakaway union. I strongly opposed that, arguing that they had to remain in the NUS and complete what they had already started.

At the end of the year, Tom Yates retired and his protégé, Jim Scott, was elected general secretary. Liverpool seamen gave him a good vote but he failed to reform the union. In 1962 Scott died and Jim Slater, Paddy Neary and one or two others who had been expelled were allowed back into the NUS. Bill Hogarth became the general secretary. In 1962, the NUS annual meeting finally agreed to the NSRM demand for shipboard representatives. Hogarth said, 'This union which not so long ago projected an image of weakness and dissension and seemed out of touch with the seamen's needs, has become a family again ... It may be that we shall all be forced to take strong action.' This was a reference to the employers' attitude and 'strong action' was indeed taken in 1966. By then I was an MP and played some part in the Commons and on TV on behalf of the seamen. I will return to that later.

Because of my part as mediator, the Dock Board paid my wages in full, as it was delighted that the strike was settled. I refused to take the money, since I had acted only on behalf of the seamen. I think they were surprised. With the strike over, I was pleased to get back to the city council. I was particularly active on the Libraries and Arts committee. Doris and I enjoyed the theatre and good films – especially Italian and French ones. We were members of the Merseyside Film Institute, liked visiting art galleries and reading books on the subject of art and society. I felt, probably because of my Stalinist past, that genuine art should be an essential part of the people's everyday life. I was much influenced by Tolstoy, especially his *What is Art?* I found myself in some conflict with the proposals of the arts director to buy abstract art and in agreement with a correspondent to the *Liverpool Post* who said, 'The public as a whole does not ask for masterpieces: it just wants good paintings which can delight the eye, not pictures which conform to some obscure standard of technical perfection appreciated only by a group of art critics.'

On the arts sub-committee I argued that there should be a special show of working-class art. The exhibition should be a regular event involving those: 'who because they work in industry or have lived in the environment of industry, reflect clearly the life around them, and in this sense marry art genuinely with society'. My view was considered as being too narrowly working-class orientated. I did, however, persuade the committee to agree to have an Industrial Arts Exhibition which took place in 1965 and which I was asked to open and address.

One of the features of art in Liverpool was the John Moores Exhibition. John Moores is well-known as the founder of Littlewoods, the football pools organization; he began life in a terraced house and became fabulously rich. The competition first began in 1957; its aim was to give Merseyside the chance to see a national exhibition of painting and sculpture, embracing the best and most vital contemporary work and to encourage living artists, particularly the young and progressive. I personally did not like all the paintings, but an immense array of talent was brought together. Over the years, such artists as John Bratby, David

Hockney, Sam Walsh and Arthur Ballard were exhibited.

Arthur Ballard had spent some time in Paris in 1957 under a scheme run by the Liverpool Corporation which allowed teachers to study abroad. He is a genuine Liverpudlian, son of a worker and an ex-student of the College of Art (the same college that Stuart Sutcliffe, the 'Fifth Beatle', attended). Arthur strongly supported Liverpool art and objected to the Moores Exhibition because it was too *national.* At Hope Hall one evening he and Arthur Dooley came to blows over the issue of working-class children getting into the college of art. Arthur Dooley argued that the college system favoured too many 'doctors' daughters'. Dooley is also a Liverpudlian and the son of a docker. He had been in the Irish Guards and worked at Dunlop's factory before becoming a self-taught sculptor. I once helped him to organize an exhibition of his work at the House of Commons and he failed to turn up on the day. His beautiful bronze figures for the stations of the cross at St Mary's Roman Catholic church at Leyland are quite wonderful and I never tire of studying them. Arthur called himself a Catholic and a communist, and was obsessed with the question of education. He went to school in Upper Park Street, Toxteth, where there was no art teacher and all the pupils were given by way of 'art' was plasticine and modelling clay.

Another Merseyside artist was Adrian Henri, who was born in Birkenhead. One of his paintings was 'The Entry of Christ into Liverpool'. On the picture it says, 'Adrian Henri, homage to James Ensor 1962–64'; it features himself, Dooley, George Melly, Pete Brown, Charlie Mingus and many others. At the foot of the picture are the words, 'Long Live Socialism'.

Jack Braddock was taken ill at the prizewinners' dinner for the 1963 John Moores Exhibition. He made a very forward-looking speech but as he sat down he slumped over the table. An ambulance was called and Councillor Frank Burke and I went with him to the hospital where the doctor told us he was dead on arrival. When we got back to the dinner, I learned that Bessie had already been contacted at the Commons. The following morning I met her in Dale Street and she said she was glad that I had been with him at the end. I thought that perhaps the hostility she had shown to me and to the left in Liverpool would now be buried with Jack. However, later, when I got to Parliament, she was just as ferocious. Hostility is something I have long learned to live with. I certainly had many political differences with Jack but I had grown to like and respect him. He was a capable person, not looking for personal gain. He lived simply, and was modest and polite.

Jack made one decision that was to exercise a powerful influence on my life. After I had been on the council a couple of years, Labour won a majority and took control. Jack proposed that I chair a new Direct Works Department which would build houses, flats and municipal buildings of all kinds, as well as carry out maintenance. It was a real challenge and I was delighted to accept. The establishment of a Direct Works Department was part of our municipal programme, an initiative which my union had advocated for years. I had often spoken on the subject at municipal policy conferences. Jack obviously believed I would make a success of it.

The first thing I did, after being confirmed as chairman, was to work out a list of things the new department should do. Then I consulted the town clerk. He suggested, of course, that none of it was possible. In the end, I asked him whether my proposals were against the law. He was cautious: 'They are inadvisable'. I ignored this and got down to the job. We established the Works Committee and the next task was to select our director and deputy director. Stephen Stone, who had been the director of the Sunderland Works Department and who had a great success story behind him, became director, and Bert Graham, another North-East man, became his deputy. I discovered later that he was, or had been, an active member of the Labour Party. Stone was a good man. After I went to Parliament and the Tories took over, he was crucified by them and a successful department was brought to its knees. He retired a sick, broken man.

We visited Manchester, Sheffield, Glasgow and other places where successful departments were operating and learned a lot from them. But we also noted their weaknesses. I felt our department should be run as a publicly owned business. We were faced with competition from private enterprise and we had to prove that we were better. But we had overheads which the private sector did not have – the conditions of employment for workers employed by the Direct Works Department were far superior to those of private contractors.

When we took over the maintenance department employed in housing and education, I thought it a good idea to call together all these workers, explain what our plans were and ask for their co-operation. Then I made my big mistake. I suggested that the meeting be held on a Friday afternoon after the men had had lunch and got their pay. They turned up, but some had downed a few bevvies. They were somewhat noisy and at one stage things got a little rowdy. The local press made the most of that. The meeting, however, ended enthusiastically with the workforce pledging its full support.

Examining the maintenance work I realized that changes had to be made. There was no real incentive for the workers and, with their agreement, we introduced a bonus scheme and created workshops out of old

corporation buses which could be driven to the housing estates. We also
adopted a policy of planned maintenance which, in the long run, saved a
great deal of money for the city. Stage by stage we developed a new
building department. Once we got it off the ground we built houses, flats
and all types of municipal buildings. We made good money for the city.

We ensured that our personnel was 100 per cent trade union. There
were shop stewards for all trades, committees on all sections and a
central stewards' body which had negotiating rights (together with the
trade union officials) with the city council. Bernard Levin wrote that,
because of our 100 per cent trade union agreement, I should have a
block of concrete tied around my neck and be dumped into the Mersey.
After I became an MP I saw him at a party and went up to speak to him.
He obviously thought I was going to have a go at him and he shrank
away.

As I go around Liverpool I still see examples of our department's
buildings. They required little maintenance afterwards, something that
could not be said of those built by certain private companies. After I left
the council I fear a deterioration took place and, once the Tories and
Liberals got control, the department was wound up. Public ownership
can be more efficient than private enterprise, if it has the right people in
charge.

It was during these four years on the council that *the planners* arrived
in Liverpool with grand schemes for transforming the city. Like many
others, I was prepared to welcome them. Jack Braddock was not.
Looking back on it, he was right and people like Bill Sefton and myself
were wrong. Bill became Leader after Jack Braddock died and was very
much sold on the ideas of the planners. We had city plan after city plan
put before us. It all seemed very exciting. The bulldozers appeared and
parts of the city were pulled down. The whole place became a construction site. Buildings were demolished but little was put in their place.
In the end, both the Labour and Tory Parties lost support due to the
state of the city and the Liberals became the major party in the city. It
was because of their activities that the city was nicknamed 'toy town'.

Graeme Shankland, a Londoner, was the city's planning consultant
and an ex-communist like myself, a fact that he drew to my attention.
Despite his politics, looking back I feel it would have been better if his
firm had never been employed by the city and Liverpool had re-
developed itself in its own way, based on the desires and feelings of its
own citizens. I continue to believe that civic planning, like art, must arise
out of the life of the people and not be imposed from above.

The Labour Party had defectors from the city council. Vincent Burke,
a dapper young man, joined the Tories. He had been an opponent,

supposedly from the left, of Bessie Braddock, and had given support to those who tried to get her removed as MP. In fact, an Irish member of the Labour Party stood against her in one general election and was expelled from the party for his pains. I remember he issued a leaflet, 'What Mrs Braddock Stands For – Please Turn Over'. The other side was blank.

Some of the characters on the city council are worth recalling. One was Les Hughes, who became Lord Mayor. Les lived in a small terraced house and on his way home from civic functions in the Lord Mayor's car, he would often get his driver to stop at a fish and chip shop near his home where he would buy some for his driver and himself. When Lord Mayors retired they were presented with a portrait of themselves. Les said that his took up almost the whole of one wall in his house.

Whilst I was vice-president of the Trades Council and Labour Party the issue again arose as to whether or not it should be split into two bodies: a Trades Council and a separate Labour Party. Sara Barker, Labour's national agent, was very much in favour, as were some on the TUC. Over the years, we had quite a few rows with the NEC. On one occasion, an enquiry into the Trades Council took place under the chairmanship of Ray Gunter, and the entire EC, right, left and centre were so angry at his attitude that we all stood up to walk out. Anyway, by our efforts, we delayed the break-up which did not take place until later when I was safely out of the way in Parliament. Gunter, in fact, opposed my name for the panel for parliamentary seats and I'm told I only just scraped through to be accepted by the NEC.

It was during the sixties that Liverpool became the city of pop music. According to Bill Harry, the editor of *Mersey Beat*, when he launched the magazine in 1961 there were already 280 beat groups in the city. The Liverpool beat scene was fundamentally working class; Bob Wooler, the disc jockey at the Cavern, was a former railway clerk. Working people appeared to be coming into their own at last. It was their youth who were writing, playing and recording the music you could hear in every club and pub. The *Liverpool Echo* began to give the pop scene prominence in its columns. Bootle had given Gerry and the Pacemakers a civic reception and I suggested that Liverpool did likewise for the Beatles. The town clerk said 'What about security and crowd control?' I admit that I was naive. I thought the Beatles would simply turn up at the town hall and that would be that. I had not anticipated that thousands would turn out in the streets to see them.

The film *A Hard Day's Night* had its premiere in London in July 1964 although many thought that the opening night should have been in Liverpool. Six days later, however, it was shown at the Odeon Cinema,

London Road. We decided to combine the Liverpool premiere of the film with the civic reception. The Beatles arrived from London by plane; from Speke Airport their route was lined with people. The enthusiasm was tremendous. Around the town hall the streets were packed and Doris and I had real difficulty getting there. Inside, the Beatles were mobbed and I saw people old enough to know better behaving like teenagers. In the end, the Beatles had to go up to the Minstrels' Gallery to avoid the crowds and they spoke to us from there.

Ringo Starr was the only Beatle who had not gone to a grammar school. Paul McCartney and George Harrison went to the Liverpool Institute and John Lennon to Quarry Bank High School. They were all, however, from working-class families. Such exceptional talent, from lads whose background was the same as theirs, went right to the hearts of the people of Liverpool. John Lennon, as we are now all aware, had strong anti-war, egalitarian ideas. It is also significant that, on the eve of the 1964 general election, Brian Epstein sent Harold Wilson a message: 'Hope your group is as much a success'. Epstein, it is said, voted Labour all his life.

During the general election campaign I would often sing snatches of Beatles songs such as 'If There's Anything That You Want' from my platform. There is no doubt in my mind that the astounding Merseybeat boom had a big effect on the outcome of the general election. The groups were young, vibrant, new. They were in tune with the desires of the people. They asserted working-class values, they looked to the future. I believe they made a powerful contribution to Labour's victory without recognizing it.

In 1964, I was again elected as president of the Trades Council and I chaired the great Eve of Poll Rally at St George's Hall where Harold Wilson was the main speaker as leader of the party. The next day was the beginning of a new chapter in my life.

ELEVEN

Adopted Liverpudlian

A representative person is one who will act in a given
situation in much the same way as those he represents
would act in that same situation. In short, he must be of
their kind. They may not know the facts as he knows
them. Indeed, they cannot expect to do so. In our
complicated society there must be division of labour,
but that division will operate in an atmosphere of
confidence only if those working it are of like mind.
Thus a political party which begins to pick its personnel
from unrepresentative types is in for trouble.
Confidence declines.

ANEURIN BEVAN, *In Place of Fear*

I was selected as Labour candidate for Walton in 1963. The shortlist
comprised Hugh Dalton, chairman of Walton CLP, George McCartney,
the candidate in 1959, John Hamilton, treasurer of the Trades Council,
and myself. I wrote a speech and, before leaving for the meeting, read it
to Doris. She suggested I put it on the fire – it didn't sound 'natural'. I
did. As I left the house, she said, 'Do your best and don't forget, be a
good loser and congratulate whoever wins'. We were both certain Hugh
Dalton would be selected.

At the meeting I was asked by Dick Crawshaw, later MP for Toxteth,
and a delegate to the CLP, whether I believed in God. I replied that
during the war in one camp hut the airman in the adjoining bed was a
member of the Salvation Army. Every night he went down on his knees
to pray. Many of those in the hut, with their religions displayed on their
cards at the foot of their beds, (I had 'atheist' on mine), would jeer and
throw boots. I always protested. The man was sincere. 'All I would want
from the CLP is to be treated as I treated that airman.' I am told that
clinched my selection and on the first vote I received more votes than all
the others combined.

The election could take place at any time in the next eighteen months
to two years. Our voluntary secretary/agent, Laura Kirton, rightly felt

that we had to strengthen our organization to win the arguments for Labour and so we began a process of regular propaganda. She was, and is, a very good agent. She used her van as a travelling office and in the evenings and at weekends toured the constituency, canvassing and giving out leaflets. I issued regular press releases and was able to get good publicity because I was also a councillor in the constituency. My press agent was journalist Bernard Falk. He was part of a PR organization working for the Labour Party and was a dynamic young man, full of energy and ideas. At first, he wanted me to participate in gimmicks but, after I protested, he concentrated on getting sound political coverage. Later Bernard worked for the BBC on radio and television and served a short time in jail in Northern Ireland for refusing to disclose his sources. He was a typical Liverpudlian, humorous and decent, and his death was a great blow both to us personally and to journalism.

The sitting MP was Sir Kenneth Thompson with a majority of 5,034. He was a Conservative and a Unionist (his house was named Boyne Lodge). Today he would be called a 'Tory Wet'. It was thought that the other Liverpool seats could be won but that Walton would be more difficult. Laura Kirton designed an excellent poster which was colourful, eye-catching and most effective. All our election material was very professional and on election day every party member and supporter worked consistently from dawn to dusk. I had learned to drive in time for the election, having bought a Ford Cortina from Cyril Taylor, my doctor. I used it all day taking people to the polls, getting Labour's message across through the loudspeaker and running errands. I was a real menace on the road. I honestly believe that the licence should be provisional for a further year after passing the driving test. As I drove to the count and pulled in, I bumped the car in front. The driver was furious. He got out, then recognized me and said, 'My God, and to think I voted for you.'

During the campaign I visited just about every street in the constituency. A group of (mainly women) supporters would give out leaflets while I spoke over the loudspeaker and took questions. It was a most effective way of getting our policies across. We did that in every election from 1964 onwards. We also had huge wall posters which could cover the end wall of a terrace. We asked a man who lived in a house at a crossroads for permission to put one up. He agreed. His wife, who was a Tory supporter, had also agreed that the Tories could use the wall. We put up our poster. The Tories covered ours with one of theirs. We returned and put up another one of ours. They tried to cover ours again but, by then, we had stationed supporters at the site and won the battle. Passengers on buses must have thought they were seeing things.

Before the count, my agent said to me privately, 'We have won, we shall have a majority of about 2,500.' We actually had 2,906. It was a moment to savour. We received more than 50 per cent of the votes cast. Labour also won Toxteth, Kirkdale and West Derby. Four seats – the size of Labour's majority in the Commons.

The original Walton constituency was formed in 1885. It did not then include the township of Walton-on-the-Hill and virtually encircled Liverpool city, taking in West Derby and Toxteth. It had an electorate of 7,683. Today, after the latest boundary changes, Walton includes some of the oldest parts of the inner city. Prior to 1983, the electorate was approximately 52,000. It is now 73,532 and the intended redistribution of the electorate to even up the constituencies has clearly gone awry. Although it includes a very small section of Aintree Race Course, there are few salubrious residential areas. After 1983, the Labour city council built a sports centre close to Walton Park which attracts unemployed youth in great numbers. It is a serious attempt to offer a real alternative to petty crime, drugs and alcohol.

Walton's first MP was a Conservative, J.C. Gibson. He represented the constituency until he became an Irish Judge in 1888. The next five MPs were all Tories and the Conservatives were not defeated until 1945 when Walton was won by Labour. The most famous of them all was the brilliant but reactionary F.E. Smith. Known locally as 'Frothy Fred', he fought strenuously against the Liberal government's Trade Union Bill of 1906. He was born in Birkenhead, educated at Birkenhead School and Wadham College, Oxford and became Lord Chancellor and Baron Birkenhead. From 1928 until his death in 1930 he was a director of Tate & Lyle.

F.E. Smith's support was basically from the Protestant electorate for he was a strong Unionist. When I first stood for Parliament in 1964, small pockets of Protestant Unionism still existed. I remember going to one house and a very old lady came to the door, saying she did not vote Papist. I said I was Labour and she slammed the door, saying, 'That's what I mean, I don't vote Papist.' Even in 1970 when I was speaking in the street using the loudspeaker, a man came to his door, shouting out that he intended to vote Protestant. I pointed out that my Conservative opponent was Jewish, that I was an Anglican, so I was not sure what he should do. He slammed the door.

Can Walton be described as beautiful? Taking it as a whole, the answer must be no – except for its people. There is a fierce pride in being a Liverpudlian, but to be a Waltonian is even better. Walton was a thriving town with its own town hall long before Liverpool was in existence. It was a separate entity until 1895, when it was finally incorporated into the city of Liverpool. Walton is mentioned in the

Domesday Book as part of the West Derby Hundred. In the parish church of St Mary's Walton-on-the-Hill, there is an old Saxon font which is perhaps the oldest relic of Walton, and opposite the church there still remains the ancient seal of Walton, a figure with the church in the background.

Liverpool was actually part of the parish of Walton at one time. Marriages and funerals took place there and tithes were paid to the rector of Walton. It began to develop slowly as a port and in the 1640 English revolution, it sided with Parliament against the King. Liverpool was one of the places used by Cromwell and his troops to embark on the shameful subjection of Ireland; an event which still rankles with thousands of Liverpudlians because of their Irish origins. Walton has both Everton and Liverpool football grounds within its boundaries. They are almost cheek by jowl in an area where, at one time, sectarian politics were very strong. It also has a very large overcrowded prison which overlooks Walton Park Cemetery where James Carling (1857–1887), who was a Liverpool Irish artist and the writer Robert Tressell (1870–1911) are buried. Carling was the illustrator of Edgar Allan Poe, and as a seven-year-old pavement artist was arrested in Lime Street and given a six-year sentence for begging in 1866. He died in the Brownlow Hill Workhouse and now lies in a pauper's grave. Robert Noonan, a fine sign-writer and house-painter, wrote *The Ragged-Trousered Philanthropists* under the name of Robert Tressell. In 1977, a stone was laid on Noonan's grave and trade unionists, including a large contingent of construction workers, held a memorable meeting and march to commemorate his memory. Engraved on the stone are the words of William Morris:

> Through squalid life they laboured
> In sordid grief they died.
> These sons of a mighty mother
> These proofs of England's pride,
> They are gone. There is none
> Can undo it, nor save our souls
> From the curse
> But many a million cometh
> And shall they be better or worse?
> It is we must answer and listen
> And open wide the door
> For the rich man's hurrying terror
> And the slow foot hope of the poor.

Also engraved on the stone are the names of the twelve other paupers

111

buried in that same grave. Noonan was on his way from Liverpool to Canada, but died of TB in one of the Liverpool workhouses. Today at the entrance to the now closed cemetery, there is a Robert Noonan Museum.

Over the years Walton has produced many prominent political figures. Jack Jones, Secretary of the T&GWU who fought in the International Brigade in Spain, was once a Labour councillor in the Walton constituency, as was Bob Edwards, MP. Bob also fought in Spain – he was a member of the ILP contingent in the POUM Militia and friendly with George Orwell.

Walton, like every other constituency in Liverpool, has been badly affected by the decline of the port. Nevertheless, many of the slums in the area have been pulled down. Walton now has some new housing estates a little like those in television's *Brookside*. Some have excellent views overlooking the Mersey where, on a clear day, you can see the Welsh hills. Since 1983, the Liverpool Labour council has done a good job, even if serious problems remain.

My Liverpool colleagues who had won seats for the first time were Eric Ogden (West Derby), James Dunn (Kirkdale), and Richard Crawshaw (Toxteth). Years later, they all defected to the SDP, and subsequently lost their seats to Labour. The day after the election I was interviewed by national television, appearing in programmes with Roy Hattersley, who had been chairman of the Direct Works Department in Sheffield. I remember we were both referred to as 'up and coming – people to watch'.

My attitude to the Parliament I was about to enter has not substantially changed to the present day. I never regarded the parliamentary road to socialism as the *only* route, but equally had never rejected the idea that socialists should participate in Parliament. I accepted the view that Parliament should be a platform for socialist ideas but I was less certain that a Labour government could bring about a fundamental change in our society. Although Labour had ensured the working class benefited from legislation, what it had not done was destroy the power and influence of the capitalist class. Britain under Labour was as much a class society as under the Tories. It was also true that the power of the working-class movement could wring concessions from Tory as well as from Labour governments.

But, like it or not, the only serious way forward was through the Labour Party. The mass of workers considered Labour as their party. Their unions created it and it represented them. Also it had built the NHS and created the welfare state. Its MPs had a good percentage of working-class people in the ranks. Most people believed that if socialist advance was to be achieved only Labour could do it. Personally, I had few illusions – even about the Bevanite left. Some of them were too Stalinist orientated and others, even to the left of Bevan, were for socialism from above. This was also the general view of the Labour government. But I could not see any way to advance socialist ideas except through the Labour Party. That did not mean that I had rejected my basic socialist views. I would fight hard for socialism in Parliament. But I believed that strikes, demonstrations and extra-parliamentary activity were also essential if we were ever to get it. In that mood and with those ideas, I entered Parliament determined to do all I could to protect and develop the interests of my constituents. They had received a bad deal under the Tories and deserved full employment, decent homes, a good education, security of employment and more rights.

After the seat had been won, Doris and I discovered that I would not receive an allowance to employ a secretary. Doris gave up her job at Sefton General Hospital (she was deputy supervisor of the medical office) to work with me without pay. We were doing two jobs for one salary and we then discovered there were no allowances for living accommodation in London. For four weeks we were able to stay with my old aunt Em in Fulham Road, and then we managed to get a rather grotty furnished flat in a Pimlico basement for seven pounds seven shillings a week.

Once established at the Commons we found we had to pay for every postage stamp and for all telephone calls to Liverpool. The amount of stationery we received was also limited and we had to pay for any excess. I was given vouchers for train or air journeys between Liverpool and London and, if I used the car, a car allowance. There were, however, no vouchers for my secretary. When I claimed tax relief for this it was refused on the grounds that I could get a secretary in London. That I could not afford to pay anyone in London and that my wife had given up her job to do the work for nothing cut no ice. In fact, we had a difficult time financially and even when the salary was later increased things remained fairly difficult. We lived at a lower level than when in Liverpool. We had two homes to maintain and not enough money to meet all our overheads. In order to save the train fares for Doris I usually drove down to London on Monday mornings and back to Liverpool on Friday afternoons. Once we had a serious accident on the M6 when the car turned over in a snow storm. We were lucky not have have been injured or killed. The police got us to Stafford railway station and we picked up the London train from there. Simon Mahon, Labour MP for Bootle, was on the train and he looked after us as we were badly shaken. He was a kind, decent man.

I literally entered the House of Commons with Norman Buchan; we walked up the steps and through the corridors together. Like myself, he had once been in the CP and knew Harry McShane well. We talked at some length and became close friends. He became a minister of state in the Scottish Office, then in Agriculture, and resigned on a matter of principle. In opposition, during Neil Kinnock's leadership, he was spokesman on the arts and wrote an excellent policy document. He was subsequently sacked after he had the temerity to disagree with Kinnock. Norman was one of the founder members of the Tribune group and his widow, Janey, is an MEP. One of the best speeches I have ever heard was her report to a Labour Party Conference of a trip she had made with fellow MEPs to investigate the situation in South Africa.

I spoke in the House on the first day. By that I mean I interrupted a Tory MP who was speaking and put a question to him. I made my maiden speech on the second day. I concentrated on the plight of areas like Merseyside with high levels of unemployment and urged my government to do everything possible to create new industries in such areas. No punches were pulled and I did not follow the convention of making a non-controversial speech. I attacked the Tories with gusto and urged our people to carry out socialist policies.

I threw myself into the life of the House. I did not feel overawed but felt, as Nye Bevan did, that I was entering a great church. I think it was George Brown who said the House of Commons was like a monastery with a few nuns about. I already knew some of the left MPs because we had met at conferences. I knew Harold Wilson, and Bessie Braddock had introduced me to Jim Callaghan, but people like Roy Jenkins, Tony Crosland, Tony Benn and Dick Crossman were part of the distant landscape. The Tribune group was formed early on in the session. There was a discussion at the first meeting as to what the group should be called and I think it was me who suggested the name Tribune. The group contained Michael Foot, Ian Mikardo, Sydney Silverman, Konni Zilliacus, Emrys Hughes, Leslie Hale, Will Griffiths, Lena Jaeger, Tom Driberg, Julius Silverman and Frank Allaun, as well as new members like Stan Orme, Norman Buchan and Norman Atkinson whose wife, Irene, was our excellent unpaid secretary.

Prior to the election Stan Orme and Norman Atkinson and their wives, the two Irenes, had come to our house for dinner. Both had inherited good safe Labour seats and were already discussing what they would do in Parliament. As it worked out, all three of us were elected and we all joined the Tribune group together. We worked closely as an effective team for many years. Stan became a cabinet minister and chair of the PLP and Norman went on to become national treasurer of the

Labour Party. I was sorry when he was de-selected by the Tottenham CLP. I had heated arguments with some of the black section comrades as he had such a good record.

It was clear that the left in Parliament did not intend to play a passive role and was determined that the manifesto be implemented. We recognized that with a majority of four this would be difficult and that the right of the party would drag its feet on the more socialist policies. Labour's manifesto had called for 'A new Britain – mobilizing the resources of technology under a national plan; harnessing our national wealth in brains, our genius for scientific invention and medical discovery; reversing the decline of the thirteen wasted years; affording a new opportunity to equal, and if possible, surpass, the soaring progress of other Western powers while Tory Britain has moved sideways, backward but seldom forward.' The manifesto also demanded full employment, a sensible distribution of industry throughout the country, an end to chaos in transport and a brake on rising prices. Much of it was mere words, but it contained the concept of a national plan and, to us, that meant democratic socialist planning.

Under the national plan Labour would set up a Ministry of Economic Affairs. Each industry would be expected to have its own plan and public ownership would make a vital contribution. The railway workshops would be free to seek export markets and the National Coal Board would be able to manufacture any equipment it needed. The steel and water industries would be taken fully into public ownership. New hi-tech industries would be established and developed either by public enterprise or in partnership with private industry. A Ministry of Technology would be established. Plans would be drawn up for the regions, for transport, for training and mobility of labour, and for tax reform. There were also targets for stable prices and growth of incomes, and for the modernization of the social services. Land for building would be made available by public acquisition. There would be lower interest rates, and greater support for owner-occupiers by providing 100-per-cent mortgages. Labour would repeal the Rent Act and restore security of tenure to tenants. It would carry out a new programme of modernization of houses, increase the building of new houses, both for rent and for sale, and improve the health service. There would be a new role for Britain in the world. Labour would end colonialism and improve prospects for peace.

Unfortunately the Labour cabinet charged with carrying out this programme was, with the notable exception of Barbara Castle, drawn from the ranks of the centre and the right of the party. One of the first big arguments between the government and the left took place over the

115

issue of social security benefits. We were told that increases were to be delayed until March 1965 because records were not computerized. Some of us refused to accept that argument, believing it to be an excuse. Meanwhile it was proposed that MPs' salaries be raised from £1,750 to £3,250. Although the increase was probably justified, it was still an embarrassment as it was to take effect at the same time as old age pensions were pegged. Protests grew at the failure to increase pensions immediately but Harold Wilson refused to meet a delegation of back-benchers. When the issue came up in the House the Liberals put down an amendment to bring forward the increases. Michael Foot, Ian Mikardo and John Mendelson spoke in support of the amendment which, however, was not put to the vote. What I did not know then was that Michael Foot had assured Ted Short, the Chief Whip, that, although he and his colleagues would stir it up, they had no intention of voting for the amendment. Short noted that NEC elections were soon to take place.

Liverpool OAPs came to London to lobby for their pension increase to be brought forward. When I met them, one of them said, 'It's all right for you, Mr Heffer, living in the lap of luxury'. I felt like taking the pensioners round to see our Pimlico flat, but they were right and the government was wrong.

Meanwhile there were severe problems with the economy. The balance of payments deficit by the end of the financial year would be £800 million (in those days an enormous figure) and the Bank of England had to support the pound constantly. The government imposed a 15 per cent surcharge on imports in October and the press reported a sick economy for which Labour was to blame. EFTA countries were angry at the surcharge. The government was pressed by the City and the Tories to carry out a policy of substantial deflation. This was rejected but the bank rate was increased by 2 per cent. The governor of the Bank of England urged that all proposals which were controversial, including the capital gains tax and the corporation tax changes, should be dropped. Speculation grew to fantastic proportions. Harold Wilson wrote, in his book *The Labour Government 1964–70*, 'It was hard to feel in our position that there was not a great deal of political malice ... behind some of this advice ... Strikes against the national interest are always to be condemned, strikes of capital are no less, and in certain circumstances are infinitely more, damaging.' I believe there was a deliberate run on the pound. The object was to destroy us at the outset. I have long held the view that the first act of a Labour government must be to bring in enabling legislation to control capital, the banks and the sabotaging of the economy. The Tories brought in legislation to control and weaken the unions, Labour should be prepared to do the same to its financial enemies.

At the height of the economic crisis Jim Callaghan addressed the FLP economic group and outlined the government's response. It was a well-attended meeting. I asked why we did not also devalue the pound. There was a stunned silence; then Callaghan said, 'We don't talk about such matters.' I felt as if I had stood up in church and shouted during the prayer of consecration. When we filed out of the meeting I was treated like a silly little boy. My reason for asking was that I had read that, when Labour ministers had faced the economic crisis of 1931, they really did not know what to do. Afterwards they admitted that they could have taken other action, but no one had suggested alternatives. I had hoped Labour had got beyond that stage.

The Labour Party annual conference was at Brighton in December. I drove down with Emrys Hughes, Tam Dalyell, Doris and another MP whose name escapes me. There was a thick fog and I spent most of the journey with my head out of the window. Emrys didn't help by saying, 'Be careful, you have the government's majority in here.' At the conference Harold Wilson had to deal with arguments about the old age pensions. Although it had not been announced he had come up with the idea of a four-pound Christmas bonus to all of those on National Assistance and, at the same time, sanctioned the biggest increase in National Assistance scales ever known.

In the Queen's Speech it had been made clear that the government intended to nationalize steel. Fred Lee, Minister of Power, produced a White Paper outlining the proposals. It came before the Commons for approval in May 1965. Two right-wing Labour MPs opposed it, Desmond Donnelly and Woodrow Wyatt. George Brown wound up for the government. Wyatt only voted for the White Paper because of an assurance from Brown that he would listen to proposals from the industry for less than 100 per cent control by the government. Donnelly and Wyatt were not the only Labour opponents. Fred Bellinger and some other ex-ministers were campaigning against the White Paper and, according to Ted Short, a cabinet minister and a minister of state in the government were also involved. The alarm bells went off for us on the left of the party. Because of the difficulty in getting the Steel Bill through, Harold Wilson finally decided to wait until after the next general election. It could not be long in coming and a bigger majority would ease the bill into the statute book.

The weekend before the vote, I had made a speech saying we must keep to our policy. During the vote George Brown approached me and got hold of my jacket lapels, saying that it was 'either him or me'. I tried to ignore him but he was persistent; 'tired and emotional' I think the phrase is. I told him to get his hands off me or he would soon be on the floor. It was turning nasty. At that moment I was literally lifted away by Norman Buchan and Sir Geoffrey de Freitas. They had each put a hand under my elbows and raised me. Norman Buchan, a slight figure, could never quite believe it happened. It did and trouble was avoided. After the vote I complained to the Chief Whip. Ted Short was sympathetic, saying that we all had our crosses to bear and that George Brown was one of his.

One of the great victories for progress between 1964 and 1966 was the bill to abolish hanging. The sponsor was Sydney Silverman, the left-wing MP who was born in Liverpool. During the First World War he joined the No-Conscription Fellowship. He became a conscientious objector, refused to serve in the army, was arrested and fined five pounds which he refused to pay. He ended up in Preston jail. A solicitor, Sydney was a great friend of the Braddocks during their left-wing days and defended Jack when he was jailed in 1932. It was his idea that Jack, who was in Walton Prison, should stand again for the Everton ward. Braddock's election address was framed in such a way that it argued his case for appeal. The electors responded by giving him a majority of 2,200 and he was duly released on the basis of mistaken identity.

After campaigning ceaselessly against hanging Sydney moved the second reading of the Abolition of the Death Penalty Bill in December 1964. There was a free vote and it was carried by 355 votes to 170. When Sydney was once asked why he was so passionate an opponent of capital punishment, he said: 'When I was a young man I read in a news-paper a story about another young man. He had, in a moment of emotional despair, shot and killed the girl he was in love with and with whom he had quarrelled so that his world had crashed about his ears ... So he shot himself but he did not die ...' After the medical authorities had got him well again, 'They took him out and hanged him, artificial eye and all. I thought that was horrible. It was perfectly legal. He was guilty .... It was my first experience of that cold, remorseless, inexorable logical savagery of legal thinking and I have never forgotten it. It seemed so hopelessly uncivilized.' Sydney's bill remains on the statute book to this day.

In December 1964 George Brown managed to get employers, the TUC and government to sign a 'Declaration of Intent on Productivity, Prices and Incomes'. Subsequently there was talk that a bill was being considered which would include compulsion in the fixing of prices and incomes. That was not acceptable to the left and it was decided to send a delegation to see Ted Short. Ian Mikardo, Stan Orme and myself warned

that we would oppose statutory powers. The government did not go
ahead with such a policy until after the 1966 General Election. Ted
Short does not record our meeting in his memoirs.

Between October 1964 and the 1966 General Election, we new MPs
were slowly finding our feet. We learned how to use the place from such
parliamentary procedure experts as Sydney Silverman, Emrys Hughes
and John Mendelson. We also learned how to make speeches which
people would listen to and had the examples of Michael Foot, Ian
Mikardo and Konni Zilliacus before us. Meantime, we agonized on issue
after issue. How could we stay true to socialist principles yet not bring
the government down? We did speak out on Vietnam. The Tribune
group was opposed to the Vietnam war – some of us wanted a Vietcong
victory, whilst others demanded peace. We were united, however, on the
need to oppose US policy. The US had bombed North Vietnam because
in February 1965 the Vietcong-North Vietnam forces attacked an
American airfield at Pleiku. It was clear that the US wanted the Labour
government to support its policy. In *The Labour Government 1964–70*,
Harold Wilson notes, 'George Thomson, the Minister of State at the
Foreign Office, with strong Foreign Office pressure behind him, tried to
get me to take a much more committed pro-American line on bombing
in Vietnam. I refused.' Harold makes it clear that the Americans were
obdurate in their refusal to negotiate, but defends Michael Stewart, the
Foreign Secretary, saying that his critics 'were wrong in their mis-
interpretation of what he was seeking'. Harold said that Michael had
made untiring efforts to obtain negotiations. I do not go along with that.
Michael Stewart lined us up in support of US policy. It would have been
worse had Harold given the US material support as well.

Ted Short admits the most troublesome problem he had from backbenchers was over the Vietnam war and that, although the government
was nominally neutral, it was, in fact, pro-American: 'Our reliance on
United States support for sterling forced us to refrain from any overt
criticism.' Sydney Silverman put down an Early Day Motion protesting
against the war which received fifty signatures. Zilliacus got signatures
on a telegram of protest to President Johnson. Harold Wilson said that it
was now a war by North Vietnam on the South, and that the US would
only withdraw their forces if the North stopped aggression. That reply
infuriated us. From then on we never gave up on the issue. We
constantly bombarded ministers with questions, sent delegations to the
US Embassy, put down Early Day Motions and spoke against Labour
government support for the US, all over the country. Some said that we
should not have done this as it would spoil our chances of re-election.
Such suggestions we brushed aside. The issues were too important and

we were not prepared to accept what ministers were saying. Looking back on it, Harold played a very clever game. On the one hand, the government gave verbal support to President Johnson; on the other, it took great care not to get more involved and constantly called for nego-tiations between the two sides. The prime minister sent Harold Davies to the area to mediate. Without qualification, I was on the side of the North Vietnamese; they had a right to their independence and as a socialist I had to support them.

Meantime, to my surprise, I had been nominated for the delegation to the Council of Europe and the Western European Union. The Council of Europe met in Strasbourg and the WEU in Paris. In those days the delegation was appointed, not elected, and was a cross-party selection from the Commons and the Lords. The Whips had a considerable say. With some misgivings I accepted. The other Labour delegates included Bob Edwards, Maurice Edelman and Renée Short. I had corresponded with Bob Edwards long before I was in Parliament. He advocated a United Socialist States of Europe – a position I supported myself. He did not join the Labour Party until after the Second World War and for years had stuck with the ILP, fighting a number of Parliamentary seats on its behalf. I also knew Renée Short. She was a Tribune left-winger and had contacted me when she was seeking a Parliamentary seat. Maurice Edelman was an historian and a novelist of some distinction. Whenever I wrote anything, he always gave me encouragement even if he disagreed. At the end of the war he had been on the left but, like so many over the years, had moved rightwards.

At home we were edging towards the 1966 general election. It was obvious that little could be done with such a shaky majority. Right-wingers were obstructing manifesto policies and left-wingers were obstructing legislation – like a statutory prices and incomes policy – which was not in the manifesto. I was quite convinced that Labour would win the election, providing we kept to our policies. Reinforcement for this view was provided in January 1966 when we won the Hull North by-election with an increased majority. During the election campaign in Liverpool we put up a tremendous fight. We increased our majority to over 5,000 in Walton and it was a clear sign that we would have a safe Labour government. The final result showed forty-nine gains and one loss (to the Liberals); our overall majority was ninety-seven. When we got back to the Commons there was nothing to prevent our legislative programme from being carried through except those on the right who were determined to make sure that socialist policies would not be accepted. The left would no longer be fighting the Tories but the forces of reaction within our own party.

120

TWELVE

'Huyton Man'

Whenever the Labour Party has made a mistake, it has
not been in consequence of pursuing its principles too
roughly or too far, but by making too many concessions
to coventional opinion.

ANEURIN BEVAN, *In Place of Fear*

The left's first serious clash with the government in the new Parliament
concerned the issue of the seamen's strike.

After discussions with the TUC and employers' organizations,
George Brown had established a National Board for Prices and Incomes.
The government proposed that the norm for wages and prices – with the
emphasis on wages – should be no more than $3\frac{1}{2}$ per cent. Because of
poor wages and conditions endured in the past, the National Union of
Seamen had demanded an increase of £60 a month and a forty-hour
week. The employers countered by offering 3 per cent – a figure lower
even than the government's norm. This was rejected by the NUS. The
employers then proposed that a forty-hour week (both at sea and in
port) should be implemented over three years. Overtime would be paid
for Saturdays and Sundays whilst at sea.

The NUS negotiators recommended the offer to the executive
committee (now expanded to include rank and file delegates). They
were not impressed and the package was turned down unanimously;
they knew what they wanted and knew that the employers could afford
to meet their demands. In consequence, seamen were advised not to sign
the Articles of Agreement on or after 16 May 1966. It was clear that, as
British ships returned to their ports, they would tie up and union
members would strike.

Harold Wilson and Ray Gunter reacted with horror. Gunter proposed
that the employers' offer be accepted. He urged the strike be called off
and he promised a full-scale enquiry into the shipping industry if that
happened. The NUS rejected Gunter's proposal and the strike began on
16 May. Harold Wilson went on television and said that whilst he had

sympathy with the seamen the NUS's demand would breach the dyke of the incomes policy: 'This is a strike against the state, against the community. . . .' In my view that was a very stupid thing to have said. The seamen were unmoved and within three days 410 ships were tied up and 11,885 NUS members were on strike. By the end of May 891 ships were tied up and 26,000 members were on strike. It was a great show of unity and trade union strength.

On 22 May the government declared a state of emergency and Ray Gunter announced a court of inquiry with Lord Pearson as chairman. It proposed a forty-hour week over two years, and thirty-nine days' leave against the thirty-six proposed by the employers. The NUS wanted a forty-hour week immediately. Under pressure from the government the TUC advised its members not to take sympathetic action. Meetings were held between Harold Wilson and trade union leaders, and in the Commons on 20 June, he said: '. . . a few individuals have brought select pressure to bear on a select few on the executive council of the NUS who in turn have been able to dominate the majority of that otherwise sturdy union. It is difficult for us to appreciate the pressures which are being put on men I know to be realistic and responsible, not only in their executive capacity but in the highly organized strike committee in the ports, by this tightly knit group of politically motivated men.' A week or so later, a debate on the state of emergency was held. In his speech Wilson named Bert Ramelson, Dennis Goodman, Jack Coward, Roger Wood, Gareth Norris, Jim Slater and Joe Kenny (a member of Walton CLP) as the undemocratic ringleaders of the dispute. I was furious about this red baiting and in the debate made an emotional speech: 'In 1960 my honourable friend the member for Bootle [Simon Mahon] and myself were appointed by the Liverpool Trades Council and Labour Party to be the mediators in that unofficial strike. . . . We said to the seamen, "We think that your case is right, but it is wrong for you to act outside of your trade union. Your job, your responsibility, is to get into your union and make it work." The seamen did precisely that. They went into their union. They decided to make it a democratic body. They have succeeded in that. Some people say that to have forty-eight members of an executive is ridiculous . . . But the seamen must decide that. If there are forty-eight democratically elected representatives coming from all the major and minor ports obviously they are reacting to the demands of their rank and file who have elected them. . . . I appeal to the government not to dash in once again and give the impression that it is the seamen who are wrong in every sphere of the argument. Put the pressure . . . on the shipowners. If they will not respond, do what it is possible to do under the emergency powers. Take over the shipping industry, run it on

behalf of the nation and make certain that the seamen get a square deal.'
We did not vote against the Emergency Powers Act. We should have
done so and I have always felt guilty about this.

In his memoirs, Ted Short says, 'We had suffered internal dissent
about government action – or inaction – in the last Parliament, but
nothing approaching the degree of condemnation by such members as
Eric Heffer and Michael Foot.... Looking back on the whole dismal
episode I asked myself how much substance there was in the strictures
... about the government's handling of the strike.... I doubted whether
Ray Gunter ... had either the ability or flexibility to deal with it ... I
doubted whether Harold's television broadcast on the first day of the
strike was wise, making it a strike against the government from the start,
though at the time I fully supported it.'

On 1 July the strike was called off. The executive of the NUS, by 26
votes to 17, agreed the following resolution: 'That this EC being aware
of the hardship caused to the citizens of the UK accept the shipowners'
improved offer of 28 June. Therefore in the knowledge that a court of
inquiry will fully investigate our other grievances and so allow further
negotiations to take place, we adjourn the strike action for a period of
twelve months to allow the inquiry to proceed.' The militants argued that
their full demands would have been met but for the shilly-shallying of
their officials. After the strike, Jim Slater became NEC secretary and
Sam McCluskie, who had been active in the Reform Movement, special
organizer.

The government had done itself a great deal of harm and laid the
basis for defeat in 1970. It was the beginning of conflict with the trade
unions and an example of how Labour governments can turn friends
into enemies. Because of the doctrine of collective responsibility, most of
us had no idea what was happening in cabinet. Was there any opposition
to Harold – who were the hawks and who were the doves? We had to
wait until ministers published their memoirs to find out. Dick Crossman
reveals, for example, that both George Brown and Jim Callaghan
wanted to fight the seamen to the death and that only Dick Marsh
disagreed, saying the strike was no issue to fight on and the men had a
good case. Crossman lamented: '... it is we the Labour government who
have prevented the shipowners from surrendering to the seamen, simply
because a surrender would have made nonsense of the 3½ per cent
norm and given the men a big increase. We are paying a high price for
George Brown and his policies.'

Barbara Castle records on 28 June that Harold Wilson and Frank
Cousins clashed: 'Frank said icily, "I thought I was the only one in
cabinet who wanted to negotiate on extra days." Jim Callaghan got fed

up: "It is a little trying for the cabinet to be continuously put in the wrong." To which Frank retorted, "You are in the wrong on this."'

Tony Benn in his diary for 28 June records: 'Back to the Commons, where I sat almost all through the debate on the seamen's strike. Harold Wilson began by naming the communists who had intervened. It made me sick and reminded me of McCarthyism. The left attacked him almost unanimously with powerful speeches by Michael Foot, Eric Heffer and Ian Mikardo ... we were afraid that by going in for these tactics, he [Wilson] would make the anti-communist smear a weapon that every Tory could use against us in the future.'

It was obvious we were in for a further battle around the Prices and Incomes Bill. Frank Cousins had clearly indicated opposition and the Tribune group was opposed to any ideas of compulsion. On 20 July Harold Wilson announced proposals for a compulsory six-month stand-still on wages, salaries and other income. This was to be followed by a further six months of severe restraint. The statement led to protests from Labour backbenchers. Forty-seven of us put down an Early Day Motion condemning government policy. The TUC began to have reservations and Frank Cousins stated that the T&GWU would not observe the freeze. There was a rough PLP meeting. George Brown, it was rumoured, intended to resign, but he did not do so. The compulsory freeze clauses were tabled on 29 July. When the vote took place we on the left, along with some others, abstained.

Since our return to Parliament with an increased majority, the Tribune group had become more militant. The younger trade unionists were beginning to lead the way. We had spent years on the shop floor and were not cowed by government whips. I wasn't worried about being reported to my CLP. It would have been disappointed had I not abstained or voted against government policy. A *Guardian* reporter once phoned my agent and asked if she was aware I had abstained so many times. She said she was disappointed (his interest quickened) that I had only abstained and that it would have been better had I voted against (his interest collapsed).

At Tribune group meetings we agonized over tactics – should we vote against or abstain? Could we get our own amendments accepted by the Speaker, so that we voted for our *own* policies? On 2 March 1967, Harold had addressed the PLP and attacked those of us who had rebelled against the government's defence policy. Denis Healey had published the 1967 Defence White Paper in which he said that cuts in defence spending were being made, military commitments were being reduced in the Far East and further reductions were on the way. It was hoped that the paper would buy off our opposition. It did not. It was our view that in the July 1966 economic crisis, high defence spending had been a central factor. When the vote was taken on the White Paper there were sixty-two abstentions. Harold later reprimanded those of us who failed to support the government: 'All I say is watch it. Every dog is allowed one bite, but a different view is taken of a dog that goes on biting all the time. If there are doubts that the dog is biting not because of the dictates of conscience but because he is considered vicious, then things happen to that dog. He may not get his licence renewed when it falls due.'

The Chair of the PLP, Manny Shinwell, would not allow any questions or discussion despite my demand to reply. Harold made sure that his views reached the press. In response Sydney Silverman issued a now-famous open letter to the prime minister which dealt with four policy issues referred to by Harold (Vietnam, the Common Market, Wages Policy and Defence) and declared his opposition on the basis of socialist principles. He concluded: 'These are all matters to which the government and the prime minister is pledged to Parliament and people alike. Of course, it is the duty of a government to govern. Of course it is the duty of its supporters to sustain it in Parliament in doing so. But it is the duty of the government to govern as it promised the people it would govern. It is the duty of those elected to support it to see that it does and to withdraw their support when it does not. That is what I have done and will continue to do. Finally, I would remind the Prime Minister that there have been many socialist tragedies in Europe in our time. This may be our last chance to avoid another and the greatest.'

Sydney read his letter to the Tribune group. Some thought he had gone too far but I did not and said so. The London *Evening Standard* published it on the front page and both the *Times* and *Guardian* ran leading articles saying that Harold Wilson had ignored the reputation of Parliament by likening MPs to dogs trained to respond to the crack of the whip. The *Daily Express* described Sydney as a bold man. The editor said that Sydney, 'a tiny man physically', had taken his place among 'the political greats'. John Silkin, the Chief Whip, wrote to Sydney, saying that he had been misinformed, but that everyone recognized his sincerity and passionate beliefs. Sydney responded by saying, 'Thank you for your letter, and particularly for your kind personal references. The only "memorial" I would value is that I have given a lifetime of service in the Labour Party's continuing efforts to establish a socialist society under a Labour government in our country.' Within a year he was dead.

After Sydney's death Emrys Hughes stayed with Doris and myself when he was collecting material for his book *Sydney Silverman – Rebel in Parliament*. During his stay he would get up early, have a cold bath and then practise yoga in the living room. He was a vegetarian and before leaving gave me a 'Teach Yourself' book on yoga. In it he wrote, 'To Eric – 30th April 1968. Do the exercises in this, take a cold bath every morning, swim when you can, stop eating pieces of burned animals and you'll soon be 50 per cent more aggressive and enjoy the routine of the gabble shop as much as Yours Aye, Emrys.'

In June 1967, the Six-Day War took place. As usual, the major imperialist powers had their fingers in the pie and although they were not directly involved, they took sides. A war between the Arab States and Israel had long been on the cards. During May the Egyptians massed their army on the Sinai and the Straits of Tiran were blockaded against Israeli shipping. President Nasser issued a declaration: 'The waters of the Straits of Tiran are our territorial waters. If Israeli leaders and General Rabin want war, hail and welcome, our troops are waiting for them.'

Inside Israel a fierce public political struggle raged. There were demands for the government to resign and for the return of Ben Gurion. General Moshe Dayan was under great pressure to be minister of defence, despite opposition from Golda Meir and Prime Minister Eshkol, and on Thursday 1 June he accepted. War was declared on the 5th. It lasted only four days. On the first day the greater part of the Egyptian army was defeated. The old City of Jerusalem was captured, so were the West Bank, the Gaza Strip and the Golan Heights. The Israelis had defeated the Egyptians, the Jordanians and the Syrians; Greater Israel had become a fact.

As soon as the war was over the Labour Friends of Israel decided to send a group of MPs to study the situation first hand. I was invited to lead the group, which comprised David Marquand, Paul Rose, Ted Rowlands and Maurice Orbach. We arrived in Tel Aviv four or five days after the end of the war. There was still a war atmosphere and considerable tension. We met officials who explained Israel's attitude, visited the West Bank up to the destroyed Allenby Bridge across the River Jordan, went into the Gaza Strip and travelled around the Golan Heights. The Israelis were triumphant, believing they were unbeatable. I did not like that at all. The authorities said that the newly acquired territories would be used as a bargaining factor for an agreed peace. I emphasized that unless this was done quickly, Israeli fundamentalists would demand the annexation of the territory; also that eventually, the Arab population would revolt. I think they thought I was crazy.

In Gaza we saw captured Palestinians in a trench in the blazing sun. David Marquand rightly protested. It was already clear that the people of the occupied territories were sullenly accepting temporary defeat; but it was also obvious that the PLO would gain greater numbers of adherents. At the time I believed that Israel only wanted peace and secure borders, that as a nation it was not basically aggressive and that early socialist Zionist ideas were still influential. I was particularly impressed by the kibbutz system.

Many communists and left Labour Party members felt a special responsibility towards the Jews and when Israel was established in 1948 all my sympathy was with its people. The Soviet Union was the first country to recognize the state of Israel. We were blind to the fact that the Arab Palestinians, whose land was engulfed by the new state of Israel, also had rights.

Wherever we went in Israel I could not but be reminded of the Bible and its stories. The whole country made religion real. Although I had left the church and turned my back on religion at the age of fifteen, its attractiveness to me never entirely disappeared. I would often go into churches, Anglican or Roman, and meditate on the problems and issues of the day. I read religious as well as free-thought literature and at times would be wracked with doubts. I never made a big thing of it – it was a private matter and remains so.

During our visit, some of us went to the Church of the Holy Sepulchre, the site of Calvary, the burial place of Christ, and then walked along the Via Dolorosa which led Christ to his crucifixion. It seemed to me as if everything I had ever believed in my childhood was coming alive. The very street was telling me that the story I had once believed was true: Jesus was crucified because He took the side of the poor. His message is as valid today as it was then. My old beliefs overwhelmed me and after visiting the church, I once again accepted Christianity. I have never since had any great doubts about it.

When the delegation returned from Israel we gave reports to MPs and to the Labour Friends of Israel. I remained a 'Labour Friend' for many years and spoke on their platforms at Labour Party Conferences. Time has changed my views. Today I firmly believe that the Palestinians have a right to their own state and that Israel is simply a client of the US. Such socialist idealism as existed in Israel has now been more or less destroyed.

There is no doubt that the Six-Day War had a detrimental effect on the British economy. I was not convinced that Jim Callaghan had any real answers. His was a traditional approach: he attempted to get a loan from the US. His budget speech was, as he put it, in *Time and Change*, 'an unexciting homily' and 'not much red meat for an expectant House of Commons'. He argued that our existing measures were doing what was needed and that we should avoid sudden switches of policy. I was unhappy.

In August 1967 Harold Wilson asked me to see him at Number Ten. I was left waiting in a room on my own for almost an hour and when I was finally called into the cabinet room my first words were, 'Now I know what it feels like to be in solitary confinement.' Harold asked me if I would join his government in the Ministry of Technology with Tony Benn. I told him that I was not keen, but that I'd think about it over-night. Tony Benn, in his diary for 27 August noted: 'Harold phoned me to say that he had offered Eric Heffer a job in the Ministry of Tech-nology as Parliamentary Secretary, but that he had turned it down on the basis that he didn't have confidence in the government's economic policy and unless Jim Callaghan was dismissed from the Treasury, he wouldn't take it. I admired him for that.'

By October the economic situation had markedly deteriorated; the pound was devalued in a panic decision by the cabinet. Harold Wilson blamed industrial unrest and strikes. Sterling speculators had already ensured that there was a run on the pound and before devaluation the press was saying that Britain was seeking a loan which would entail conditions unacceptable to backbenchers. Jim Callaghan made a state-ment to the House and met with a hostile reception from the left. We were strongly opposed to a loan with strings attached.

The government announced devaluation in November. With it went other measures, described as 'opportunities': the base rate was to be increased to 8 per cent, hire purchase regulations were to be tightened on cars, defence expenditure would be reduced the following year, other public expenditure, including capital expenditure, would be reduced by £100 million, the IMF would be approached for more standby arrange-ments and this, with assistance from overseas central banks, would help stabilize the currency. Wilson made a broadcast explaining the devalu-ation. He said imports would cost more, which meant higher prices, even for some basic foods.

In December, Jim Callaghan moved to the Home Office. I par-ticularly remember that because Harold was the guest speaker at a Press Gallery luncheon. I had been invited by a lobby correspondent and was having a pre-lunch drink when Harold arrived. He called me over and told me privately that Callaghan was leaving the Treasury. 'So,' he said, 'you've got what you wanted.' The journalists were intrigued and wanted to know what was up. I said nothing – the announcement had not yet been made public.

During this period the government decided to apply to join the Common Market. After a series of cabinet meetings Harold got a majority for application and proposed that the PLP should have three meetings to discuss the issue. George Brown opened the first and Harold

Wilson made the closing speech at the third. When I spoke at one of the meetings I clashed with Michael Foot. I was one of the few on the left who supported the application, and Roy Jenkins congratulated me on a fine speech. Since I disagreed with him on just about everything else I was deeply embarrassed. Years earlier I had debated the issue with Michael Barratt-Brown in the US socialist journal *New Politics*. My speech to the PLP echoed that debate. I said that I had long argued against Britain's becoming a US or Soviet satellite and for its membership of a Socialist United States of Europe. As for the Commonwealth, it was disintegrating and its members would increasingly seek political and economic alliances elsewhere. The Common Market was not socialist but it offered a vision of a socialist Europe. We could work for a socialist federation and an end to European wars within it.

In the Commons debate thirty-five Labour MPs voted against the application. I was not one of them, but it was academic anyway because on 16 May 1967 General de Gaulle blocked our entry to the EEC. One British newspaper said de Gaulle had given the 'Velvet Veto'.

Before the general election of June 1970, however, I had changed my position. In April 1970 I wrote an article for the *New Statesman*, entitled 'Europe: My Change of View'. When Labour Party members in Walton saw it they were delighted. We had agreed to disagree for many years; at one party conference, I made a pro-entry speech and the Walton delegate, Don Hughes, spoke against. The local press tried to make mischief about our disagreement. Don Hughes replied saying that I was not a constituency delegate at Conference and had as much right to speak for entry as he had to speak against. The members of Walton CLP had always known my views on the issue but I was never put under any pressure by them and I changed my mind after studying the facts. Membership was a bad deal for the country in general and for Liverpool in particular. In the article I still argued for the widest possible unity of Europe: 'In the past the idea of a United States of Europe has had powerful socialist advocates.' I referred to Leon Trotsky and Rosa Luxemburg. 'Those of us on the left who had supported entry 'never advocated that this should be taken without regard to cost.... Until recently I have been convinced that the cost need not be too high, but certain developments have given me cause to think again. I had hoped that the Common Agricultural Policy could be radically changed.... That hope has now vanished.... I am not suggesting that the British government should break off discussions and withdraw the application. The application is in and the discussion must go ahead, but it should be made clear from the start by our negotiations that if the Six are not prepared to welcome Britain without forcing her to accept the EEC

Agricultural Policy, then the discussions will prove fruitless.'

I made regular speeches at the Council of Europe and at the WEU urging agreement between the European Economic Council and European Free Trade Association (EFTA) and requesting invitations to speakers from Eastern Europe. In Paris I got to know Reuters' Harold King. He was a friend of de Gaulle. I had said in a speech that in a sense I was a Gaullist without a bomb. By that I meant I supported a united Europe from the Atlantic to the Urals. That intrigued him and he invited Doris and myself to dinner. Every time I visited Paris after that I would see him and I learned a great deal about the French government from these meetings.

On one occasion at Strasbourg I had prepared a careful speech about the EEC and EFTA and the need for a socialist perspective for Europe as a whole. A Gaullist deputy attacked Britain in a very chauvinistic way and, riled by his remarks, I scrapped what I had originally intended to say and instead pointed out that during the war, our troops had died fighting Hitler on French soil, that my father had been wounded twice in France and that I had an uncle who was killed and buried in France. I also pointed out that I had been in the RAF for four years. Looking back on that speech I fear I was being as chauvinistic as the Gaullist.

On May Day 1967, Stuart Hall, Raymond Williams and Edward Thompson issued a May Day Manifesto: 'For nearly eighty years the international labour movement has taken May Day as a festival: an international celebration and commitment. On this May Day 1967, as we look at our world, we see the familiar priorities of money and power, but now with one difference; that their agent in Britain is a Labour Government.'

I went to the meeting at which the manifesto was discussed. With regard to the Labour left, the manifesto took a critical view: 'Thus we welcome some of the stands and speeches made by left Labour MPs, but for all the courage and sanity of many individual members, what is being shown is a whole process ...' A great deal of the manifesto I agreed with, especially when it said: 'For, just as the Labour Party has been a compromise between working-class objectives and the existing power structures at the national level, so the traditional Labour left has been a compromise between socialist objectives and the existing power structure at the party level.'

I had got to know Edward Thompson in the days when I was in Liverpool, prior to becoming an MP. I had a great respect for him but I felt the way ahead was through the Labour Party. I was prepared to work with people outside the party. But I was not prepared once again to concentrate on building a movement away from what I felt was the mass organization of the working class in Britain.

In October 1967, a dock strike took place in Liverpool with some support in London. Harold Wilson later blamed the subsequent devaluation of the pound on the strike. Once again he failed to recognize the real grievances of the workers involved. He considered it the work of an unholy alliance of communists, neo-communists and Trotskyists. Harold met Frank Cousins and Jack Jones of the T&GWU on the night of 18 October at Number Ten and Jack Jones made it clear he believed the men had a genuine case. Jack Scamp was appointed as the mediator in the dispute. The Liverpool employers refused to accept Scamp, but after pressure from the national employers, they eventually agreed. Scamp spent days seeking a settlement with the various parties in Liverpool Town Hall. Harold arrived in Liverpool and, as usual, stayed at the Adelphi Hotel. I was asked if I would make myself available to help achieve a settlement of the strike. I agreed but was never summoned.

Harold, Scamp, the employers, trade union officials and the unofficial strike committee worked out a proposed settlement at the Adelphi. This was put to the rank and file dockers at a mass meeting in Liverpool boxing stadium. They said they would sleep on the proposal. They did, for almost a week. They had to be thoroughly convinced that Harold's efforts did not mean a sell-out. What had happened to the seamen was certainly not forgotten by the dockers. The men went back to work on 27 October.

On 7 December 1967, I asked for an emergency debate in the House on the issue of Rhodesian sanctions. I was turned down by the Speaker. Then I had a stroke of luck. I was sitting in the library near David Weitzman, MP, when I overheard a Labour whip talking to him about his adjournment debate. She said he should get ready because it would soon be on and asked whether he would take long. David said no, that it was purely a constituents' issue. I noticed that it was then about 5.40 p.m., and remembered that Emrys Hughes told me once that if an adjournment debate finishes early, it is possible for anyone to apply for a second adjournment. I did precisely that and applied for an adjournment on Rhodesia.

By 7 p.m. David's debate was over and we had three-and-a-half hours of prime time in front of us. We focused the debate on the government's refusal to prevent a British tanker from docking in an East African port. It was carrying 12,000 tons of crude oil for Rhodesia. Sanctions were being broken. Arthur Bottomley, Secretary of State for Commonwealth Relations, was to reply for the government. The House filled up for the debate and some members, hearing about it on the radio, decided to return. The cabinet's position was that it was pointless to halt the tanker because Rhodesia was already getting all the oil it needed. I was not prepared to accept this view and felt that the government had deliberately confused matters by saying Zambia's economy would be affected if the embargo were tightened. I said that if an airlift could be organized for Berlin, why not for Zambia?

Arthur Bottomley was on a sticky wicket because, only a fortnight earlier, the government had supported a UN resolution which, in addition to other sanctions, had called for an oil embargo. In his reply, he appeared to go further than government policy, and the press made the most of it. I always felt that Arthur, had he not been hemmed in by government collective responsibility, would have been more aggressive towards the Smith regime.

Revolts by the left against the government continued in 1968. In January Harold Wilson outlined a package of economic measures following devaluation. It included increases in prescription charges. Lord Longford was the only cabinet minister to resign. The debate on the statement took place on 17 and 18 January. The reaction from left-wingers was predictable. Twenty-six of us abstained. John Silkin, the Chief Whip, wrote to us all saying we had 'endangered the existence of the government' and would be suspended from all party activities which included attendance at party meetings and specialist groups. Silkin's ruling was countermanded by Harold Wilson but out of this came new rules for the PLP, so that 'defaulters' could be dealt with.

In May the government published a new Prices and Incomes Bill which continued existing statutory powers and extended for twelve months the period in which a standstill order could be effective after a reference to the Prices and Incomes Board. Harold made it clear that the issue of the Prices and Incomes Bill was a matter of confidence. Despite that, when a vote took place on government policy, forty-two Labour members in the PLP voted against. In the debate on the Prices and Incomes Bill in the Commons in the following week the second reading was carried by 290 votes to 255 with thirty-five Labour abstentions.

Barbara Castle was now the Secretary of State for Employment and Productivity and I asked to see her to discuss the Prices and Incomes policy. We talked for about half an hour. I told her I was not against a genuine socialist Prices and Incomes policy but was opposed to a compulsory one. It was obvious that the government had made a rod for its own back, but a compromise could be worked out. I told her that if she persisted with a compulsory policy, she would be crucified. I admired her and did not want to help knock the nails in. But if I had to, I would. In her diaries, Barbara records our meeting and also says she met a delegation from the Tribune group. They too urged compromise. As the meeting ended Ian Mikardo said to her, 'You are a marvellous woman and we love you dearly, but even you can't make us think a cesspool smells like a rose.'

Barbara defended her policy with her usual wilful vigour. She got a rough ride, however, in the PLP and the trade union group in particular. The left made the running but we were by no means alone. Right-wing trade-union people came out strongly against the proposals. On 29 January I wrote an article in the *Guardian* stating my position: 'The door to legal sanctions has been opened. The question arises, why has the government come up with such proposals? Some argue that it is due to the government's reliance on opinion polls, or that they have been pressurized by the CBI, and some organs of the press, that a sop had to be given. In my opinion, there is a deeper reason. For those who seek an ordered society, the concept of legislation to put that into being is highly attractive. The bureaucratic mind has long held fantasies that the class struggle can be legislated out of existence. It is precisely that sort of thing which is inherent in the concept of the corporate state.... If tomorrow morning the government can promise to have a further look at their proposals and a bill is finally introduced which does not go beyond Donovan as the White Paper does, then the party can go forward united. If not, then I am afraid we could be in for a period of real trouble.'

When the White Paper 'In Place of Strife' was eventually debated in Parliament, Stan Orme put down an amendment on behalf of the Tribune group. It simply said, 'Rejects the White Paper "In Place of Strife" on the grounds that it contains proposals for legislation which would destroy certain fundamental rights of a free trade union movement'. The Speaker accepted the amendment for a vote and fifty-six Labour MPs voted against it with many abstentions.

Early in 1969 Michael Foot and I debated on behalf of Tribune with Tariq Ali and Bob Rowthorn of *Black Dwarf*. The Methodist Central Hall in London was packed to the doors, mainly with students. Despite our opposition to 'In Place of Strife' Michael and I got a very rough reception. The *Black Dwarf* speakers said that 'In Place of Strife' was proof that social democracy was the agent of capitalism and, although opposing, I was inclined to agree. Clearly, it was ridiculous trying to convince the meeting that a Labour government could bring in socialism when, at that very moment, it was making proposals which would take away rights from trade unions. Although Barbara Castle and Harold Wilson were prominent members of the old left, what we were getting, as I said at the time, was the old conservatism.

In his book *Street Fighting Years*, Tariq Ali, referring to the debate says: 'We received massive support, whereas Foot and Heffer were consistently and sometimes unfairly heckled. Heffer's attempt to utilize his working-class origins to defend his case ("Four years ago I worked at a bench.... I know more about the class struggle than 90 per cent of the people here") was drowned in laughter'. In fact, it wasn't just laughter, I was booed. Doris, who was in the (mainly student) audience, turned to those near to her and said, 'Why are you doing that? What he says is true'. They replied, 'That may be so, but he should never have said it.' Earlier I had said, 'in the future, no doubt some of you, perhaps a lot of you, will be working in the City, will be bankers and capitalists of all kinds, with your bowler hats and rolled umbrellas. I know what I will be doing, I shall be fighting for my class and for socialism.' I wasn't too far wrong.

After Tariq had spoken he left the platform and walked around the hall talking to people. I thought that pretty arrogant but during the course of the meeting, Robin Blackburn, an LSE lecturer later sacked and nowadays a friend of mine, as is Tariq, stormed into the meeting and said the gates of the LSE had been torn down. I got the impression they thought the revolution had taken place and they were storming the Winter Palace as in 1917. I leaned over to Michael and said, 'It will take a lot more than pulling down some gates at the LSE to defeat British imperialism.'

Despite my reception at the Central Hall debate I attended as many student meetings as I could. Most weekends I spoke at university labour and socialist clubs. At times I received a rough reception, but I thought it important to go: firstly to try to understand what the students were thinking and secondly to try to influence them to join the Labour Party and fight for socialism inside the party. It was not an easy task.

In August 1968 Soviet troops and tanks appeared in Prague and there was fighting in the streets. Committee offices were taken over. Dubček and other Central Committee members were arrested and taken to Moscow – supposedly to negotiate. Huzak took over and freedom was stifled. These developments had a profound effect on democratic socialists in all parts of the world. It was now clear that the Soviet bureaucrats would not allow freedom to exist in any of the satellite countries. They recognized that if genuine freedom developed and took root in Eastern European communist-controlled countries it was the beginning of the end of their role.

British students now had two clear enemies. The US government and its supporters, and the USSR bureaucrats and their supporters. Their movement grew in strength, as did their hostility to the Labour Party. They did not differentiate between government leaders and the left of the party. That did not stop me from doing what I could to help students who got into difficulties with the authorities through sit-ins and other direct action in Liverpool. Two of the students involved were Ian Williams, who became Neil Kinnock's speechwriter in the 1987 general election and a strong opponent of Militant and the left in Liverpool, and Jon Snow, the Channel 4 newscaster.

During the first Wilson government, I brought in a bill to abolish live hare coursing, defended the building workers in their fight for higher wages, opposed changes in British Standard Time, introduced a bill to end the Lump (the system of labour only subcontracting on building sites), fought hard for more council housing, and supported Direct Labour Departments. In the 1969–70 session, I participated in forty-four debates, either by making speeches or by asking ministers questions in the debates. I also asked around a hundred questions at question time.

The 1966–70 Labour government, despite its backslidings, did some beneficial things for working people. Against that, it became increasingly right wing, backed the US in Vietnam and brought in a Prices and Incomes policy which controlled wages only, and not the prices or incomes of the rich.

The compulsory element put forward in 'In Place of Strife' had upset the entire trade union movement and it was obvious to me that we would lose votes in the general election. We did. I lost a thousand in Walton. In other places Labour seats went down like ninepins. I had told Tony Benn this could happen when I spoke to him at the Party Conference at Scarborough the previous autumn. He wouldn't believe me. I urged Harold by letter not to go to the country in June but he chose to do otherwise. At the eve of poll meeting in Liverpool he asked me what I thought would be the outcome. I told him we in Liverpool would hold our seats but that we would lose nationally.

As predicted, I now faced a Tory government under Ted Heath. It was going to be a hard fight – but one for which I was ready and prepared.

135

THIRTEEN

'Selsdon Man'

In many ways Heath played Kerensky to Mrs Thatcher's
Lenin. Perhaps he would prefer to say that he played
Lenin to her Stalin since she rejected his New
Economic Policy as soon as she replaced him.

DENIS HEALEY, *The Time of My Life*

When I entered Parliament Alec Douglas-Home was leader of the
Conservative Party. It should be remembered that he lost the 1964
general election by only four seats. Just after I was elected I happened to
be walking down Whitehall as he was on his way to the House of
Commons. He stopped to ask how I was getting on. I was amazed that
he noticed me and had a niggling worry that I was being enticed into the
aristocratic embrace described by Nye Bevan. I think not. Over the years
I got to know Lord Home quite well and he was just being his civilized
self – friendly and never arrogant.

Alec Douglas-Home had been persuaded to stand down in 1965. He
was succeeded by Ted Heath. I suppose Heath could be classified as a
centre-left Tory. He had supported the International Brigade in Spain
during his undergraduate years and had never been on the right wing of
the Tory Party. He had been Chief Whip 1955–59, Minister of Labour
1957–60, and Lord Privy Seal with Foreign Office responsibilities 1960–
63. He had experience in government as well as in leading the Opposition. He could be ruthless but in opposition he had not shown great
leadership qualities and had always been well down on Wilson in the
poll ratings.

One thing was certain, a Tory version of 'In Place of Strife' would be
introduced by Heath. The Tories had published 'A Giant's Strength', a
very anti-trade union pamphlet and, under Heath's leadership while in
opposition, 'A Fair Deal at Work'. In April 1970 Ted Heath, speaking at
the Conservative Trade Unionists Conference in London, endorsed 'Fair
Deal at Work': 'Without it, all our plans for tax cuts, for expansion of
output, for new help to the schools, to the aged, to the homeless ...

would go out of the window'. Although in the 1970 general election the Tories presented somewhat vague proposals on industrial relations they had drawn up detailed plans for dealing with the trade unions in a meeting at Selsdon prior to the campaign. After this they were referred to as 'Selsdon Men'. During the election 'Selsdon Man' went missing but after the Tory victory he returned with a vengeance. The Queen's Speech in July revealed: 'A Bill will be introduced to establish a framework of law within which improved industrial relations can develop and a code of practice will be prepared laying down standards for good management and trade union practices'. The Tories obviously intended to charge through the door which Barbara Castle and Harold Wilson had opened for them.

The government said it intended to hold talks with the TUC and the CBI and issued a consultative Green Paper. It was almost identical to 'Fair Deal at Work'. The TUC proposed talks on a voluntary scheme but the government turned them down. After the Green Paper was published I wrote in the *Liverpool Echo*: 'Mr Robert Carr is currently the darling of the Conservative Party ... his view is that the Bill is not anti-trade union, that it is only directed against those who are acting unfairly and irresponsibly in our society.... My view is that it is unfair, and despite his honeyed words, it is directed against the trade unions. For too many years now, voices have been raised against the trade unions, against shop stewards and against the British working man ... a lot of harm has been done to our image abroad, as well as to industrial relations at home. This in turn seriously affected our trade'. It was clear to me that Labour would have to put up a united fight against the Bill.

Once back in Parliament I was persuaded by Tribune group members to stand for the Shadow Cabinet. I came 14th in the ballot. In those days there were only 12 members. Approaches were then made to Wilson suggesting that I should be a spokesman on the industrial relations Bill. Harold agreed. The first debate on the Tory proposals was in November Robert Carr and Geoffrey Howe were opposed by Barbara Castle and myself. I ended my speech by saying that on Labour's return to office: 'We will eliminate this piece of class legislation if Hon Gentlemen opposite are silly enough to go foward with their proposals'. Barbara Castle made a brilliant speech but was handicapped by her previous commitment to 'In Place of Strife'. Her presence weakened our case and it looked as if the Shadow Cabinet was half-hearted about the repeal of the Act.

The Tribune group issued a statement: 'The Industrial Relations Bill ... is a device for shifting the balance of power in industry, and therefore

137

in society, still further away from working people. The Bill will not contribute to harmony in industry. That was never the intention of its authors. The government cannot be interested in industrial peace or it would not have consistently provoked conflict since June 18.... The Bill is anti-working class, produced at a time when working people are reaching out for rights which they have been denied hitherto, and are intent on safeguarding those rights for which they have fought success-fully.... The workers' answer to the threat posed by the growth of new business empires is a clear demand for the devolution of power from the boardroom to the shop floor. The trade union movement, on the threshold of its most radical period ever, is capable of leading this campaign to victory. So it is the trade union movement that the Tories have selected for their first major attack.'

The second reading took place in December and I spelt out very clearly that we would repeal the Act. Ted Heath opened the debate for the Tories: 'It was left to Mr Heffer to say last night that if his party is returned to power ... it will repeal the whole of the Bill. It is a little unusual to allow such an important announcement to be made by one so newly on the opposition front bench'. Douglas Houghton spoke next. He read out the resolution passed at the PLP which said, 'We call upon the NEC in conjunction with the PLP and TUC to develop our constructive alternative to the Tory Bill which will ensure that a workable accord between a future Labour government and the unions and their members can be put before the electorate as a firm basis for the repeal of the Industrial Relations Bill before Parliament.' I was not entirely satisfied with that statement but proposing an alternative accord was a necessary concession to ensure the support of the PLP in opposing the Bill. After all, some leading lights had agreed with 'In Place of Strife'. The committee stage of the Bill was taken on the floor of the chamber. The Tories thought that they would get good publicity by doing this. They failed – our arguments were well aired outside Parliament and we won widespread support once people understood what we were saying.

We fought the Bill clause by clause. We had a great deal of help from Professor Bill Wedderburn, whose knowledge of industrial law is second to none. I got to know him during that struggle and he has remained a friend ever since. The real struggle, however, was outside Parliament. Workers all over the country held mass meetings, rallies and demon-strations and I spoke at many of them during the campaign against the Industrial Relations Act. Since the beginning of 1971 I had spoken at Birmingham, Blackpool, London, Guildford, Corby, Liverpool, Flint, Croydon, Watford and Cowley. On 21 February the TUC speaker was Vic Feather and his speech, in particular, was interrupted by demands for a general strike. There is no doubt that many of the rank and file of the movement were prepared to support one.

When the Bill was guillotined by the government the Tribune group, and others, held an emergency meeting. We decided to try to hold up proceedings and cause a Parliamentary rumpus so that people would know that the government was flouting parliamentary democracy. Thousands of workers had downed tools to demonstrate against the Bill and we had to show them that we were just as committed in our opposition. Tom Swain thought of seizing the mace but the last MP to do this had become a fascist. We wanted to defend parliamentary democracy not vandalize it. Norman Atkinson proposed that we should enter the lobby to vote but refuse to pass through so that the procedure of the House would be undermined. The trouble was that this would happen out of sight and the press might not understand what was going on. Finally it was decided that, just before the vote, we would assemble in front of the mace and refuse to sit down. We anticipated being suspended by the Speaker and that then each member could have his or her case discussed by the House. This would occupy the whole night and possibly the next morning. At a later stage, other MPs might follow our example. At the Tribune meeting, Stan Orme agreed to lead the way. We were delighted that ex-Ministers and many other members who were not of the Tribune group were prepared to join us. I told Barbara Castle we were planning a demonstration and that I would take part. She urged me not to and phoned Harold Wilson. He was not in the House but some of the shadow cabinet met us. It was a brief meeting and Joe Ashton bluntly told those present that our minds were made up.

As Robert Carr neared the end of his speech I watched Stan with nervous anticipation as he prepared to make his move. Momentarily, I did him an injustice and thought his nerve had failed. I decided there and then that I would do it if I had to. I need not have worried. Stan got up and was followed by Ian Mikardo, Frank Allaun, John Mendelson and Jim Sillars. Others, including Tom McMillan and Reg Freeson, also joined the crowd gathering in the centre of the chamber. Hansard did not capture the atmosphere but recorded the episode: '9.50 p.m. Mr Speaker, Order – (Interruption) Order. If hon. members defy the Chair – (Interruption) Order – Throughout the debate, I have allowed opportunities for a reasonable expression on the motion. The conduct of hon. members is very disorderly – (Interruption). Order. This is getting almost as boring as a standing ovation – (Interruption). I really must ask hon. members – (Interruption). I understand their strength of feeling, but I must ask hon. members to leave the front of the table and return to their seats – (Interruption). If hon. members persist in challenging the authority of the Chair in this way, I shall suspend the sitting for fifteen minutes. Sitting suspended.'

Once the House resumed we again assembled before the mace but the Speaker decided that there would be no martyrs and just ignored us. We were outflanked and felt a little foolish. When he called the vote, it seemed as though we had no choice but to go into the lobby and record our opposition. On the next day the morning papers urged Harold Wilson to sack me. Journalists asked if I'd been carpeted. I had not. On Wednesday, however, Harold sent for me and Reg Freeson separately. We had a talk about the situation and Harold's press officer issued a statement. The papers reported that Harold would ask for an assurance that we would never do such a thing again and, if we failed to give it, we would be removed from the front bench. In fact Harold asked for no such assurance and I told the press later that night that if he had I would have refused to give it.

I still believe the demonstration was right, despite the attacks on us. We had shown our solidarity with those workers who had lost pay by demonstrating against the Bill – we would have lost our Parliamentary pay had we been suspended – and we had helped to create an atmosphere of militancy in the PLP. The battle lines had been drawn. The guillotine ended our debates on 28 January and we voted from midnight until 4.45 a.m. – voting twenty-four times.

My book *The Class Struggle in Parliament* tells what happened next. It is not recorded in Hansard: 'Some of us had urged that as a way of showing our defiance, something should be done. But what? In fact, the dilemma was automatically solved. As we began to line up in the "No" lobby to cast our final vote in that series, some of the Welsh miners' MPs began to sing "The Red Flag". It was taken up on all sides. We filed through singing and we continued to sing in the chamber. We went back to our seats, standing up in front of them, and sang "The Red Flag" as I had never heard it sung before. I had never really liked the song, especially when sung in desultory fashion at the end of the Labour Conference. But this was different. This time, it was being sung with a fire and fervour unknown to me in the past. It was wonderful and very moving. Even as I write now I am moved by the event.'

Despite all our efforts and those of the workers, the Bill was finally made law. At the end of July, however, events took a dramatic turn. The official solicitor Sir John Donaldson, on behalf of the National Industrial Relations Court, ordered the arrest of five London dockers for contempt. Despite a court order they had continued to picket the Midland Cold Storage Company at Hackney Marshes. Bernie Steer, Cornelius Clancy, Tony Merrick, Derek Watkins and Vic Turner were

NEVER A YES MAN

gaoled in Pentonville on Friday 21 July. The effect of the arrests was precisely as the Bill's opponents had forecast. Dockers throughout the country went on strike in support. As the week progressed, more and more workers from other sectors came out on token or indefinite strike. Even the Midland Cold Storage workers, who were in dispute with the dockers, took strike action.

The Labour Party front bench was divided on the arrests. Reg Prentice said the arrested dockers were 'absolutely wrong to organize picketing and blacking without the support of their union. They are even more wrong to defy the order of the court. They have been looking for martyrdom for weeks. I have no sympathy for them and I do not think they deserve the support of other workers.' On the other hand, Tony Benn compared them to the Tolpuddle Martyrs and Barbara Castle spoke with passion about their arrest at a meeting at Tolpuddle called by the Agricultural Workers Union.

Norman Atkinson, Tom Driberg, Dennis Skinner, Ian Mikardo, Stan Orme and I tabled a motion in the Commons. It was signed by seventy MPs and said: 'This House supports the five dockers condemned to imprisonment for expressing conscientiously and non-violently, their contempt for the Industrial Relations Court; considers that their action is in the true tradition of democratic resistance to evil and stupid laws; recalls the warnings by opposition members, contradicted by government spokesmen, during the debates on the Industrial Relations Act, that this Act would lead to the imprisonment of trade unionists; and calls on Her Majesty's Government immediately to release the five imprisoned men, without requiring any apology or promise from them, and to repeal the Act.'

The dockers had a great meeting at London Bridge and decided to march to Pentonville Prison. Dennis Skinner and myself were present. The TUC called a national one-day general strike – for the first time since 1926. Meanwhile, the print workers struck; the only sources of news were radio and television. The country was heading for a serious industrial crisis. The government kept stressing that only 170,000 workers had struck out of a workforce of twenty-four million. But the dispute was gathering pace. Ten million affiliates to the TUC were due to become involved by Monday 31 July. The jailed dockers were visited by the Official Solicitor but refused to apologize. They were supported by Vic Feather. Shortly afterwards they were released from prison to an ecstatic reception from the entire trade union movement. The government claimed to have had no hand in this but their protests were not credible. Working-class solidarity had inflicted its first major defeat on the Heath government. It was not long before it struck again.

141

In July 1971, in the face of progressive inflation, the NUM had demanded a pay rise of approximately 47 per cent. When this was turned down, the union imposed an overtime ban and called for a national strike the following January. The strike took place, resulting in serious power cuts. The government eventually realized it would have to compromise and a committee of enquiry under Lord Wilberforce was established. The miners were offered 22 per cent which was reluctantly accepted. The Tories were furious with Heath. Many of them believed he had surrendered to the miners.

Britain's entry into the EEC was voted on by the Commons in October 1971 with 364 for and 244 against. The Labour Party was split with Roy Jenkins leading sixty-eight Labour MPs into the EEC lobby. I had been in favour of entry but I had been wrong about one vital issue. I had previously believed that the Treaty of Rome was negotiable. But it was made absolutely clear that if Britain joined it would have to accept the treaty as it stood. I realized that Liverpool could decline further as a port, that unemployment would increase and that our trade slump (because of the rules of the Common Market) would stop us from building up industries as we wanted to.

In July of 1971, the party had a special conference on the Common Market at Central Hall, London, at which I spoke. Harold came out against the market and the Labour vote split in the Commons. In fact Harold played both ends against the middle without giving away his true position. At the Annual Conference in October 1972 a resolution moved by Danny McGarvey, for the Boilermakers, was carried. 'This Conference declares its opposition to entry to the Common Market on the terms negotiated by the Tories and calls on a future Labour government to reverse any decision for Britain to join unless new terms have been negotiated, including the abandonment of the Common Agricultural Policy and the Value Added Tax, no limitation on the freedom of a Labour government to carry out economic plans, regional development, extension of the public sector, control of capital movement and the preservation of the power of the British Parliament over its legislation and taxation ...' It was a very clear statement. Later, Harold appeared to be backing out of the policy and Tony Benn declared firmly that the Conference decision should be respected. I fully agreed with him and thought Harold was wrong.

In January 1972 thirteen people were killed in Northern Ireland. The event became known as Bloody Sunday. I said in the House that, at that moment, I was ashamed of being an Englishman. I was very distressed; in fact when the soldiers were first sent in – ostensibly to defend the Catholic population – I was the only Labour MP in the House to query whether this action was right. I felt it would only be a matter of time before the troops were defending the status quo against the demands of the civil rights movement. The day after the shootings in Londonderry, I was sitting next to Bernadette Devlin when Reginald Maudling, for the government, claimed that the troops had fired in self-defence. Bernadette called Maudling a 'bloody hypocrite', got up from her place, crossed the floor and slapped his face. There was uproar in the House but I fully understood how she felt. For thirteen people to have been shot dead in cold blood was criminal. She proved to be a young woman of determination and guts.

Later that spring, I visited Chile with a delegation of British MPs invited by the Chilean government. I was keen to see the achievements of the socialist Popular Unity government there. Harold Wilson gave me a personal letter to be handed to President Allende. I was delighted at his support. Although the British Embassy laid on a cocktail party to greet our arrival in Santiago, the ambassador seemed reluctant to arrange a meeting with Allende. After a few days I showed my impatience, pointing out that I had a personal letter for the president from the leader of the opposition. Eventually, we were told he would see us at the palace for half an hour. I gave my brand new Labour Party tie to the president. You would have thought I had given him a million pounds, he looked so pleased. (Later I learned he collected ties!) After our talk he asked if we could stay for lunch. Before any of the others could say anything, I accepted. Although we had an arrangement with some Radical Party politicians, I felt they would not mind deferring to the president. Before lunch, Allende told us he was meeting a delegation of disabled people outside the palace and asked if we cared to join him. I was delighted to and he showed great compassion, asked questions and took notes. There was obviously a mutual trust and affection between Allende and his visitors. During lunch Allende said Chile's revolution would not be like Russia's: no vast repressive bureaucracy, but freedom, democracy, music and dance. Then he added: 'If they let us.' Later, when I heard of his murder by Pinochet's army, I remembered those words. We stayed at the palace for approximately two-and-a-half hours and discussed Popular Unity's programme and the government's vision. Rear Admiral Morgan Giles asked the President whether he was a Chilean first or a Marxist. The President said that there was no contradiction. He loved his country, but believed progress could only be made through socialist policies.

Whilst in Chile we saw a number of newspaper editors. The extreme right-wing *El Mercurio* continually called for the overthrow of the President. Even the *Daily Express* and *Daily Mail* would not have gone so far. Yet the papers were allowed to print their attacks and were not suppressed. Almost every day there were panels of MPs discussing the issues of the day on radio and television. We travelled the country, often accompanied by right wing senators who fed us with anti-Popular Unity propaganda. It was obvious that the right was becoming increasingly bold.

We did not know then, but do now, that the CIA deliberately undermined the goverment and destabilized the economy. It helped to destroy the most democratic country in Latin America. Elections were to take place in March and it was obvious that Popular Unity would increase its support. It duly received 44 per cent of the vote and a mandate of similar proportions to that with which Margaret Thatcher ran Britain for a decade.

A coup of extreme brutality took place in October 1973. Allende was trapped in the palace and had to take up arms personally to defend himself. He was murdered. I wept unashamedly at the news, for an attempt to achieve socialism through the Parliamentary process had been murdered too. The Americans were not prepared to let socialism become a reality. Chile joined the list of countries in which democracy had been destroyed to maintain the capitalist system. I have felt sick about what happened ever since. The ruling classes only believe in democracy when it supports them. When it doesn't, they destroy it.

The philosophy of the Heath government was not to support lame ducks and to phase out direct government subsidies to private industries. To deal with the threatened collapse of Upper Clyde Shipbuilders, the government set up a committee. 'The Four Wise Men' (Alexander McDonald, Chairman of Distillers, Sir Alexander Glen, a shipping magnate, David MacDonald, Director of Hill Samuels and Alf Robens, ex-Chairman of the Coal Board and ex-Labour MP) decided: 'Any continuation of Upper Clyde Shipbuilders in its present form would be wholly unjustified, and would cause serious and more widespread damage.' The workers took immediate action to save UCS and six thousand jobs. They staged a work-in which received tremendous support and rallied the entire labour movement to their cause. In August 1972 over 80,000 people (supported by TUC top brass) took part in a demonstration in Glasgow. Tony Benn played a big part in this campaign and Jimmy Reid made great anti-capitalist speeches: 'The workers are getting up off their knees, getting on their feet and asserting their dignity, asserting their abilities, asserting in a determined and disciplined way that they will have a say in the decision-making of this country ...'

Many years earlier Reid had come to Merseyside seeking support from fellow shipyard apprentices for the apprentices' strike. He was a very different man then from the poacher-turned-gamekeeper he has become.

In June 1971, Tony Benn had sponsored a Bill in the House called 'Upper Clyde Shipbuilders (Public Ownership)'. I gave it my support but was sceptical about those who, in opposition, were in favour of public ownership, but who did little for it when in office. The Bill had no chance. However, it spotlighted the struggle of the workers who, in the final outcome, partially won. It was announced that Govan Shipbuilders would incorporate the three Glasgow yards and would be provided with £17 million to cover losses and £18 million for further capital development. It was a step in the right direction.

In April 1972, I was joint twelfth (with Barbara Castle) in the Shadow Cabinet election. I was pressed not to let it go to another vote and to allow Barbara in, as she was a woman. I refused, saying that it was a political question. Barbara got 111 votes, I got 89. The right and centre had voted for Barbara. Tony Benn's diary notes that he voted for me.

The same month, Roy Jenkins resigned as deputy leader because the party had accepted Tony Benn's plan for a Common Market referendum. The resignation was part of a campaign to halt the party's move to the left. Since the 1970 election there had been a definite shift. The struggle against the Industrial Relations Bill, the work-in at UCS and the resolutions passed at Labour Party Conference all demonstrated that the movement wanted Labour to support the working class and fight more consistently for socialist policies. In the deputy leadership contest in 1971 Roy Jenkins based his campaign on the EEC. His challenge to Harold Wilson was clear. The left's candidate was Michael Foot and Tony Benn also stood. Jenkins got 140 votes, Foot 96 and Benn 46. Jenkins had made it clear he would not necessarily vote with the party if it opposed entry to the EEC. In fact, he did not support the party anyway and left Parliament to become an EEC commissioner.

As Tony Benn was not in the Tribune group and had not identified himself with the left over 'In Place of Strife', I supported Foot, although I recognized the weaknesses in his position on a number of issues. In essence he was an old-fashioned liberal rather than a class-orientated socialist.

Labour's move to the left continued at the Party Conference in October 1973 and a progressive programme was accepted for the next general election. The public ownership debate was opened by Harold Wilson. He seemed somewhat hesitant but Tony Benn's reply was positive and well received. In *The New Politics – A Socialist Renaissance* Tony wrote: 'Workers are not going to be fobbed off with a few shares.... They want real workers' control ... that is what is being demanded and that is what we had better start thinking about.' Tony was moving rapidly to the left. I spoke with him and Jack Jones at the Tribune Rally and called for trade unions in the armed forces to prevent a Chilean situation in Britain. In his speech, Michael Foot urged that Tony Benn should be re-elected to the Shadow Cabinet. He duly was.

Meanwhile the 1972 Industry Act had created sweeping new interventionist powers and the government took further action to control pay, prices and dividends. We fought them vigorously and some Tory MPs, who had opposed Labour's statutory policy on Prices and Incomes, joined us. Pay policy met with strong opposition from the trade unions and Heath had his own 'Winter of Discontent' well before Labour. The old alliance against statutory policy was back in business.

At the end of that year the miners came out on strike again and by December a three-day week had been imposed on industry, to save energy. The government also announced cuts in public expenditure. There was talk of a government of National Unity. According to Tony Benn, Jim Callaghan said that he would welcome such a proposal and, at a TUC Labour Party Liaison Committee, Reg Prentice said, 'We must look for national unity when we attack the three-day week ... the miners' action is not justified; they are aggravating and inflicting hardship on millions of workers and weakening the national economy and it should be called off.' I was on the front bench with Reg Prentice for quite a time. He was absolutely right wing and, although a T&GWU member, had an inbuilt antagonism to the workers. It was no surprise when he went over to the Tory Party – he was always a Tory in Labour's ranks.

The atmosphere in the country became very tense. MI5 was very active and Heath believed we were on the eve of revolution. There was also talk of SAM missiles, to be fired, possibly, at Heathrow. It was bizarre. Reg Prentice went out of his way to attack Mick McGahey of the NUM; then Harold Wilson, Ted Short, Douglas Houghton, Bob Mellish and Eric Varley put down an Early Day Motion also attacking McGahey. I was horrified by their attitude. It was the seamen's strike all over again, only this time we were not even in government.

During those years, 1970–74, I had begun to write much more for newspapers and journals like the *New Statesman* and *Spectator*. I had written for *Tribune* for many years. On one occasion I covered the Tory Conference for the *New Statesman* with the excellent Christopher Hitchins. At the Conference I attended a meeting of the Monday Club which made my hair stand on end. The Monday Club was flourishing. John Biggs-Division MP claimed that, 'Under the creeping socialism of a generation we have been stripped well nigh naked of our monetary, military and moral defences. The threat to our kinsfolk and partners overseas is matched by the threat to domestic economy and social order.' I wrote: 'There were times last week when I could have been forgiven for thinking I was at Ripley's Odditorium "Believe it or Not" on Blackpool seafront, rather than at the Conservative Party Conference at the Winter Gardens. An advertising blurb about Ripley says that "he made his money with stranger-than-fiction cartoons. The more people disbelieved him then the happier and richer he became".' I also wrote: 'Although Ted Heath got his standing ovation at the end of the Saturday rally speech ... the thing that amazed me was the strength of the attacks on the government and Ted Heath in particular, in private, in the bars and at the informal gatherings.... One Tory ... was very happy to tell me that the quicker Heath went the better, and he had great hopes that when Ted went to China, he might never come back.'

He didn't have long to wait. Heath panicked and called a general election.

147

FOURTEEN

No Minister

This above all: to thine own self be true,
And it must follow as the night the day,
Thou canst not be false to any man

WILLIAM SHAKESPEARE *Hamlet*

Labour won the general election with 301 seats; the Tories gained 296.
The Liberals did well by getting 20 per cent of the vote, although they
only won fourteen seats. Ted Heath suggested that the Liberals join him
in a coalition. His proposal was rejected. After further discussion with
his cabinet colleagues, Heath resigned on 4 March 1974. Harold Wilson
again became Prime Minister.

The Tory manifesto had talked of great dangers both from within and
outside the country: 'it is essential that the affairs of this country are in
the hands of a strong government, able to take firm measures in government with a renewed mandate from the people ...' Labour's manifesto,
'Let us Work Together', reminded voters: ' the aim of the Prime Minister
is to continue the scourge of the three-day week until he has secured a
political victory over the miners.... The folly of this type of politics
passes description.' It also made clear that the Labour Party opposed
British membership of the EEC on the terms negotiated by the Tory
government. If renegotiations were successful then a referendum of the
people would be held. The Pay Board set up by the Tories would be
abolished and the Industrial Relations Act would be repealed as a matter
of urgency. An Industrial Democracy Act would be introduced. A Royal
Commission would look into income distribution and a non-
Governmental Conciliation and Arbitration Service (ACAS) would be
established. Labour would bring in a new Industry Act. There would be
a system of planning agreements. Shipbuilding, ship-repairing and
marine engineering, the ports and the manufacture of air-frames and
aeroengineering would be publicly owned. We would take over profitable firms either on a sectional or individual basis. A National Enterprise Board (NEB) would be established. The intention was to socialize

existing nationalized industries. There would be new regional planning machinery and a National Labour Board would be established. The NHS would be improved.

The manifesto had begun by declaring that its aims were socialist. 'It is our intention to bring about a fundamental and irreversible shift in the balance of power and wealth in favour of working people and their families.' It ended by urging greater democracy and the restoration and development of institutions such as the House of Commons, trade unions and local authorities. This was a comprehensive, reasonably radical policy to deal with a serious economic and political situation.

Once Harold was in Number Ten he asked me to join the Department of Industry, working with Tony Benn. I accepted, though not without some reservations. The department would be responsible for the Industry Act, for setting up the National Enterprise Board (NEB), for extending public ownership and also for regional policy. As I had been on the committee which drew up these plans I felt I had a responsibility to see them through. I had not been sure that the NEB was the way to proceed but, when Tony Crosland opposed it, I began to see its merits. Crosland's attitude suggested that he and his friends did not really believe in public ownership and their argument for competitive public ownership was a diversion. Now their bluff would be called.

Doris and I had talked about the situation. We had agreed that, although our financial position would improve, we should not become too dependent on a ministerial salary. I might at some stage find it right to resign or leave the government. When I did make a stand, the financial situation was not given a second thought. Thank goodness I was married to Doris instead of a pushy woman who wanted me to 'get on'.

The Ministers in the Department of Industry were Tony Benn, Secretary of State, myself and Lord Beswick as Ministers of State, and Gregor Mackenzie and Michael Meacher as Under Secretaries. It was with some trepidation that I entered the building on my first day in office. Although it would not be plain sailing I was determined to get party policy carried through. That was easier said than done. As could be expected, I had quite a few letters from people on my appointment. One was from Dick Crossman. He was ill when he wrote to me 'Have you started with a burst of jubilant activity or are you already up against the civil service and fuming at their methods of quiet sabotage?' Dick was right about quiet sabotage. The first or second day we were in office, there was a party for senior civil servants and ministers. It was a revealing gathering. One woman civil servant asserted that ministers were soon tamed or they left. I said little, but took note. In Peter Shore's book about the role of civil servants, he calls them the 'permanent politicians' and those of us who are elected the 'transient' ones. We go; they stay and more or less rule the country. Most of them are natural conservatives. The TV series *Yes Minister* is not far off the mark.

Each morning I had a meeting with Tony Benn in his large office. On the end wall he had an old trade union banner and on his desk a paper-weight bearing the words 'Workers of the World Unite'. He also had a map of Britain on the wall, upside down, so that we could study the development areas easily. Tony was a great one for consultation. I noticed, however, that it was his view which usually prevailed. If he failed to carry you at first he would raise the same thing again under different circumstances. He generally won in the end. We had many arguments and at times he could be somewhat naive. But he was honest and he passionately wanted what was best for working people. One of the first things he did was to make sure that every civil servant of importance had a copy of the manifesto. There were times when I informed Sir Anthony Part and others in no uncertain terms that our policy was in the manifesto and had to be implemented.

Every day I would meet delegations from trade unions, shop stewards, employers' organizations, local authorities and, of course, MPs. I would make sure that they were heard quickly. I had often been angry in the past at the cavalier attitude some ministers had adopted towards myself and my Merseyside colleagues. I wanted us to tackle issues together and for the department to give all possible assistance to those it dealt with. Some civil servants were very helpful, others put every obstacle in your way. To a large extent I was dependent on their advice. I believe ministers should have their own advisers who are not civil servants. In that respect we could learn from the US system. The personal private secretary allocated to me was a highly intelligent young man; nevertheless, for someone from my background and experience, I found it surprising that I was given a secretary I did not choose. There should be a system which allows ministers to select from among a number of suitable people.

After meetings, delegations, official lunches, and so on, I went to the Commons to vote, or sometimes to participate in debates from the front bench. Junior ministers handled adjournment debates which often took place in the early hours of the morning. At the end of a long day I would deal with the red boxes. I had quite an argument with the civil servants about these; I did not want them filled with extraneous material which would deflect me from important issues. In the end, I got what I wanted and I would often write to the Prime Minister giving my views. That, I was told, was unusual for a minister of state. You were supposed to accept policy without argument.

Some civil servants would have had you travelling all over the country and the world, if you had let them; if they got you out of the office you couldn't interfere with their work. To such people a good minister is one who does as he or she is told. I was a real nuisance. I found that the constituency side of my work was of no importance to them; my wife, as my constituency secretary, often had difficulty getting through to me on the telephone until I absolutely insisted that she be put through immediately.

Early on one civil servant tried to work a 'flanker' on me. As I was leaving for a lunch appointment, he dashed up and asked me to sign a couple of letters. He said they were only routine. I told him I would see them when I got back. They were not routine. They proposed transferring responsibility for Barrow-in-Furness from the North-West Regional Offices based in Manchester, to the Northern Regional Office based in Newcastle. I said that we must consult the local authority, the local unions, the employers and the commercial organizations and ask them for their views before that was done. After consultation, the transfer was dropped. I was told that when I left the department the areas were transferred, despite the opposition of local people.

New ministers must go to the palace to meet the Queen. I queried whether this was essential and was informed that it was – otherwise I would not be confirmed in office. We duly lined up at the palace and eventually the Queen came in to meet us one by one. It was the first time I had met her although I had seen her in her finery in Parliament, delivering the Queen's Speech. When she reached me she said she had often read my speeches and agreed with me about British Standard Time. It was obvious the Queen took her job very seriously.

Tony Benn soon asked me to chair the committee to draft the White Paper on the new Industry Act covering planning agreements and the establishment of the NEB. The committee comprised two senior civil servants, Alan Lord and Ron Dearing, Tony Benn's political advisers, Frances Morrell and Francis Cripps, and Michael Meacher and Stuart Holland, who had played such a constructive part on the party committee. Meetings were held sometimes three or four times a week, and the work made real but slow progress. I wanted the outcome to be totally in line with the party's policy document. I was also made responsible for regional policy, something that really concerned me, because I represented Merseyside.

In his book *How to be a Minister*, Gerald Kaufman says that there are two dangerous diseases a minister must beware of: ministerialitis and departmentalitis. I was determined to suffer from neither. I took an interest in the whole of the government's policy and the wider political and international issues. That interest led me into quite a bit of trouble. My first serious argument took place the day I was to answer my first parliamentary questions. A civil servant, Murdoch Maclean, brought me the answers, all nicely typed out. I said I did not agree with many of them and would answer in my own way. A few eyebrows were raised but I felt that some of the civil servants rather liked my attitude. I did not want to give replies which cut across my basic beliefs – nor did I want to give anodyne replies which meant nothing at all.

My attitude as a minister, however, was always a positive one and, following a request from Harold Wilson that ministers should try to explain government policy, I spoke in my constituency in March. I said that the government had settled the miners' dispute by allowing free negotiations, and had got the miners back to work. It had put the country back on a five-day week, frozen the rents of council tenants and of those living in privately owned accommodation, and had announced a subsidy on bread. 'This has all been done in less than three weeks and is a remarkable achievement'.

I was, however, soon in trouble with the PM. It was apparent that the government was going to continue to supply warships to Chile. I recalled the attitude we had taken in opposition. In the Commons debate Judith Hart had made an excellent speech on behalf of the party against the Pinochet regime. She had demanded a boycott of such arms. It seemed to me that the government had said one thing in opposition and another in government. I wrote to the PM voicing my opinions. In March, Tony Benn raised the issue with Jim Callaghan at the NEC: if the warships were delivered there would be an outcry in the party. Michael Foot agreed with Tony. Callaghan said that the Chile policy was in line with what was done over South Africa, that he had mentioned it to Harold and had been told he should go ahead. Tony pointed out that many MPs were concerned, including Eric Heffer. Callaghan said I had better be careful. I had been seen in the lobby arguing about the matter. Was I a member of the government or not?

On Friday 12 April I called in at Number Ten, on my way to Liverpool, and left a copy of the speech I intended to deliver the following night. I had already met Tony on the Wednesday and read out the main points. On the Saturday, at lunch time at my mother-in-law's house, I received a phone call from Number Ten and the text of a letter that the PM intended to send was then read over. It said my proposed speech was incompatible with my position as minister. I was about to tell the PM to get stuffed when Doris put a restraining hand on my arm. I told them I would give Harold a reasoned reply in good time. My speech received wide publicity and I awaited the phone call of dismissal. It was a holiday weekend and the warships made every news bulletin. Jim Callaghan was interviewed and said that I was a young man and he recognized my sincerity. He hoped Harold would not sack me. The truth is, at fifty-two, I was not so young! Still, after watching Jim I felt that no action would be taken. In his diary for 16 April, Tony Benn noted: 'The papers this morning were still full of Eric Heffer. *The Times* had a leading article. Generally speaking he has done extremely well.... Of course there is widespread support in the party and I think it could well put him on the NEC and I personally would be pleased if it did.'

The issue came before the NEC on Wednesday 24 April. Jim Callaghan tried to justify his position. Michael Foot said we would never have sold arms to fascist governments before the war. The government should review the situation. Tony Benn followed Michael: 'We have to accept that ministers do hold collective responsibility but should not use it as an excuse for fending off criticism.' Walton CLP backed me all the way.

During the argument on Chile, Tony Benn told me that my choice of Parliamentary Private Secretary (PPS), Caerwyn Roderick, had not been immediately accepted, probably for reasons of security. I was very angry. Caerwyn was a good left-wing MP, but to suggest that he was a security risk was absurd. In the end he was cleared. He was a first-class PPS and friend. 'Now don't pull any punches,' I told him, 'If you think I'm wrong, or handling something badly, then tell me. You are a friend, not a sycophant.' I'm pleased to say he took me at my word.

The situation between Number Ten and ministers in the Department of Industry became extremely tense. Harold became convinced that we were a pocket of 'loony leftists'. Joe Haines, the Press Officer to Harold, constantly fed stories about the department to Fleet Street. Tony Benn was portrayed as a 'commissar'. We were 'Soviet agents', we were against democracy. This used to madden me, but it was to be expected. Our department was trying to carry out the manifesto. That made us dangerous. We intervened to save jobs. We agreed with workers' co-operatives and believed that, if money could be granted to private enterprise, it should be granted to workers' co-operatives too. Any argument between Harold and Tony Benn was therefore given great prominence in the press.

One of the major disagreements we had was about the document concerning collective responsibility of ministers. I thought it was ridiculous. For example Harold was once on a visit to Moscow and I was told that I could not appear on television without his agreement. I telexed Moscow. He did not send an immediate reply, so I went on. On another occasion I was instructed not to continue to write my weekly column in the *Walton Times*. I pointed out that I had written it since I was elected. It had helped Labour retain the seat and I would continue to write it. Nothing happened.

Meanwhile, the Industry White Paper was transformed into a Green Paper. That is, a paper for discussion rather than action. I was not happy. As far as I was concerned, the White Paper contained all the policies in the manifesto. Even though it was couched in civil service language, I was not particularly bothered. What was important was that it contained the *policy*. Cripps, Morrell and Meacher said very little in committee but when the paper was completed they told Tony that it was not radical enough in language and it was changed. I was furious. Why had they not spoken up at the time or come to see me personally?

The whole question was discussed at the Industrial Development Committee of the cabinet in June. Denis Healey said he preferred a mixed economy which was profitable, and Jim Callaghan backed him up. Harold Wilson said he agreed with the manifesto but could not support an NEB outside the control of ministers. He resented some ministers suggesting that they were custodians of parts of the manifesto. As I had feared, Wilson took the paper into his own hands and decided that it should be re-written and discussed. I knew that was the end of the policy as laid down in the manifesto and at that point I thought of resigning.

The Department became involved in rescuing companies which had gone, or were about to go, bankrupt. One such was the old Fisher-Bendix works at Kirkby, Merseyside. In 1971, Jack Spriggs had asked me to enlist Harold Wilson's support to help save the factory. He did – through his efforts the factory was sold to Thorn Electric. Now, however, 1,200 jobs were at risk. Jack Spriggs and Dick Jenkins, the two senior shop stewards, went to see Tony and the firm went into the hands of a liquidator, Kenneth Cork, who thought that the factory could employ 240 workers but not more. Tony Benn felt that they should have six months to get the factory back on its feet. The department would help them to do that. The workers formed a co-operative. I was in constant touch with Jack Spriggs and Dick Jenkins and did all I could to help. In January 1975, Jack asked for £2 million to get the co-operative working. There was a great deal of opposition from other ministers and civil servants. Much was made of the original grant being 'once and for all'. That was not true and right-wingers were using the situation to promote their own views against ours.

When Tony and I had met Jack and Dick we had been much impressed by their proposals for the Kirkby factory. They were being transformed by their experiences into real worker-managers. We addressed a mass meeting. It was an important event. The workers were very enthusiastic over the support they were receiving from Tony and myself. I'm sorry to say that, after we left the department, the co-op was allowed to fail.

Another of the problems we faced was British Leyland. The company came to the department for cash. Donald Stokes said that £240 million was required. Some of the cash, he believed, could be obtained from the banks, but the rest he needed in equity. British Leyland, unfortunately, came under the umbrella of the NEB. I was very unhappy about the situation, as I knew a great of money would be directed away from our projects. I thought British Leyland should be publicly owned, and that separate government money should be made available. It was too heavy a burden on the department and I made my views known at the time.

Meantime, factory closures multiplied. It was a nightmare. Weekly, sometimes more often, I was seeing shop stewards and union representatives as redundancies were being announced in every part of the country. I was sickened by the thought of all those workers being thrown out of work. We did our best to save jobs but I fear some of our civil servants in the department saw only numbers, not people. When Bear Brand tights faced closure in Liverpool, I discussed the situation with the workers. They needed £350,000 or 500 jobs would be lost. I had some very serious arguments with my old friend Joel Barnett, threatening to resign if the money was not found. Joel records this in *Inside the Treasury*: 'I felt I could not allow our friendship to influence me and I fought as hard as I had ever done. But I lost ... I do not know if Eric would have resigned if I had won, but knowing his feelings for Merseyside, I believe it was not an idle threat'.

Another general election was held on 10 October 1974 in an attempt to increase Labour's majority. Labour won the election but only managed to win a few more seats. Harold sent me a letter through Sir Robert Armstrong, the cabinet secretary, informing me that I had been re-appointed as minister of state in the department. I was, nevertheless, very unhappy with the government. I would have to play my part in getting the now toothless Industry Act through. There would also be an argument over the Common Market referendum. At the first PLP meeting, Harold was elected leader without opposition. He said there would be no retreat on policy. I listened with scepticism. After a meeting with the CBI to discuss our industrial policy, I took Tony Benn aside; I told him I would stay for the session and then return to the back benches. A motion was moved at the NEC about Simonstown, the naval base in South Africa. Tony Benn, Joan Lestor, and Judith Hart, all ministers, voted for it. Harold was very angry, saying that their actions were against collective responsibility and they must comply with the rules. Such rules, he said, applied at meetings of the NEC as well as in the Commons or elsewhere. If they did not accept this it would be assumed they did not wish to remain in office.

Neil Kinnock and Ian Mikardo told Benn not to resign. For some reason he did not talk it over with me. Finally he sent Wilson a letter: 'Dear Prime Minister, In my last letter I made it clear that I accepted the principle of collective responsibility and hence all the requirements that flow from it. Yours, Tony Benn.' After that Harold assured him the matter was closed.

When Tony showed me his letter I was disgusted: 'Look, you have grovelled to Harold. I am sorry to say it, but you have grovelled.' I threw down his letter and left the room immediately. I don't think Tony realized the effect his letter had on me. He was obviously under pressure from Michael Foot and some on the left who wanted to keep the party together until the Industrial Relations Act was repealed. I understood all that but I would have acted differently – whatever the cost to myself. I felt very unhappy.

The second reading of the Industry Bill took place on Monday 17 February. Tony Benn moved it and Michael Meacher wound up. I am glad I did not as it was a shadow of what it should have been. Meacher was one of those responsible for Wilson taking the Bill over and it was fitting that he should defend the watered-down version in the House. Meanwhile, Tony Benn was being increasingly attacked in the press. Other ministers, too, were stepping up the fight against him and the department because we were trying to keep to our manifesto commitments. I became even more unhappy and ill with stomach trouble which had developed because of my concern over closures and redundancies. I told Tony: 'This is a most reactionary government and I am living a lie by giving it credibility. I would like to get out.' I found that I was handling most of the work on the Industry Bill Committee. Amendments were being put forward by Labour members with which I agreed but, because of collective responsibility, I had to oppose them. I became more and more fed up with the situation and told Tony Benn I could not tolerate it much longer. He got somewhat tetchy and I felt he was losing patience. I'm afraid I had already lost mine.

The Common Market was the last straw. The cabinet held two meetings in March 1975 on the issue. Jim Callaghan tried to convince the cabinet that great progress on re-negotiation had been made. I felt we were being conned. After hearing about the cabinet debates, I decided I really had had enough. As Harold would not agree to even one minister speaking for us against the Common Market and for a 'no' vote, I decided I would do it myself. The cabinet decided by sixteen votes to seven to stay in the EEC and support a 'yes' vote. Some cabinet ministers decided to agree to differ publicly. They were Barbara Castle, Tony Benn, Michael Foot, William Ross, Peter Shore and Eric Varley. Guidelines were passed around the cabinet as to how ministers should behave. In cabinet Tony Benn supported the right of ministers to speak in the Commons against the government's majority view. Harold replied: 'It is quite unheard of for a government not to have the majority support of its own party'. John Silkin agreed with Harold: 'We cannot have ministers speaking against the government in the House. It would be a shambles.' I wrote to Harold Wilson in April: '... we dissenting ministers must have the right to speak in the debate (if the Speaker decides to call us) and I feel it right to approach the Speaker accordingly.' Harold replied: '... Ministers unable to accept the government recommendation are free to dissociate from it and to campaign in the country during the period of the referendum. It was never envisaged as a licence to ministers to express views contrary to the policy of the government in the House.... [this] is a cabinet decision. There is no question of the cabinet changing it'.

I did speak from the back benches. The Speaker kept me waiting and the longer I waited the more nervous I became. It was not a good speech. The Press Gallery was full as was the Chamber. The next day the press were not very flattering. As expected, I was sacked by Harold: 'Dear Eric, Your deliberate decision to speak against the government's motion in today's debate, although you had been informed of the cabinet's decision that ministers who dissented from the government's recommendation should not speak in the debate, makes it impossible for me to retain you in the government. I am therefore informing the Queen that you have ceased to be a minister, and I shall recommend a new appointment in due course. I should like to thank you for all your services to the government and the party over these recent years.'

One of the first letters I received after my dismissal was from the Tribune group: 'Dear Eric, All the members of the Tribune group – and, we feel sure, many other members of the PLP as well – want to express our thanks for all the fine work you did as a minister, notably in connection with the Industry Bill. We understand that it couldn't have been easy for you to face the choice you have had to make, and we'd like you to know that we are solidly with you and behind you. Yours sincerely, Jo Richardson, Secretary to the group.'

The next day I issued a statement outlining my unease: 'For some time now I have found myself increasingly concerned with certain aspects of government policy, such as the failure to cut defence expenditure in line with Labour Party Conference policy, the failure to release the Shrewsbury pickets, the way the Social Contract is being handled as a method of wage control, the restrictions on ministers and the style of government decisionmaking, the need for a more positive socialist economic strategy, the fact that the Industry Bill has fewer teeth than is necessary, as well as my opposition to the Common Market. I shall of course continue to support the government and fight for the full implementation of the manifesto. I shall also work hard to ensure that the Labour Party sustains and develops its internationalist principles.'

Tony Benn issued a statement: 'I greatly regret the dismissal of Eric Heffer. He has worked hard and loyally for the Labour government over the last year and his contribution as a minister in the Department of Industry has been outstanding. He has served the Labour movement faithfully and well.'

The Labour movement seemed to agree. Letters and telegrams of support poured in. I received a letter from Ebbw Vale CLP and a telegram from Archie Lush, who had been Nye Bevan's agent: 'Nye would have been delighted with your stand'. Muriel Nicol, the MP for Bradford North in 1945–50 also wrote. My cousin Lt. Col. F.W. Heffer, OBE, said in a letter: 'I agree neither with your politics nor your stand as an anti-marketeer. Having said that I must express my admiration for your courage in sticking, at no small cost, to your principles in this matter.... I was always proud to speak of my cousin who was a minister of state. I am much prouder to refer to you as an MP with guts.'

The National Union of Students expressed their full support. So did Patrick Moore, the astronomer: 'From the far-right, I salute you.' Arthur Ballard, the Liverpool artist, sent a telegram, as did Clive Jenkins, General Secretary of ASTMS. I had telegrams, too, from the Joint Construction Unions on Merseyside and from the Rolls-Royce Hillington Shop Stewards' Committee. Joel Barnett and Bill Wedderburn wrote from the LSE. James Cameron, the journalist, wrote the shortest letter: 'Dear Eric, Thank you. James.' Enoch Powell wrote: 'Dear Eric, Welcome to the club. No political career is worthwhile without one resignation. We are all the better for your decision. With good wishes. Yours ever, Enoch.' I also received letters from Ron Dearing and from my personal private secretary. Joan Dean, my department driver, was very upset, and Frances Morrell, Tony's adviser, was in tears.

FIFTEEN

Lucky Jim?

There is nothing at which the civil service is so skilful as
in persuading a minister who is vague about his policy
that it is much better to let sleeping dogs lie. Unless he
enters office knowing definitely what he wants to do, he
will either do nothing at all, or do merely what the
department wants.

HAROLD J. LASKI, *The Labour Party and the
Constitution*

I resumed my role on the back benches as an active member of the
Tribune group. I was asked to work closely with Ian Mikardo, particularly on prices and incomes, the economy and industrial policy. In
June 1975 the economic situation had again reached crisis proportions
and on 1 July the cabinet discussed the situation. Denis Healey had
stated that the pound was crumbling, and the Chairman of the Bank of
England believed that only a wage-freeze could stop the rot. Public
expenditure and the borrowing requirement would have to be tightly
controlled.

My sacking as a minister must have had an impact on those ministers
on the left who were still in government. On 3 July some left-wing
ministers and others met in Tony Benn's room and discussed the possibility of resignation. In his book *Backbencher*, Mikardo recalled: 'I
thought the behaviour of the ministers was both incomprehensible and
gutless, and I said so more than once in short sharp words of four letters.
But they wouldn't move – except that Judith Hart showed the rest of
them up by resigning.'

In cabinet, the draft White Paper 'The Attack on Inflation' was
discussed. In effect the government was adopting Ted Heath's
deflationary policies. Cuts and unemployment were bound to follow.
Harold Wilson made a statement in the House on 11 July. Tony Benn
noted in his diary that Ken Coates of the Institute of Workers' Control
had urged him to resign. Finally, he decided not to, even though he had

159

been transferred to Energy and Wilson had made it clear that the previous policy of the Department of Trade and Industry was dead. The government had said there would be no compulsory powers regarding wages but then announced its intention to publish a 'Reserve Powers Bill' as a form of wage restraint. It was a bombshell and the left was furious.

In February 1975, Mrs Thatcher had defeated Ted Heath in the first ever ballot for the Tory leadership. After a decent interval, she began putting her people into strategic positions. It has been said by political pundits like Hugo Young that Mrs Thatcher was not elected on a right-wing ticket. I do not believe that. For years Sir Keith Joseph had argued that Tory policy since 1951 had been 'creeping socialism'. Thatcher fully agreed with him but she was clever enough not to change the Shadow Cabinet in one fell swoop. At her first Tory Conference as leader, she proclaimed: 'Britain and Socialism are not the same thing, and as long as I have health and strength they never will be ... Let me give you my vision: a man's right to work as he will, to spend what he earns, to own property, to have the state as servant and not as master: these are the British inheritance. They are the essence of the free country, and on that freedom all other freedoms depend.' Mrs Thatcher thought Heath had been too easy with the unions. She was a hawk in her attitude to the unions as well as to other issues. Norman Tebbit, the 'skinhead from Chingford', became one of her advisers. She also looked to George Gardner, another ultra-right supporter, and Nigel Lawson was taken into the fold. Things were certainly changing in the Tory Party. Mrs Thatcher's advisers outside Parliament were the ex-communist Alfred Sherman and John Hoskyns – both from the hard right.

After the death of Bill Hambling in March 1975, Labour's majority was reduced to one. The government was in a shaky position and the left had no intention of helping the Tories by bringing it down. However, we believed that we should fight for our own amendment to the Reserve Powers Bill. A Tory amendment to reject the bill was defeated by 320 to 260; it got its second reading by 294 to 16. The Tories abstained. The committee stage began the next day. I moved an amendment on behalf of the Tribune group which was defeated by 229 to 39. Enoch Powell and a handful of Tories voted with us. The press accused us of being a party within a party. The committee stage went on through the night but by 1 August the bill received the royal assent.

Eric Varley and Gerald Kaufman had taken over from Tony Benn and myself in the Department of Trade and Industry. When Eric Varley accepted the job of Secretary of State for Industry he clearly repudiated Tony Benn and the party programme. He had moved a long way as one of Harold's 'high flyers' – I recalled an interview we had given together on first entering the House in which he had sounded far more left wing than me.

In 1978, the government introduced an Industry Bill which was very different from the one Tony and I had drafted. As the *Financial Times* said, in a survey in January 1979: 'Two years ago the NEB was the City's enemy: today Barclays, Midland Bank, Rochschilds, United Dominion Trust and Finance for Industry are only some of the private institutions which are working in partnership with it.' And why not? – It was no longer a threat. I agreed with the analysis of Victor Keegan in the *Guardian* of 12 June when he wrote: 'Industry can congratulate itself on the success of the campaign to have Mr Benn shifted.'

At the 1975 Conference Harold pointed to the achievements of Labour in office, stressing the abolition of the Industrial Relations Act and the introduction of the Trade Union and Labour Relations Act, the Health and Safety at Work Act, the National Insurance Act 1974, the Rent Act and the doubling of the Regional Employment Premium: all that in the first government in 1974. He then went on to outline the achievements of the second government: increased child benefits, the Capital Transfer Tax, the Finance (No. 2) Act (this marginally tackled 'the Lump' in the construction industry which I had long fought against), the Housing Subsidies Act, the Offshore Petroleum (Scotland) Act, (nationalizing land for oil construction), the Oil Taxation Act, the Referendum on the EEC, improved pensions, the Social Security Benefits Act, the Social Security Pensions Act and legislation helping the disabled.

Harold was quite pleased with himself. Speaking about the NEC, he said he could record a measurable period of absolute silence – a reference to his threat to NEC members who were ministers. He claimed to have dealt with the extremists, left and right: 'The left were not so much communists as an assortment of left-wing deviationists, sailing under different and frequently changed names. Had the different varieties been locked in a room without food or water until they produced an agreed policy statement, the mortality rate would have been high.' Of the right he said: 'Their group had in fact tried a putsch with much Tory press support against me in the weeks before the February 1974 election – their strength was minimal....' He regarded the right as his real enemy and went on to say that the party needed to protect itself against the activities of small groups of inflexible persuasion. Nevertheless, whilst he was leader not one member of the PLP had had the whip withdrawn and Michael Foot – who under Gaitskell had been disciplined – was now in the cabinet.

On 16 March 1976, Harold resigned as Prime Minister. It came as a great shock. Patrick Cosgrove, a Tory journalist, said in *Harold's Years* that Harold was 'Labour's Baldwin and he will, like Baldwin, be remembered as a simple man who became an enigma.' Harold was succeeded by James Callaghan. It wasn't long before I found myself in conflict with him, especially now that I was on the NEC. Jim said that, after becoming prime minister, he sat down and wrote his 'Objectives for 1980': reduction of inflation to below 5 per cent; unemployment to below 3 per cent; a manageable balance of payments; devolution within the UK; to resume our policies on housing, education, health and welfare; and to create a cohesive society. Admirable objectives – but never carried out.

At the 1976 Conference Tribune rally I spoke of my concern about the gulf between the government and the party: 'Too often the NEC, like the mass of party members in the country or the PLP, hears about policies through the media, rather than by face to face discussions with government ministers.... What, for example, are members of the NEC to say to a speech which today the *Daily Mail* can represent as a speech which "would have sounded well enough from any Tory Prime Minister with his back to the economic wall". Or where the *Daily Express* can say: "He then made what was, in effect, a brutal assault on the dominance of Keynesian ideas in British economic policy. Sir Keith Joseph could not have put it better." What are NEC members to say when the Tory philosophy that the way out of the crisis is to cut public expenditure is enthusiastically accepted within the movement.... If the NEC puts forward an alternative economic strategy, based upon the election manifesto, the party programme and Conference decisions, or proposes public ownership of the banks and insurance companies – also based upon Conference decisions – it must not be treated as if it were a wild bunch of irresponsibles; and the Tory press must not be given comfort in its efforts to set government and party against each other.'

The press attack on Conference delegates was being stepped up and Joe Haines, the ex-press officer to Harold Wilson, writing in the *Daily Mirror*, talked of 'bully boys' and Trotskyists. He later wrote a book which, in parts, was very nasty about Harold, to whom he owed everything. It was clear that the Intelligence Services were influencing Jim Callaghan, and he became obsessed with the notion of Trotskyists infiltrating the party.

After Conference there was constant talk of going to the International Monetary Fund for support but backbenchers did not know that the cabinet was seriously discussing the idea, or that Denis Healey was actually working out a package with the IMF. Crosland had rightly warned that if the package was put forward the TUC would pull out of the Social Contract. Tony Benn was working out an alternative strategy to the IMF proposal but noted in his diary that on 1 and 2 December, cabinet meetings were held which: 'Finally sealed the fate of the government's economic, and therefore, industrial and social policy ...' At a PLP meeting in December Denis Healey announced that the package with the IMF had been agreed and that the cabinet was united. Callaghan said that this was no time for class war and called for unity in the party. When Denis Healey made his speech in the House, I said he should resign. Callaghan in his *Time and Change* said he was unduly irritated by the remark because the cabinet as a whole had taken the decision. In his diaries, Benn says, 'It's a bloody lie' that it was united. I knew that our government then, as during the White Paper 'In Place of Strife' earlier, was laying the basis for the Tories to follow the same policies as us, only worse.

One of the main union struggles during 1977 was that of the firefighters. Terry Fields, District Secretary of the Merseyside Fire Brigades Union, came to see me and explained the position. I thought Terry (now a Labour MP for Broadgreen, Liverpool) put a very fair case and I promised to do all I could to help. I wrote to the Home Secretary warning of a possible strike. The FBU wage claim was moderate, but the government's pay policy stood in the way of a settlement. When the firefighters came out on strike I organized a whip round for them in the Parliamentary Labour Party. I collected £409 – 121 Labour MPs donated. The issue was discussed on the NEC. Although no resolution was passed, it was agreed that officers of the party should seek a meeting with the PM. They were also instructed to raise the whole question of the 10 per cent ceiling for wage increases.

When the public expenditure plans for 1977–8 were announced, a number of us made it clear we would abstain. In the event, the government Whip thought up a procedural way of not having a vote. It was then that the government, not the party, entered into an arrangement with the Liberals. After meetings between Callaghan, Steel and others, an agreement between the two parties was reached. It was strictly a Parliamentary agreement between the front benches, and it was not ratified or even seriously discussed on the NEC. It was designed to do one thing: keep the Labour government in office until it could see its way clear to winning a general election. I had strong reservations about this but I realized that good friends like Audrey Wise could well lose their seats if we went to the country immediately and I felt it right to play for time irrespective of the risks. These were serious: we could achieve very little if we had to rely on the Liberals for support. Already the agreement had included legislation for direct elections to the European Parliament, devolution – which I basically opposed – and a concession on proportional representation. The pact was to last to the end of the Parliamentary session and then be discussed again. Callaghan assured the PLP that the agreement was in no sense a coalition and it did not involve the abandonment of manifesto pledges.

Callaghan's hostile attitude to the left on the NEC is shown in his *Time and Change*: '... the usual group on the NEC was ready to carp, they were not willing to strike.... A small majority of the NEC was usually opposed to the cabinet, and some of the MPs on the NEC appeared to set themselves up as the alternative government.' It did not seem to occur to him that it was only when the government backed away from manifesto commitments, attacked the unions, or failed to really fight Tory policies, that NEC members 'carped'. In the August 1977 *Labour Leader* (a journal published by Independent Labour Publications, once the ILP), I wrote: 'In reality the pact has two purposes: to keep the Tories out: and to introduce legislation of a mildly reformist kind. If renewed, the pact will ensure the government's survival for at least another year. This would enable it to take advantage of North Sea oil, and of any economic upturn.... Ever since the Gaitskell/Bevan clash, forces have existed which wish to change the character of the Labour Party. They would delete Clause IV of the Constitution, destroy our unity with the trade unions and turn the Labour Party into a type of social democratic party. The present situation is seen by these "moderates" as a heaven-sent opportunity to achieve their goals. From our perspective, the pact may have been necessary, but it must be seen as purely temporary.... If the liberalistic elements within the party find this difficult to accept, then they are welcome to join other parties which are closer to their views.'

The first Devolution Bill had been introduced in December 1976. It did not get through the Commons. A second bill was introduced in November 1977 following the Lib/Lab Pact. In 1976 the Liberals voted against the bill. Now they were prepared to support it in exchange for certain amendments which, as it turned out, helped defeat devolution in the referenda held in Scotland and Wales in March 1979.

The time taken up on devolution in the Commons seemed endless. The issue had found its way into Labour's manifesto in 1974. It was ostensibly a response to a report from the Kilbrandon Commission. But what really determined its inclusion was the increase in support for the SNP. By October 1974, it had received 839,000 votes. It frightened the living daylights out of the Labour leaders and also the Scottish Liberals. Even Scottish Tories began to talk of the need for some type of Assembly.

The 1977 bill was divided into two with separate legislation for Scotland and Wales. The bills were guillotined on the first day. Those MPs most strongly opposed to the legislation included Tam Dalyell, Neil Kinnock, George Cunningham and myself. Cunningham moved an amendment to the Consultative Referendum for Scotland stating that if 40 per cent of the total electorate had not voted in favour of devolution, then the Secretary of State for Scotland would have to lay an Order in Parliament, wiping out the entire Act. That amendment was carried by fifteen votes. I was among the thirty-four Labour MPs who voted for it. I wrote in my weekly *Liverpool Echo* column: 'I really cannot understand why supporters of the bill are getting so upset. If the people want devolution then they will vote for it, and in high enough percentages to cover a 40 per cent voting clause'.

Why was I against devolution? My opposition arose out of my under-standing of international socialism and the ideas of the German–Polish Socialist, Rosa Luxemburg and the Austro–Marxists like Otto Bauer and Max Adler. The Austro–Marxists who led the Austrian Social Democratic party were in favour of the Austro–Hungarian Empire being transformed into a socialist unified state. It was a pipe dream. The Empire broke up into separate countries, each with its own Parliament, and the concept of a socialist federation foundered. Luxemburg was particularly opposed to the Poles having a separate national government. I feared that devolution for Scotland and Wales would weaken Britain as a united economic unit and be detrimental to socialism in the UK as a whole. I accepted that the various peoples who made up the UK had cultural differences which had to be respected but, I argued, this was no reason for devolving the UK. Tom Nairn, the left-wing author of *The Break-up of Britain* thought I was wrong but accepted that my argument was a respectable socialist one. In the Commons I made speeches drawing attention to what the Austro–Marxists and Luxemburg had argued. They cut little ice.

When the referenda were held on 1 March 1979, the Welsh people decisively rejected the Welsh Act – Neil Kinnock and those Welsh Labour MPs who had fought the bill were proved correct. In Scotland there was a very marginal majority in favour of the Act, but as 40 per cent did not vote in favour it failed. Today the subject of devolution is still a matter of importance and I have changed my mind on the issue. In *Socialist Scotland* (Summer 1990) I wrote: 'I first went to Scotland during the Second World War. It was then that I began to discover another people and I learned that their law and customs and the cultural heritage were different from those in England. We were united by the fact that we believed in the struggle for a socialist Britain as part of a

165

socialist world. The struggles of the Scottish working class were as important to me, an English socialist, as were the struggles of the English working class to my Scottish friends.... The fact, is, however, that in Scotland the working class has not succumbed as easily to Thatcherite concepts and policies ... because of the unrepresentative nature of the Tory government the mood is for a Scottish Assembly or Parliament with real powers ... unless action is taken in the next Parliament, sooner or later Scottish nationalism will increase and then UDI could eventually be declared ... national rights cannot be ignored, and if they are, they are ignored at peril. That is something that Gorbachev is beginning to fully appreciate in the Soviet Union. The nationalist question can also get involved in class issues and that is what is happening in Russia and to some extent in Scotland.

'Proportional representation will also not go away.... In the long run it could be helpful to the future of socialism, not just socialism in Scotland but in the whole of Europe. Democracy and socialism must be synonomous. The struggle for democratic rights, for the vote, for Parliamentary elections, for the Charter in the 1830s, was a proletarian demand, not a bourgeois one, and the struggle for a vote not tied to property and incomes was one conducted by the working class with some middle-class allies ... but if the system is not able to be used effectively in our class interests ... perhaps it is Arthur Scargill who is right on this, and not us who, up to now, have been opposed to electoral change. Anyway, I certainly am beginning to have definite second thoughts. Not for the reasons that are advanced by Charter 88, the SDP or the SNP but because, in the long run, socialism can gain by a change.'

The Winter of Discontent in 1979 was the final nail in the coffin of the Callaghan government. It arose because, whilst the government had managed to win the TUC to its policies on pay, union members were becoming impatient. Jack Jones ran into trouble at the T&GWU Conference in the summer of 1978. The government seemed oblivious to the problems they were creating and despite the warnings, fixed a pay norm of 5 per cent. When it was announced in the Commons, I told the government that it had just lost the next election. Workers were putting in claims well above 5 per cent. They had suffered restraint for two years but their loyalty was being taken for granted. Strikes developed on a large scale. Fords settled for 17 per cent. The government tried to impose sanctions against the company. Five left-wing Labour MPs abstained. Moss Evans, the T&GWU General Secretary, said that he would, if necessary, appeal to the Labour MPs to oppose the government. Stan Orme, by then a loyal minister, urged Tribune members not to defeat the government. We went to see Callaghan. Some of us argued that this was the final parting of the ways. We had put down an amendment and would ask the Speaker to call it. Michael Foot said that if we voted against the government we would be falling into a Tory trap. We said if our amendment was not called we would abstain on the Conservative amendment. We urged the government to suspend the policy but Callaghan said that this would make it a laughing stock. The Speaker refused to call our amendment and the government was defeated by 285 to 283.

The number of workers involved in strikes increased dramatically. In Liverpool, the gravediggers came out. I said nothing publicly but pressed union officials and shop stewards to find a way for burials to take place unhindered. I was concerned that action of that kind would alienate those who genuinely supported the workers.

The government was responsible for its own unpopularity, and certainly laid the basis for its defeat. After a summit meeting in Guadelupe, Callaghan came back to strike-torn Britain and was reported to have said, 'Crisis? What Crisis?' The press had a field day. He had been expected to call a general election in September 1978. Instead, at the TUC conference, he sang a verse of the song 'Waiting at the Church'. I was amazed when I watched him on television and phoned my agent who had begun to make preparations for the election. I knew it was a monumental mistake for the government to go on.

In his book *The Time of My Life*, Healey says: 'The Winter of Discontent was not caused by the frustration of ordinary workers after a long period of wage restraint. It was caused by institutional pressure from local trade union activists who had found their role severely limited by three years of income policies agreed by their national leaders.' The activists to which he refers *are* the workers. The colossal arrogance of party members like Denis Healey annoys me. He has little real understanding of ordinary working people. Perhaps if he had listened to rank-and-file workers, rather than those in the City or right-wing trade union leaders remote from their own membership, things might have gone better. His economic strategy, like Callaghan's and Jenkins' before him, was a disaster, yet he complacently blames all the problems on the left.

Despite all this, Healey differs from many others in the leadership of Labour's right wing in his genuine interest in political ideas. Perhaps he never entirely forgot his days as a student communist when, he recounts, one of the favourite topics of discussion was, 'Who will do the dirty work under socialism': in later life he discovered it was him – an uncharacteristically honest appraisal.

After the referenda rejecting devolution, the government could find no satisfactory solution to the problem. The Tories thought about a vote of no confidence: in the end, the Scottish Nationalists put down a vote of censure. The Tories immediately supported it. It really was a cliff-hanger. No one could predict with certainty how that vote would go. Alfred Broughton, a Labour MP, was seriously ill, and was brought in to vote. (He died shortly after.) Gerry Fitt, the SDLP Member for Belfast, decided to vote against the government. He rightly opposed the Ulster Unionists getting more seats from future boundary changes. The government was defeated by 311 votes to 310. The Callaghan government had proved to be its own worst enemy.

SIXTEEN

Committee Man

Anyone can make marvellous speeches and write
excellent pamphlets, and I assure you it is very easy to
be a Right Honourable, and carry a red box, and have a
ministerial car, but if you are not on the right side when
it matters, you are not much use to the movement.

TONY BENN, *Fighting Back*

I was elected to Labour's National Executive Committee in 1975 – the
year I was sacked as Minister of State for Industry. I replaced Denis
Healey. My first NEC meeting was at Conference at the end of
Wednesday's business. I was elected to the CLP section alongside Frank
Allaun, Tony Benn, Barbara Castle, Michael Foot, Joan Lestor and Ian
Mikardo. Jim Callaghan was Treasurer, the Leader and Deputy Leader
were Harold Wilson and Edward Short, respectively. The General
Secretary was Ron Hayward and the National Agent Reg Underhill. By
1976, I was contributing to the work of the Organization, Youth, Press
and Publicity, Home Policy, and International committees. Thereafter I
served on a wide range of committees, subcommittees and study groups
and became Chairman of the Organization Committee, which was a key
position. I also served on the TUC-Labour Party Liaison Committee and
often chaired the International Committee.

Shortly after I joined the NEC, the Labour government proposed
cutting subsidies for council housing, something I could not accept. I
fully supported the NEC resolution which placed on record 'the belief
that cuts in council house subsidies would have disastrous consequences'.
As a former construction worker and member of UCATT, I spoke regularly on housing in the House and at the NEC I put forward a resolution
which urged the government 'to give priority to restoring cuts in house
building and improvements, both by local authorities and housing
associations, in view of the serious need for more homes, and of the
growing unemployment in the building industry ...'

At the 1977 Conference, the document 'Building Britain's Future' was debated. I had chaired the committee which drafted it and I was delighted that when Danny Crawford of UCATT spoke, he noted the document 'demonstrated a depth of understanding of the industry which has been lacking in the past within the party.' In my reply to the debate, I insisted that casualization must end, and that construction workers needed job security, decent working conditions and improved safety. In the long term we needed a Public Procurement Agency to ensure a regular flow of work. We should push for more Direct Labour Departments. The party should call for the establishment of a National Construction Corporation which would take over one or two major companies. 'Building Britain's Future' was carried overwhelmingly. Construction employers then began a campaign known as 'CABIN' (Campaign Against Building Industry Nationalization). They said that Labour intended to nationalize the *whole* industry. Afterwards I thought we might just as well have gone for all-out public ownership in view of the overheated attitude of the Tories, the employers and the press.

In the economic debate, both Denis Healey and Neil Kinnock spoke. Denis, in 1975, had justified his policy of going to the IMF for a massive loan. This time he justified the general policy of the government on economic matters, arguing that it was working and that all that was needed was more time. Kinnock weighed in very strongly: 'What [Healey] is saying of course is that he and the IMF are so despairing at the depth of depression in the capitalist world that any means must be used to try to stimulate the Western economies or disaster faces; and the fact of the matter is that there is a dole queue twenty million long in the other manufacturing, industrialized, advanced countries of the Western world ... as the TUC has said in two successive years, as this Conference said last year, as I think this Conference is going to say this year – the only way to fight our way out of this crisis is to see that the state, the government, stimulates where capitalism has not, and will not, stimulate. That is the request of this Conference.'

The NEC statement on the abolition of the Lords was also debated. A resolution from the T&GWU was taken at the same time. It called for an efficient single-chamber legislating body without delay, with abolition to be in the manifesto backed up by a national campaign. The resolution was in line with NEC proposals. Ending his speech, Jack Jones said, 'We want to revive the ideas of socialism, and I ask you to vote overwhelmingly for the motion in the spirit of one of our great founders, Keir Hardie, who would have damned to death the House of Lords, and so should we.' In his reply for the NEC, John Forrester said, 'Comrades, I say to this Conference what we cannot mend we must now determine to end ... if Conference accepts the T&GWU resolution the NEC will

170

gladly endeavour to have the intention contained in the resolution included in the next election manifesto.' On a card vote it was carried by 6,248,000 to 91,000. The NEC statement was also carried. As the majority for the resolution was well over two thirds, the Party could expect the abolition of the House of Lords to be in the manifesto.

An excellent statement was carried on international big business, and a resolution was also carried deploring the continuing disqualification of twenty-one Clay Cross Labour councillors and demanding a government bill to remove disqualification forthwith. A resolution calling for Labour to close down all nuclear bases, and another on the reselection of MPs were remitted. That meant their fate was in the hands of the NEC. A strong resolution against the Common Market was also remitted whilst the NEC's statement was carried. It was clear these issues would come up again. Conference was very radical in spirit, and I was again elected to the NEC with a good majority.

At an NEC meeting in November 1977 Ian Mikardo proposed that, as the resolution on reselection had been remitted to the NEC, a working party be established. His proposal got through on the chairman's casting vote and a working party was set up. Mikardo pointed out that although the CLPs would support reselection it was possible that the trade unions would use their block votes to crush the proposition. That would cause a great deal of pain in the CLPs and develop serious antagonism between them and the trade unions. He therefore made a proposal which became known as 'The Mikardo Compromise' – where a CLP wanted reselection they could have it, but they were not compelled to reselect. It was accepted by the majority on the committee. The Campaign for Labour Party Democracy (CLPD) considered that Mikardo had reneged on mandatory reselection and opposed his membership on the NEC. He was defeated and Neil Kinnock and Dennis Skinner were elected. Norman Atkinson was elected Treasurer. Because of the election of Kinnock and Skinner the press declared that the NEC was now left-wing dominated.

Neil Kinnock was an active member and a staunch supporter of CLPD, but I did not join for many years. My doubts about some of the issues it raised suggested I might lose its support too. As I had never really supported the Tribune slate either I did not miss any sleep over this. I had stood on the Tribune slate for years but it was my stand on Chile and the EEC which won over the CLPs and saw me elected to the NEC.

Because it was clear that a general election was not far away, a series of joint NEC/Cabinet working groups were set up. I served on Housing and Land, Government Machinery, EEC and Unemployment. It was

171

later claimed by enemies of the left, that such joint committees were first established under Neil Kinnock. That was a straightforward lie; the working parties we established prior to the 1979 election were genuinely joint bodies; the Cabinet had half the membership and sometimes more. The Cabinet and government were also fully represented on all the NEC working parties.

The working groups were established on the basis of resolutions formulated and discussed at Party Conference. A resolution which had originally come from a trade union branch or CLP ward, could go to the EC of the union or CLP, could be discussed at the full CLP meeting or conference of the trade union, then if agreed could go to the Labour Party for inclusion on the annual Conference agenda. The NEC working parties would examine the resolutions passed at Conference and work out policies based upon them. The humblest party member could help formulate policy; it meant the most widespread membership involvement at all levels. Then reports would go to Conference for debate and voting. It was socialism from the bottom. As I write, proposals are afoot from the party leadership which will change all this. The Conference will be downgraded and a new body will be established to consider policy.

Following the 1978 Conference the left consolidated its position on the NEC. Tony Benn was Chair of the Home Policy Committee, Joan Lestor of the International Committee, Joan Maynard of the Youth Committee, Frank Allaun of the Publicity Committee, and Norman Atkinson was Treasurer. I became chairman of the Organization Committee. I was now well and truly involved in internal party affairs.

The general election was called for 3 May 1979 and I attended the Clause V meeting of the NEC and cabinet members to finalize the manifesto. It was clear that radical policies carried at Conference were not welcomed by Jim Callaghan and that he intended to keep as many as possible out of the manifesto. A draft NEC manifesto had been drawn up by Geoff Bish. Jim Callaghan got one of his aides to produce an alternative document and a joint meeting of some cabinet members, including Callaghan and NEC members, took place at Number Ten in the early hours to try to bring the two together. It was one of the most painful meetings I have ever attended.

Jim was determined to make sure the manifesto would be without any commitment to radical policies. The real crunch came on the question of the abolition of the Lords. The conference resolution had received over a two-thirds majority and should have been automatically included. Jim said that if it was he would resign as party leader. At first I was dumbfounded and then very angry. I asked him who did he think he was? He was a party member like the rest of us. There was an acrimonious exchange but he refused to budge. We were therefore faced with the possibility of two elections: the general election already announced, and the election of party leader. This was sheer blackmail. It was because of that exchange that the demand arose for the NEC to draw up the manifesto and for a rule that the leader could not operate a veto. At the NEC Home Policy Committee on 16 July 1979 I moved the necessary resolution. It was seconded by Neil Kinnock.

The matter came before the Party Conference in October that year and the NEC supported a motion moved by Stuart Weir (later editor of the *New Statesman*), the delegate of Hackney and Shoreditch CLP: 'This Conference is deeply disturbed at the continued failure of success-ive Labour governments to advance the realization of the party's long-term objectives. It regrets that policies approved by Conference, and recommended by the NEC for inclusion in the party's general election manifestos, are often omitted because some members of the Labour government/Shadow Cabinet object to them, such as the abolition of the House of Lords. Conference therefore instructs the NEC to submit to the 1980 Labour Party Annual Conference constitutional proposals which would lay down that the NEC alone, after the widest possible consultation with all sections of the movement, would take the final decision as to the contents of the Labour Party general election manifesto.' In his speech, Stuart Weir said, 'At the last election we hardly recognized the manifesto we were supposed to be fighting on ... what happened? When it came to the crunch, Mr Callaghan presented an entirely new draft from 10 Downing Street which became the basis for the manifesto.... Then finally at the Clause V meeting, the meeting of the full NEC and Cabinet, the meeting which is supposed to have the final say, Mr Callaghan suddenly produced a constitutional amendment, the leader's personal veto.' The resolution was carried on a card vote by 3,936,000 to 3,088,000; a reasonable majority. The matter would be up before us again at the 1980 Conference.

At the 1979 Conference, Tony Benn and I published a statement, 'Unity Through Democracy'. In it we stressed that many trade unions and constituency party members were disappointed with the way the party had been operating and the basis of our recruitment of new members ought to be that their views would really count both in making policy and in seeing that it was carried out. We believed that the party's elected leadership must be accountable to the policy decided at confer-ence and that patronage too must go. We supported the NEC decision to put all these matters to Conference and argued that Conference should support mandatory reselection of Labour MPs; an electoral college to

173

choose the leader; and the demand that Conference decide the contents of the manifesto.

To back up our views we issued three supporting documents: 'The Party and the Unions – A strategy for Close Co-operation' (approved by the Organization subcommittee on 10 September 1979); 'The Future Work of the PLP' (a paper discussed at three PLP meetings in July and a PLP working party set up to consider it after Conference); and 'The Labour Party Manifesto and How it Should be Prepared' (a paper approved by the Home Policy Committee on 10 September 1979). Tony and I worked closely on these issues and our documents were genuinely joint efforts.

Although Labour lost seats in the 1979 election it did not lose votes. The mood in the party, however, was one of real unhappiness. In 1979, the NEC set up the commission of enquiry. As chairman of the Organization Committee I explained to Conference that we were urged by the unions to set it up. In September 1979 we met them and agreed to their request. The terms of reference were very comprehensive. The Commission was to deal with the finances of the party, to consider ways of improving political education, and to review the policy-making process, the relations between Conference, the NEC, the PLP and the constitution. The pressure for this commission came mainly from right-wing trade union leaders. They were clearly alarmed at left-wing support in the party which was diminishing their influence. They had problems in their own organizations where the rank and file had also moved left.

They focused their attention initially on problems about party finance and the opportunity was taken by the right to undermine the Treasurer, Norman Atkinson. They did not want Norman and stressed the financial problems, more or less blaming him. It was very unfair. Today, with the new right-wing non-socialist party under Kinnock, the party's finances are far worse. Some of the proposals of the Commission were useful but, in practice, they were already being implemented by the NEC with the help of the rank and file: for example, the need to build up the circulation of the *Labour Weekly* (which the right wanted to get rid of and eventually did under Kinnock) and the establishment of a theoretical journal, something for which I had long argued. The journal was established, the *New Socialist*. It began well but after a period seriously deteriorated. The Commission, in my view, was a waste of time and energy. It was a deliberate diversion and its existence caused the party a great deal of harm. It created an atmosphere of confusion and paved the way for our further defeat in 1983.

On the Friday morning of the 1980 Conference I made the last speech on behalf of the NEC on the political education section of the

Commission's report: 'Irrespective of what the press have said, and I read the editorials in the *Guardian* talking about our entrails being in the mud and all that sort of thing, this party is in good heart. When I go around the country like other MPs, Tony Benn, Joan Lestor, Dennis Skinner and the rest of us, speaking at party meetings and rallies, I find that our members are absolutely determined to democratize the party and at the same time to get the Tories out and to build a socialist society.'

The Conference decisions on the economy included the restriction on the export of capital, and an extension of public ownership, a substantial cut in arms expenditure, the immediate introduction of a wealth tax, selected import controls and a thirty-five-hour week without reduction of pay. With regard to unemployment, closures and redundancies had to be opposed, overtime reduced, and the retirement age reduced. There was support for workers' alternative plans, such as Lucas Aerospace, support for workers' co-operatives and for using public ownership to create employment. We had to defend and expand retraining of older workers. On issue after issue, much as on the EEC and defence, the Conference decisions were socialist and radical. Mandatory reselection for MPs was carried as was a constitutional amendment on the principle of the election of the leader. There had been considerable confusion on the issue, two alternatives being rejected. The NEC had come up with a further proposal that was also lost. A special rules revision conference was to be held in three months' time. Conference also carried the NEC draft manifesto but it could not become the election manifesto unless changes were made in Clause V of the constitution.

During Conference Callaghan made his last speech as party leader; he resigned on 15 October. As Chair of the Organization Subcommittee I urged the PLP not to go ahead with an election under the old rules. I began my speech by quoting the NEC resolution: 'This meeting of the NEC, having taken account of the decision of Conference that the leader and deputy leader of the party should be elected on a wider franchise, calls on the PLP to suspend its normal practice so that the elections for the forthcoming session are deferred and so that the officers and the Parliamentary committee for the 1979–80 Session continue until the Conference decision has been carried out.' I continued: 'Let me say from the outset that the NEC does not regard the Shadow Cabinet's proposal to go ahead with the election of a leader or deputy leader as illegitimate or illegal. The PLP are perfectly entitled to go ahead with the election and the Shadow Cabinet are fully entitled to propose or hold such an election if they so desire. I therefore do not agree that it is illegitimate, but it is ill-advised. It can cause really serious and difficult problems for the party. I say that because of the decision of Conference.

The first and main argument against suspending standing orders is that we need a new leader now. The truth is that the deputy leader can carry on. He has proved his worth in debate and Parliamentary procedure and organization against the Tories in the House and he can continue to lead without any great difficulty. Secondly, if a new leader were elected he would not have the authority that it is said he would have because the Tories would say, "What about the forthcoming Conference and the new election?"

'In conclusion, let me say I do not believe in threats; I do not believe that the PLP has no rights; on the contrary, I believe that the rights of the PLP must be upheld. Equally, the NEC has rights; we are the custodians of Conference decisions and we believe that the election should be postponed. I also ask that the views of trade union leaders like Moss Evans and David Basnett as well as dozens of CLPs should be listened to. It is not in our view too much to ask the PLP and I hope they will support the plea of the NEC and suspend standing orders.'

It was obvious that if an election were held the front right-wing runner would be Denis Healey. The right wing was determined to go ahead, and the PLP rejected the NEC appeal. The Denis Healey of 1990 is not the same as the Healey of the 1970s or the 1980s. Today, he is charm itself, with a hail-fellow-well-met bubbly good humour. Then he was, or could be, very belligerent indeed. Peter Shore and John Silkin fancied themselves to beat Healey. I thought that was impossible. For some reason, Michael Foot decided to support Peter Shore. Peter was not left-wing but had that reputation because he was anti-Market. Shore, in my view did not have a cat in hell's chance of defeating Healey. When I heard that Michael Foot had endorsed Shore, I telephoned him urging him to reconsider and stand himself. I felt he should do this on an interim basis until the new leadership electoral college was in being when Tony Benn could stand. I reckoned without his ambition – once elected Foot had no intention of standing down under the new rules.

Clive Jenkins and Ian Mikardo, I now learn, had also phoned Foot. Michael had a dinner party in his house to discuss the situation. Those present included Moss Evans, Alan Fisher, Clive Jenkins, Bill Keyes, Alec Smith and Arthur Scargill. Clearly, the object was to influence the MPs through an elitist group of trade union leaders, most of whom turned out to be dicey allies of the left; in any case, they couldn't vote in the leadership election.

I supported Foot because I felt that he was the only one who could beat Healey. Shore and Silkin stood, and in the first ballot Healey got 112, Foot 83, Silkin 38 and Shore 32. Both Silkin and Shore dropped out. On the final ballot, Foot got 139 and Healey 129. Foot was now the party leader. At the PLP Healey congratulated Foot and said that he would be happy to serve under him as deputy leader. At that stage no one in the PLP challenged Healey. After the Shadow Cabinet elections on 5 December 1980, I issued the following statement: 'The elections to the Shadow Cabinet this year after Michael Foot's election as leader were of immense importance to the Labour Party. There was a real need for a truly balanced Shadow Cabinet. Michael Foot requires people around him prepared to fight hard for the political policies he supports. I had hoped to have been one of the elected twelve to do just that. After the Shadow Cabinet elections last year, I said that I would not take a Shadow job unless elected by the PLP. I believe the principle of election to Shadow Cabinet posts is the correct one, irrespective of who the leader is. To have responsibility without any real say by voice or vote on the elected committee in my view is wrong. I have decided therefore, despite my support for Michael Foot as leader, not to accept a Shadow post. I will support Michael and help to conduct the fight against this disastrous Tory government from the back benches.'

A special Party Conference to decide on the procedure for electing the leader and deputy leader was held in January 1981 at the Wembley Conference Centre. The electoral college it proposed for this gave the trade unions a 40 per cent vote, 30 per cent to CLPs and 30 per cent to MPs. From the word go I had supported one third, one third, one third. That was the decision of the NEC, but it had not been fully accepted at the Bishops Stortford Conference. David Basnet had argued for 50 per cent for MPs. It was left to Conference to decide. The USDAW vote was decisive. The AEU decided to abstain because they would not support any motion which did not give the MPs a 75 per cent vote in the electoral college.

On 1 April Tony Benn decided to stand for deputy leader. I told him I was not sure it was the best thing to do at this stage. Why not wait until the leadership became available? Tony did not agree and decided to go ahead. I made my position clear in a statement which was published in *Tribune*: 'Over the past few years, especially since the last general election, the left within the Labour Party has made tremendous and important advances.... The danger in the present situation is that if a left-wing candidate argues that he or she truly embodies the policy accepted by the party, and is then defeated, that will be interpreted by the right as a defeat of the policies rather than a defeat for the individual concerned... There is no doubt, that the recent announcement by Tony Benn, without first discussing the situation with the group, or even a proper joint discussion with colleagues who have worked in agreement with him for a period of time, has caused worry and confusion, not only in the House of Commons, but also in some parties in the country. There is a feeling that, because of the defectors, because Michael Foot is now leader, because of the media attack on the party, and in particular because of the need for a united fight against the Tories, this was not the time, or the right thing to do at the moment.

'I would urge us to keep cool, not to lose our heads, and for all of us to have another look at the situation; in the meantime those concerned as proposed candidates for the deputy leadership should be prepared to change position in the light of the problems and complexities which lie ahead for the left and the party.'

However, once Tony had decided to go ahead there was nothing we could do about it. The contest was on. Some of the Tribune group urged me to stand. I said I would consider the proposition, but would consult my CLP. I became suspicious of the motives of some of the Tribunites and it became very clear that they wanted to use me as a fall-guy. Robert Kilroy-Silk reveals in his book *Hard Labour*: 'I can remember we were urging Heffer to stand for the deputy leadership ... against Denis Healey and Tony Benn. We actually didn't want to support him, although he thought we did. We just wanted someone on whom we could waste our vote instead of being forced to vote for Benn.' I realized then that people like Kilroy-Silk, John Silkin and Frank Field had joined Tribune not out of socialist conviction but because they felt it might advance them in Labour politics. That really sickened me.

Walton CLP felt it would be quite wrong for two left-wingers to be in competition and knew I was not really in favour of any contest. In the interests of left unity they urged me not to stand and I accepted their advice.

It was during the deputy leadership campaign that I had a fierce exchange with Arthur Scargill. Speaking in Scotland at the Miners' Gala, he attacked myself and Neil Kinnock – 'so-called lefts' – for not supporting Tony Benn. I wrote to him on 15 June 1981:

Dear Arthur,
I see from some of the Sunday newspapers and today's papers that you attacked me and other comrades at the Scottish Miners' Rally.

I would like to know on what basis the attack was made. Where or when have I written about or in a speech attacked Tony Benn? ... When have I ever indicated or stated I would support Healey or even John Silkin? In fact, on television after I had decided not to stand I clearly said I would in no way be supporting Healey.

I wonder what your objectives are in making such an attack. Has it not crossed your mind that such unwarranted attacks on comrades help those opposing the policies about which we agree? ... I expect from you some clear answers to the questions I have put. I also feel you should apologize for your scurrilous attacks.

Yours sincerely,
Eric Heffer

Arthur replied to me on 19 June:

Dear Eric,

I was rather surprised to receive your letter complaining about my speech to the Scottish Miners' Gala on Saturday 13 June 1981.

I made my comments about your role in the election for the deputy leader of the party based upon well-publicized and documented fact! In the *Financial Times* on 13 April 1981, under the heading 'Heffer Joins "Stop Benn" Campaigners' it was reported that you were publicly joining the campaign to stop Tony Benn from challenging Mr Denis Healey for the deputy leadership of the party. The article went on to state that you had written to all MPs belonging to Labour's Tribune group arguing that a contested election would be against the interests of the Labour Party as a whole and the left in particular.

That statement arguing against an election under the new pro-cedures adopted at the special conference on 24 January, can only be construed as support for the existing deputy leader, Mr Denis Healey, because it is a contradiction in terms to suggest that one opposes the deputy leader on policy and yet at the same time support the argu-ments of the right wing that there should be no election.

I am well aware that after you had decided not to stand (probably taking into account the fact that your constituency party was supporting Tony Benn) you said that you would in no way be supporting Healey, but that does not detract from your earlier state-ment which was construed publicly to be in opposition to Tony Benn's decision to fight Healey in an election.

On the other hand, of course, I do not recall any statement to the effect that you would be opposing Mr Silkin and, more important, I am not aware of any public statement that you have made in support of Tony Benn's candidature, which one would most certainly have expected from someone who has consistently declared himself to be a leader of the left within the party and Labour movement.... The objective I had in mind when making any speech was to provoke the conscience of every left-wing MP into publicly declaring support and fighting for the candidature of Tony Benn.... I trust that the points made in this letter are very clear answers to the questions posed and in the light of what I have said, trust you will now come out publicly with a declared message for the candidature of Tony Benn in the contest for deputy leadership of the party.

Yours sincerely,
Arthur Scargill, President

I was disappointed at Arthur's intolerance and further exchanges took place. On 6 July I wrote a letter to Dick Clements, then editor of *Tribune*:

'Arthur Scargill's so-called reply to me is amazing. He bases his "case" on a piece written in the *Financial Times* of 13 April. The view that I had joined the "Stop Benn" campaign was that of the headliner of the piece, not mine. Arthur surely should not take everything he reads in the newspapers as gospel. He, as much as anyone in the trade union and Labour movement, should know that.

'It would appear from Arthur Scargill's letter that my "crime" was that I had sent a letter to all Tribune MPs which, although referred to, was not quoted in the *Financial Times* because in fact I did not give them or any other newspaper a copy!

'Actually, the letter was published in full in *Tribune* on the Thursday after I had sent it to all Tribune group MPs. It would seem that Arthur Scargill does not regularly read *Tribune*, otherwise he would have known the contents of my letter. Let me quote from that letter. It said, 'Now that a new method of electing the leader and deputy leader is in being, anyone in the PLP has the right to stand for either of these offices under the rules. That right cannot be denied and must be defended."

'It is true, I did go on to say: "The issue for us in the Tribune group is, should someone on the left at this stage, especially a Tribune group member, be challenging for either of these positions? Is it politically wise to do so, and if such a challenge is undertaken, on what terms should the challenge be made?" I find it amazing that the letter in any way could be construed as support for Denis Healey. Only someone who *wants* to believe that could interpret it in that way ... Once an election was clearly on, and I had personally decided not to stand, my vote was never in doubt. I shall be voting for Tony Benn, despite Scargill. His contribution certainly does not help ...'

It gave me no great pleasure to do what I had to do to put the record straight. Later when the miners were on strike I gave my full backing to Arthur because I felt he was right to lead the strike in the way he did. I continue to support him today and I feel he is being wrongly hounded by people who wish to destroy him because of his class politics and hatred of the capitalist system. The trouble is that people with strong views, especially if they are anti-capitalist, do not always help themselves. This is a charge that could sometimes be made against me.

At the Conference Tony Benn lost the deputy leadership vote by the smallest of margins. I felt that the left had suffered a real setback and I think time has proved me right. From that point on every effort was made by the centre and right to undermine the left which was now divided between so-called 'hard' and 'soft' wings. In time the careerists and opportunists in the Tribune group became dominant – with disastrous consequences for socialist politics in Britain.

During 1981 the NEC instigated a great campaign against unemployment. Rallies were held in Liverpool, Birmingham, Glasgow, Cardiff and elsewhere. The Liverpool turnout was about half a million – it seemed as if the whole city was there. I marched from Sefton Park with Tony Benn and made a speech at Pier Head to a sea of faces. I was proud of the Liverpool people. I phoned my brother-in-law Bob and asked if he had seen it on television. 'Seen it on television?' he replied. 'The family and I marched all the way!'

Elsewhere the numbers turning out were not so great, although Glasgow was excellent. I was not booked to speak because of my past opposition to devolution, but the crowd demanded I be given the platform and gave me a tremendous reception. However, the Benn-Healey contest haunted the demonstrations and on occasions Healey was howled down. I did not like Healey's policies but shouting him down was counter-productive and gave the right a useful weapon against us.

The attack on the left continued. In 1982 a register of groups was introduced and a committee set up to investigate Militant Tendency. The issue of Militant had first been raised on the NEC by Reg Underhill in 1977 and a subcommittee of John Chalmers, Tom Bradley, Michael Foot, Ron Hayward and myself was then set up to examine documents held by the National Agent. Our report noted 'the NEC has declared against witch hunts. It is because of our principles of democratic socialism that the NEC urges tolerance and believes that Trotskyist views cannot be beaten by disciplinary action.' We felt that the declared aims and claims of Militant Tendency should be opposed by education, not expulsion.

In 1980, Underhill had further investigated the activities of Militant and issued a statement attacking them. As Chairman of the Organization Committee I replied: 'It is surely important that this whole question of groups and tendencies should not get out of perspective. The conference made its position clear in 1977 and no really new evidence has been presented ... the publication of Lord Underhill's statement and docu-

181

ments should not be used as the occasion to commence witch hunts and embark on internal strife. . . .'

At the 1982 Annual Conference a report on Militant Tendency, drawn up by Ron Hayward and David Hughes, was moved by the new General Secretary, Jim Mortimer. He made it clear that he was not in favour of a witch hunt, but as General Secretary, he had to stress that the constitution of the party be upheld. In the debate the left's case was eloquently put by Mildred Gordon of Hendon South CLP who pointed out: 'I was in America during the McCarthy period; and I want you to remember, comrades, that once you start a witch hunt it has its own momentum . . .'

Michael Foot replied to the debate and accepted that he must take complete responsibility on the matter because he had moved the motion at the NEC to set up the enquiry. At the NEC Michael had been fully backed by Neil Kinnock, with whom I had a sharp exchange, reminding him that he had at one time associated with Militant supporters in his own constituency. Although I was chairman of the Organization Subcommittee I refused to have anything to do with attempts to outlaw groups, journals or individuals. That did not mean that I agreed with Militant, but I felt that we could not have double standards. I had fought hard against the motion and reminded Foot of what he had said in the past about *Socialist Outlook* and the Socialist Fellowship. He was not pleased, but neither was I. Michael was rejecting his own record of belief in freedom of speech and organization within the party. He was no longer the man I had grown to respect over the years.

SEVENTEEN

Mrs Thatcher Moves In

> Margaret found for the first time that she really did
> have the levers of power in her hands, and my goodness
> she was going to exercise them. From day one in
> cabinet she was very much more determined and gave a
> far stronger lead than she ever gave in opposition.
>
> JIM PRIOR, *A Balance of Power*

I will always have the picture before me of Mrs Thatcher standing in front of number ten reciting the prayer of St Francis:

> Lord make me an instrument of your peace.
> Where there is hatred, let me sow love;
> Where there is injury, pardon;
> Where there is doubt, faith;
> Where there is despair, hope;
> Where there is darkness, light;
> Where there is sadness, joy.

Time has revealed that she has not been the instrument of peace. She has not created love, she has not pardoned the unfortunate wrong-doer. She has not produced faith, except in the profit-making system of capitalism. She has not given hope to the poor, the unemployed and the homeless. She has not shed light on society, but endeavoured to get us back to outdated Victorian values. She has given joy to the rich and spread misery elsewhere.

The result of the 1979 general election led to the Conservatives winning 339 seats, Labour 269, Liberals 11 and others 16. That gave the Conservatives an overall majority of 43. Mrs Thatcher made Sir Geoffrey Howe Chancellor of the Exchequer, Lord Carrington Foreign Secretary and William Whitelaw Home Secretary. She offered Ted Heath the ambassadorship to the US, which he turned down.

In May 1977, I wrote an article for *The Times,* where I asked if Mrs Thatcher and Sir Keith Joseph would put their free market policies into

183

practice, warning that a bleak prospect faced the nation if they did so. Although 'wets' held office at first, within a very short time Mrs Thatcher imposed her personality and policies on the cabinet and the Thatcher-Joseph concepts took over. Selsdon Man was let out of his cage.

After the election, in a further article in *The Times* I argued that Labour must not tear itself apart but should seriously question why its government had rejected the alternative economic strategy of the NEC, why it had advocated cuts in public expenditure, and why it had become wedded to the futile 5 per cent pay policy. I quoted from an essay 'Forty Years On' (in *Political Quarterly*) written by my old friend, John Mackintosh, with whom I had previously disagreed on so many occasions: 'A political party capable of winning a majority of votes must be a complex and representative body. The task of socialists is not just to defeat their Conservative opponents, but to keep up discussions inside the Labour Party which go beyond the question of who wins the next election.' That view has become very unpopular with the present day leadership. But in the wake of the 1979 defeat it is precisely what the left in the Labour Party did. Because we wanted Labour to be a really serious opposition in Parliament, reflecting the swing to the left in the country, Tony Benn and I put forward a paper, 'The Future of the PLP', which argued:

The PLP meeting should be the main forum of debate and should be the final authority – subject to Conference policy – on all matters concerning day-to-day work in the Commons.

The PLP meeting should have the right to discuss all recommendations relating to the handling of Parliamentary business and proposed appointments should go before it for approval.

All principal front-benchers, as well as the Parliamentary Committee should be elected each session by open ballot. Proposed shadow portfolios should be approved by the PLP.

Subject groups within the PLP should recommend the names of other speakers from the front bench and nominate members for all committees in the House.

There should be regular meetings of the Parliamentary Committee and the NEC. Reports of such meetings should be given to the PLP.

All staff employed or funded for the work of opposition should be fully integrated with existing PLP staff.

No names should be put forward for peerages on behalf of the party.

These arrangements should remain in force when Labour is in government.

The debates on the various papers extended over several PLP meetings. I thought at the first meeting there had been general agreement on a number of our proposals; Willie Hamilton presented a paper on patronage which had definite similarities to our own. Jim Callaghan made a long speech attacking the proposals and I responded to it at the second meeting. I pointed out that he had given a false impression of the character of NEC working parties. I had chaired a number of these and they included Ministers, MPs, academics, practical people from the industries and civil service, and from trade unions concerned. It was untrue to say they were narrow, one-sided and based in London. This view originated from a hostile press rather than from party documents. Government policy had only been discussed with the PLP after cabinet had agreed it and not always then. We were told, not asked, what our policy or tactics should be. PLP members had less influence over issues than ordinary councillors had over council policy. Nevertheless, the PLP did not want the tight discipline that existed in some council groups.

There was some argument about our proposal for an open ballot. A good case could be made out for secret ballots but what was important was to have a vote rather than appointments by individuals. What we were proposing was not particularly new. The party had discussed such issues back in 1925. In 1929, the ILP Conference carried a resolution in favour of the PLP selecting the cabinet.

After I had spoken, Tony Benn passed me a note observing that there was agreement on the working party and we should try to get that formalized rather than keep going for our full programme. The wider context arguments, such as the drafting of the manifesto by the NEC and mandatory re-selection, still frightened many centre MPs and others did not understand the relationship of our proposals to the fight against the Tories. It would take time for them to be absorbed. Our initiative was to no avail. A working party was set up but the result of its deliberations was disappointing. Today, there is even less discussion and involvement of the PLP on policy and tactics and power has been removed from the NEC and the PLP, in favour of the leader.

In the meantime we were faced with a fundamentalist Tory Party and a Labour Party which at first pretended it was socialist, but soon showed its true colours. I outlined my analysis in a Lenten lecture which I gave to the Jubilee group (a religious socialist group), on 'The Changing Face of Toryism': Winston Churchill, in 1946, defined Tory objectives as: '"to uphold the Christian religion and resist all attacks on it. To defend our Monarchist and Parliamentary constitution. To provide adequate security against external aggression and safety for our seaborne trade. To uphold law and order ... to support as a general rule free enterprise and initiative against state trading and nationalization of industries." Harold Macmillan, in *The Middle Way*, refined Churchill's words: "If capitalism had been conducted all along as if the theory of private enterprise were a matter of principle, we should have had civil war long ago.... I do not propose to employ the defence of private enterprise in the fields for which it is best suited in order to condone or excuse the poverty and insecurity in the basic necessities of life.... The volume of the supply of these necessities, the prices at which they are sold, and the power of the consumers to buy them should not be left to the determination of the push and pull of competitive effort." In 1974, Sir Keith Joseph outlined the new Toryism: "... our industry, economic life and society have been so debilitated by thirty years of socialistic fashions that their very weakness tempts further inroads.... We have overestimated the power of government to do more and more for the people, to reshape the economy and indeed human society, according to blueprints. I argue that there are limits to the good which government can do to help the economy, but no limit to the harm."' It was clear that the Thatcher government intended to carry through the Joseph policies, not those of Macmillan.

In February 1980 I put the economic argument in an article for *The Times* 'The Friedman Plan – Ready for the Bin?': 'Professor Friedman is, like Mrs Thatcher's government, only up to "A" levels in his economic thinking ... one could be forgiven for believing that he looks upon the people as having a mental age of no more than fifteen or sixteen ... he rightly draws attention to the fact that a pencil is the product of co-operative labour and says it can only really be produced because "the operation of the free market is so essential, not only to promote productive efficiency, but even more to foster harmony and peace amongst the peoples of the world". It is such a simple notion that Professor Friedman misses the whole point. It is precisely because no one product can be made by one person, that co-operative effort and ownership is required. This was the message that Harold Macmillan preached in *The Middle Way*. It was the theme of Maynard Keynes' economics; it is in reality the only way to survival.' I was delighted to receive a letter from Professor J.K. Galbraith, who was staying in London at the time. He wrote: 'I've just read your piece in Monday's *Times*. Rarely, vanity being what it is, have I encountered anything I have so much wished I might have written myself. I hope we meet some time so I may tell you so in person. Faithfully, J.K. Galbraith.'

Two things happened in October 1980, which, for a period, stimulated a real fightback against Tory policies. Firstly, unemployment passed the two million mark and areas like Liverpool were badly hit as the government's policy of non-interference began to bite. Secondly, Michael Foot was elected leader of the Labour Party. The NEC launched a series of demonstrations against unemployment and pointed out that one man and one woman were being added to the dole queue every thirty seconds. Since the Tories got into office the number of unemployed had risen by 860,000. The mini-budget and cuts in public expenditure and increases in national insurance would make matters worse.

On 29 November there was a great demonstration in Liverpool. I spoke at the Pier Head and put forward a plan on which Labour should fight: to restore and maintain full employment as priority number one: to extend and develop public ownership of varying forms, on a planned democratic basis; to recognize that new technology and new investment in industry can and does cause unemployment; that it was essential to have a shorter working week, earlier retirement with good pensions and longer holidays similar to those in the professions; and that we needed to build a great mass movement to force the government out by fighting inside and outside Parliament. This, I said, was in the best traditions of British democracy and as much a part of our heritage as the Tories singing 'Land of Hope and Glory' and waving the Union Jack.

From mid-1980, Dr David Owen, Bill Rodgers, Shirley Williams and other right-wingers began working openly towards the formation of a new party. Six months earlier, Roy Jenkins speaking at a Press Gallery lunch at the Commons, argued the time had come for a political realignment of the centre. His speech was not taken up with enthusiasm. I wrote an article for *The Times* in June 1980 entitled 'Who Needs Another Centre Party?' David Alton and Cyril Smith of the Liberals poured cold water on it and Shirley Williams said that such a party would have: 'no principles, no values and no backing'. David Owen insisted: 'We will not be tempted by siren voices from outside.'

Although the Owenites were affronted by the constitutional changes, they were equally concerned about the decisions of the 1980 Conference to urge withdrawal from the EEC and to support unilateral nuclear disarmament. They had been defeated, and decided to split the party rather than to remain within it. Owen, Williams and Rodgers announced that they were organizing a Council for Social Democracy. As chairman of Labour's Organization Subcommittee I issued a statement: 'They are perfectly entitled as are the Manifesto group, Tribune group, Labour First group, and others, to form such a group. That is the basic democracy of the party. It will be a sad day when such activities cease. However, the statement also says that the Gang of Three seek a realignment in British politics. What precisely does that mean? A realignment

187

with whom? With the Liberals or Tories or possibly both? In view of the fact that the Gang of Three have so far refused to give details of their political aims, members of the Labour Party are entitled to ask this important question, and are entitled to an early answer.'

Prior to the Special Conference, I had written in *The Times*, on 12 January 1981, that some Labour MPs 'are giving Labour's political enemies succour and comfort in what is clearly an orchestrated series of speeches and articles containing threats of splits, resignations and new political alignments, all designed to blackmail or at least to pressurize delegates attending Labour's special conference on January 24th ...' For the SDP this was the pretext to leave the party.

I liked Shirley Williams and was genuinely sorry at her eventual departure. In an open letter to Shirley in *The Times* in August 1980 I had replied to hers in the *Guardian* and *Daily Mirror*:

Dear Shirley,

I am writing this letter particularly to you because I know you better and have worked more closely with you than your two colleagues, David Owen and Bill Rodgers, and because, despite our present political differences, I regard you as a friend. I also have the highest respect for your intellectual ability, honesty and integrity. I further believe that you are not likely to succumb to the blandishments of David Steel.

Over the sixteen years we have known each other we have found ourselves sometimes on the same side of an argument, and sometimes in strong disagreement; for example, when we privately exchanged views about the last Labour government's attitude to the 5 per cent norm for pay increases, and you expressed opinions indicating that you did not really disagree with my criticisms.

We have both argued for more open government and for a Freedom of Information Act; we have condemned the harsh treatment of dissidents in the Soviet Union and other East European communist states. There are many issues on which we basically agree, even on such complex problems as Northern Ireland, especially the prisons there.

You must remember that over the years the left has found itself in a minority and has had to learn to live with this. Being in a minority, as long as one can continue to fight for one's views, is also part of the democratic process.

At the last NEC, as you will recall, I moved a resolution which was carried unanimously, calling for unity around the statement, 'Peace, Jobs, Freedom' to fight the Tories and get them out of office at the earliest possible moment. The resolution also argued for tolerance, mutual respect for, and a recognition of one another's views. You did not oppose that resolution. Yet within days, you and your friends returned to an attack on the NEC, badly distorting its policy.

The future of our country is at stake, and I am sure you do not wish that future to be delivered into the hands of Mrs Thatcher for a day longer than necessary'.

Shirley replied to me in *The Times* in September:

... You and I share many socialist ideals. We want to see the removal of privilege. We want full employment and the abolition of poverty which is now so evidently increasing. We believe socialism must be international, and we both want to see a united socialist Europe, though you do not share my opinion that the way to achieve that is by fighting alongside our socialist comrades in the European Community.

You loathe and oppose, as I do, the suppression of human freedom whether in Chile or Czechoslovakia. You have never applied double standards to totalitarianism, as so many on both sides of the political divide do ... You describe 'the acceptance of democracy as the essential ingredient of socialism'. I agree with you. Yet here our differences begin.

In short, Eric, I want to see changes in the party but I believe the changes you and your colleagues propose are unwise, and could indeed erode our democratic institutions. I do not want to see 'democratic centralism', as Lenin called it, but rather democratic decentralization, a plurality of decisionmaking at local and plant level.

You say that 'strongly socialist' policies will not lose votes. It all depends on what 'strongly socialist' means. Policies that imply bureaucracy, central control and statism will surely lose votes: Labour's share of the vote has declined since the 1960s, partly because we are associated with such policies in the public mind. But policies of good public services, full employment and greater participation will certainly not lose votes....

Shirley's letter distorted my views on a number of issues including democratic centralism. I abandoned that idea when I left the CP. I also opposed bureaucracy, central control and statism, as she well knew. I followed up our exchange of views by inviting Shirley to lunch at Beotys, a Greek restaurant in London. It was a last-ditch effort to try to stop her leaving the party, but I discovered that she really did believe that Labour was going in an East European direction. That night I watched her on television and it appeared that she might be having second thoughts. Within a few days, however, she was again promoting the idea of a new party and it was clear that she and her colleagues had made up their minds. The result was that they kept Mrs Thatcher in power for years by dividing and confusing Labour supporters.

After the breakaway, Joan Lestor and myself issued a joint statement:

'As the [SDP] MPs say that they have now resigned the Labour whip and have also resigned from the PLP, it is clear that if they are the honourable people they say they are then they should resign their seats and fight Parliamentary by-elections. They were elected as Labour MPs and therefore they should be prepared to submit themselves to the public. If they fail to do this then they are clearly sailing under false colours.'

The SDP was launched in March 1981. In April and July there were riots in Brixton, London and Toxteth, Liverpool. In Liverpool, for the first time in British history, CS gas was used on the mainland. Roy Jenkins stood in Warrington and Labour's majority was cut from 10,274 to 1,759. In November, Shirley Williams became the first SDP candidate to be elected to Parliament. She won the Crosby by-election; I remember that Michael Foot and I addressed a great rally in Crosby. On the platform with us were Pat Phoenix of *Coronation Street* and Tony Booth of *Till Death Us Do Part* (whom Pat later married). The meeting was so packed and enthusiastic you could be forgiven for believing Labour would win. It was an illusion.

Meanwhile the government revealed its antagonism to the trade unions. It bought in a series of Employment Acts which replaced Labour's Labour Relations Acts. Mrs Thatcher was determined to destroy the power and influence of the trade unions and the acts were cleverly introduced, not in one piece of legislation like Ted Heath's Industrial Relations Act, but piecemeal. When they were all in place they added up to the most hostile anti-trade union legislation in the Western world. At first, the government, with Jim Prior as Employment Secretary, talked with the TUC. His approach and legislation were relatively mild, but the steel workers had gone on strike and the country seemed to be in for a period of industrial unrest as well as political upheaval. Nevertheless, Prior resisted the pressure to bring in legislation removing trade union immunities.

In the Commons, without consulting him, Mrs Thatcher went further than Prior. In future, strikers claiming social security benefit for their families (strikers could never claim benefit for themselves), would be deemed to be receiving strike pay from their union and this could be deducted from the amount the DHSS paid them. Prior wrote: 'Margaret hated the fact that she had been thwarted from taking tougher action and was determined to announce an initiative of some kind against the unions. The right wing loved it.' Prior, however, kept his bill intact. There were no serious concessions to the Tory right in it.

In January 1981, Mrs Thatcher had engaged Alan Walters as her economic adviser. He is a monetarist par excellence and an associate of Sir Keith Joseph. He had a big influence on the 1981 budget proposals and tensions inside the cabinet increased. Gilmour and Prior were very upset at the proposals and later said they regretted they had not resigned at the time. Subsequently Gilmour was sacked and Prior was sent to Northern Ireland.

The Toxteth riots in Liverpool that summer led to a very heated exchange between myself and Margaret Thatcher in the Commons. I was so incensed by her lack of understanding and genuine sympathy towards the city's problems, I called her a 'stupid woman'. Afterwards, I felt I should not have said that. It didn't help overcome the difficulties, and as I wanted help for the area, I felt it was an error. I was surprised, there-fore, when Ian Gow, her PPS, approached me and said that she would like to speak to me privately. Gow was with her in her room and she asked if I wanted him to leave. I said no and she offered me a glass of whisky. She had one herself, and began by apologizing to me. I was dumbfounded and said that I should apologize for calling her names. She said, 'Let's forget that and talk about the problems of Liverpool.' I was only too pleased to do so. In my life I have become obsessed with the fate of Liverpool and would do practically anything to help its people – especially working people. With regard to Toxteth itself, I had lived in the area, had black relatives there and had been chairman of the Toxteth CLP. I told the prime minister that Toxteth required more public money channelled through the local authority and other public agencies. Work was needed, as well as good housing. The riot had not been a totally racial one. Youths, black and white, had united; they saw society, authority, as their enemy. Merseyside, as a whole, needed special assist-ance. The port had declined, factories had closed, unemployment had leapt up. The need was for immediate government action.

Mrs Thatcher did not agree with my approach but said that she accepted that something had to be done. She said that she was sending Michael Heseltine to Merseyside to see what private enterprise could do to help. We talked for nearly an hour and a half. I made no comment to the press about our meeting, but it gave me a new view of her. I felt that she *was* worried about the situation and prepared to listen to all views in order to reach a solution. In the end I was disappointed. Heseltine's proposals were turned down at cabinet and Liverpool got a largely cosmetic package with no serious extra public money.

Following Michael Foot's election, it was clear that his Shadow Cabinet was right-wing. In 1979, as runner-up, I had been offered a job by Jim Callaghan, but turned it down, unlike Neil Kinnock who accepted the post of education spokesperson, on the grounds that I would only accept a position if I were elected.

During 1980 a vacancy arose on the Shadow Cabinet. It was only for a short period and, at first, I was reluctant to take it. However, it was an automatic appointment as I had been the runner-up the previous year. Michael Foot was surrounded by right-wingers and on balance I decided it was right to join. In the Shadow Cabinet I saw just how bullying and awkward Denis Healey could be to Michael Foot. Foot was a prisoner overwhelmed by those who did not go along with his policies on nuclear disarmament, Europe and much else. When the Shadow Cabinet elections took place I was again unsuccessful. I again refused a Shadow job issuing a statement which said: 'In my view the majority of the Shadow Cabinet does not really reflect the new spirit and views of the party in the country. In the interests of the party, therefore, it is important that these views are expressed forcibly in the House of Commons from the backbenches....'

I received a letter from Jennie Lee: 'The failure of the PLP to elect you to the Shadow Cabinet was particularly uncouth. Tony Benn's self-righteousness gets on my nerves, especially when I recall his double dealing in the 1964–70 Parliament. But for all that, you should both have been on the list of any fairminded responsible Labour MP. You know what Nye and those associated with him had to put up with. The PLP has changed but little. Nye said that the Shadow Leader, not just the PM, should have been free to choose his team as he would have to keep some kind of balance among the varying points of view and regional areas. But that is all past history. Now one can only hope for a type of electoral college that will give the same result ... don't be discouraged. I read your *Times* articles with pleasure.'

In 1981, I was directly elected to the Shadow Cabinet and given the job of Spokesman on European Affairs. Although Denis Healey was the chief Spokesman on Foreign Affairs, Europe had a separate slot at Question Time. I chose Guy Barnett as my deputy and, after he went to Overseas Development, Ioan Evans.

Conference had agreed that a Labour government would take Britain out of the EEC. In the next two years I spent much of my time putting Labour's case for withdrawal. I stressed that we opposed entry in 1973 and campaigned for withdrawal in 1975. The policy of withdrawal was carried at the 1980–81 Conference by more than the necessary two-thirds and Michael Foot had declared: 'We are committed as a party to come out of the Common Market.' The promised benefits had not been forthcoming and the pro-Marketeers had been proved to be wrong. Industrial output in Britain had dropped by 16 per cent since we entered the EEC. Unemployment had soared to three million (as I write, fore-casts are that it might again reach three million by the end of 1991). At the beginning of the 1970s, real national income per head in Britain was equal to the EEC average. By 1981, it was 6 per cent lower, and would have been worse had it not been for North Sea oil.

We had to develop real aid and trade to the Third World. The EEC had buried the Brandt Report (concerned with aid and support for the Third World), but a Labour government would resurrect it. We would open up trade by the import of its foodstuffs and the export of the goods it needed.

I began working on a document for withdrawal, helped by researchers at Walworth Road, Chris Jones my own researcher, Ioan Evans and others. Entitled 'Britain and the European Community – Labour's Socialist Approach', it was eventually published in February 1983. At the press conference at the House a large contingent attended. Most of the interest from the journalists centred on just *how* we were going to withdraw. The last part of the document stated that negotiations were likely to be in two stages. Preliminary negotiations would establish a timetable for withdrawal and the 1972 European Communities Act would be amended through a Repeal Bill. EEC law would then no longer apply to the UK: 'The Labour Party is an international party. We believe in a wider European unity. We hope that eventually the whole of Europe will be under a democratic socialist system. We are convinced the Rome Treaty is an obstacle to that and only by leaving the EEC can we work towards a Europe of detente, peace and prosperity.'

Following the 1981 Annual Conference, Liz Nash of the International Department and I represented the NEC at the Twenty-Ninth Congress of the Spanish Socialist Workers Party (PSOE) in Madrid. I had always had a great interest in Spanish affairs since the Civil War and had met Felipe Gonzalez and Alfonso Guerra, the leading lights of the post-Franco PSOE, in London. Since those days, Gonzalez had consolidated his position and had defeated and marginalized his own left wing. The other British delegate was the Spanish Civil War veteran Bob Edwards MP.

Our report to the NEC at the International Committee in November noted: 'The Congress was dominated by the attempted coup of February

ERIC HEFFER

23 [1981], when army officers and civil guardsmen stormed the Spanish Parliament, and by the prospect of general elections in 1983. Both events made the party leadership seek a peaceful congress showing the party as one of unity and responsibility.

'In those terms the Congress was successful, if at the cost of a perceptible moderating in policy. Debates were uncontroversial and low key; even party leaders were concerned that the pursuit of unity seemed to be resulting in unanimity, with 99.4 per cent in favour of the executive report presented by Felipe Gonzalez, and 100 per cent in support of Gonzalez as General Secretary of the party.

'There were few changes in the executive, no policy surprises and a reinforcement of Gonzalez's social democratic concept of the party as one opening wide its doors so that Spanish society becomes more fully represented in its ranks ... The high degree of unanimity in conference decisions, and the elimination of the critical 'socialist left' from among the delegations was partly due to two organizational characteristics which aroused considerable opposition within the party. Firstly, there is now a two-tier system of electing delegates instead of the former system of election by local group, whereby regional conferences are convened which themselves elect the delegates. The intention was to strengthen the party's federal character and weaken the power of the centre. But Felipe Gonzalez noted that the effect has been to take power away from rank-and-file party members in favour of regional officials. Also, once at congress, only leaders of delegations have the right to vote, which means that minorities on delegations go unrepresented.

'The two leaders of the party's left wing, Luis Gomez Llorente and Pablo Castellano, had argued unsuccessfully for representation of tendencies within the party and for the right of individuals to vote; as a result they did not attend the Congress and the left's voice was simply nt heard.'

The Congress reaffirmed its opposition to joining NATO, opposed foreign (US) bases and argued for a referendum on NATO. Later, Gonzalez reversed his opposition to NATO in a similar way to Kinnock's about-face on unilateral nuclear disarmament.

We concluded: 'The PSOE leadership is united, talented and hard-working, but despite its short experience in working under conditions of democracy, it is already showing signs of becoming more distant from the rank and file. Gonzalez himself regretted the oligarchization of the party and stressed the need to combat this tendency. The risk is that in perfecting the party's image as attractive for all Spaniards, the party may exert less of an appeal for socialists and working people.'

I wrote an article for *Tribune* on the Congress. Now I feel I was too

194

kind to the Spanish leadership and not sufficiently critical. I argued: 'From the point of view of the left of the Labour Party, the policies of the PSOE would be considered tame and relatively reformist and orthodox. But ... it has to be understood that democracy was not re-established in Spain by action from below, but was brought about from above through the King and his advisers, in fact from the very pinnacle of Spanish society.'

Gonzalez won the 1983 election but did little to change society in a fundamental way. I continue to accept that Spain – because of Franco's legacy – has particular problems, but Gonzalez has too readily accepted the Thatcherite solutions to its difficulties. That is why he has steadily lost support from wide sections of the Spanish working class. In Britain, this lesson was ignored by the Labour Party leadership, and in the years 1982–3 it made mistake after mistake. Michael Foot was under great pressure and did not get all the support he should have from right-wingers like Denis Healey. But he was responsible for some very serious misjudgements himself, which highlighted divisions within the party and undermined our 1983 general election campaign.

In April 1982, the Argentinians captured Fort Stanley in the Falklands. I heard the news on my way back from a wedding in North Wales and it was reported on the radio that the Commons would sit on a Saturday for the first time since Suez. I telephoned Brian Davies, the Secretary of the PLP, and said we ought to have a Shadow Cabinet meeting even if it meant members travelling overnight. Brian said that such a meeting was impossible before the sitting took place. Michael Foot did meet a small group but I was not included. The debate was a dramatic occasion. The only Labour MP who showed any doubts in his speech in the House was George Foulkes. I have to say I was horrified at the patriotic fervour demonstrated by most MPs. I thought it far worse than anything I had seen in the 1939–45 war.

The problem for Labour was that its programme contained an innocuous paragraph: 'We affirm our commitment that under no circumstances will the inhabitants of the Falkland Islands be handed over to any Argentinian regime which violates human and civil rights.' That was all – nothing about how the problem of Argentina's claim could be dealt with without war. Now we had a war and Michael Foot was as responsible for it as Mrs Thatcher. His speech was thoroughly jingoistic and I was the only one to say so afterwards in the Shadow Cabinet.

There were 1,800 people on the island and approximately 600,000 sheep. It was one of the last outposts of the old empire, now largely dead and buried. Some people suggested we could rehabilitate those islanders who wanted to come back to Britain. The response from the nation was amazing. It was as if we were back in 1939–45. Warships were withdrawn from NATO. The *Queen Elizabeth II* was requisitioned and other vessels were taken over by the government. In a matter of days, a hundred ships were assembled as a Task Force and 28,000 men were on their way to the Falklands. I even remember some crackpots saying Buenos Aires should be 'nuked'. I thought the world was temporarily going mad.

The PLP, in the main, supported the stand of Michael Foot, but some MPs were opposed, and others were very uneasy. The party in the country was very concerned too. Wherever I went members would tell me they did not like the way in which the Party had responded in the Commons. Speaking at a public meeting in my home town, Hertford, in May, I referred to a division in the Commons in which some Labour MPs had voted against government policy: 'It is clear that, despite the vote, Labour is united around the position a) that peace must be achieved by negotiation through upholding the UN Charter and b) that it does not want a full-scale war with its possible adverse consequences for world peace.' I felt that the entire Labour Party was deeply anxious. There was a dilemma at the heart of the problem. We could not allow a bunch of military fascist thugs to take over the island and it was right that the Falkland people should be able to live in peace, but neither could we support rampant jingoism and warmongering. The only reference Michael Foot made to the Falklands at the following Party Conference was to say, 'All through the Falklands crisis the phrase of George Orwell kept drumming in my ears: "I do not want to see England humiliated or humiliating anybody else". That is a good form of patriotism ...' I only wish that Michael had noted the words of Orwell when he made his speech in April to the Commons. The fact is, at that stage, Mrs Thatcher was more subdued than he was.

Another example of a massive error of judgement by Michael Foot which helped us to lose the 1983 election was the sorry saga of Bermondsey. There had been trouble and confusion in Bermondsey CLP for some time. The council leader, John O'Grady, a firm rightwinger, had been vice-chair of a forerunner of the SDP, the Social Democratic Alliance. Arguments raged about the policies of Labour councillors. Was the South Bank to be developed for yuppies or working people? Party members wanted working-class housing. The right became split and Bob Mellish's former agent left the party. The Broad Left decided to put forward its own candidates for the local election panel, excluding a number of right-wing councillors and thereby making them unavailable for reselection. At the same time the CLP elected left-winger Peter Tatchell as its secretary by thirty-six votes to twenty-nine. Mellish referred to this as a 'palace revolution'. He was disenchanted with widespread opposition to the London Docklands Development Corporation plan and decided to retire as an MP. Selection of a new candidate took place in November 1981. There were six candidates and, to Mellish's dismay, Peter Tatchell was narrowly adopted. I shall never forget what happened in the Commons. James Wellbeloved, a defector to the SDP, asked Mrs Thatcher: 'Has the PM's attention been drawn to the demand made by the Labour parliamentary candidate for Bermondsey that extra-parliamentary action should be taken to challenge the government's right to rule? Does she agree that such an irresponsible demand should be condemned by all supporters of British parliamentary democracy and should not be condoned by craven silence?'

Mrs Thatcher's careful reply did not set the place alight but Michael Foot intervened: 'Since the matter has been raised, may I say that the individual concerned is not an endorsed member of the Labour Party and, so far as I am concerned, never will be endorsed.' Later, he said, 'On a point of order, Mr Speaker, I understand that in the exchanges at the end of Prime Minister's Questions I used the term "not an endorsed member". It must be clear from the context that what I wished to say was "not an endorsed candidate".' I was horrified. It was not just a mistake it was ridiculous. I knew what he said could only harm the party. I leaned over to him and whispered, 'You've just lost us that seat'. After all his years in the Commons such ineptitude was amazing. Here was an occasion to say nothing or to attack the SDP and the Tories.

During my years as chairman of the Organization Subcommittee I had toured the country with the national agent David Hughes, trying to solve local party problems by mediation and conciliation. Now we had a potentially disastrous problem right on our doorstep. Internal arguments about the council candidates were awkward enough, but the parliamentary candidate being disowned by the leader was almost unbelievable. I did not know Peter Tatchell but I had argued for many years for extra-parliamentary activity to supplement and underpin parliamentary action; they were complementary and had been since the days of the Chartists in the 1830s.

The press had a field day, falsely suggesting that Peter was a supporter of Militant Tendency and headlining his homosexuality. The matter was placed before the NEC and the left put up a real fight on the issue. The five defeated candidates had signed a statement saying that the election had been conducted 'openly, fairly and democratically' but John Golding, seconded by Denis Healey, moved a motion of non-endorsement. It was carried by twelve votes to seven with Tony Benn, Frank Allaun, Les Huckfield, Joan Maynard, Jo Richardson, Dennis Skinner and myself voting against. Afterwards Golding and Betty Boothroyd made it clear the vote was not about Tatchell but about the direction the Labour Party was taking. Foot had played right into their hands. At the meeting I reiterated that I saw nothing wrong with extra-parliamentary activity and had argued – from the front bench – in support of it during the debate on Heath's Industrial Relations Act.

Peter Tatchell then asked to put his case before the NEC. The request was turned down by fifteen votes to four. One of those who voted against him was Neil Kinnock, who sided with Michael Foot and the right. In January 1982, the NEC decided that David Hughes and I should meet the Bermondsey CLP. I was reluctant but felt it my duty to do all I could in the interests of the party and Peter Tatchell. The CLP were very suspicious and rightly so. I urged them to accept the right-wing councillors whom they had previously excluded back on the panel in the interests of party unity. I was equated with Ray Gunter by some and Peter wrote that I was 'bulldozing' while they were being asked to give up everything for nothing in return. It was not true. I was determined he should be candidate and pointed out that even if the councillors were put back on the panel the wards did not *have* to select them.

The Organization Subcommittee, by a majority, put the councillors back on the panel but, in the end, of the eight sitting councillors, only two were selected. (Some fought as Real Labour candidates endorsed by Bob Mellish and thereby left the party.) If my argument had prevailed I fancy none would have been selected as the heat would have been taken out of the situation. With the left outvoted on the NEC I did what I could but my motives were misunderstood. I remember speaking at a fringe meeting at the London Labour Party Conference. Peter Tatchell came up to me and I asked him to trust me, saying I would not let him down. I was working on a formula which I believed would reinstate him. I had managed to get Michael Foot to withdraw his opposition, providing a new selection took place. If Peter was selected Foot would not oppose his endorsement. Tatchell remained convinced that I was paternalistic and I had treated the CLP like naughty school children. He failed to understand that unless we acted quickly an even more right-wing NEC might be more hostile in the future.

The NEC agreed to a new selection but Tony Benn moved that Peter be endorsed immediately. His motion lost thirteen to four. Tony didn't realize that I had worked hard to get a face-saving formula acceptable to Foot. A new selection was held and Tatchell was again selected with a triumphal fifty-two votes against Eric Moonman's eight. Michael Foot wrote to him: 'When the NEC confirms today's decision, you will be the official Labour Party candidate and you will have my full backing in the election.' There followed a truly appalling episode in British political history.

John Golding continued to oppose Tatchell's endorsement and Bob Mellish resigned from the Labour Party. The by-election was called for 24 February 1983 and the Bermondsey CLP printed 25,000 campaign leaflets, using Cambridge Heath Printers. It had used this company in the general election without objection but now David Hughes stepped in and had the leaflets impounded because the printshop was owned by Militant. In fact the printers were all Labour Party members, ran a trade union shop and offered a good price. All this added fuel to the claims that Peter was a Militant supporter and was in its control even though not a member. None of this was true.

O'Grady, Mellish's crony, became the Real Labour candidate. On the doorstep all kinds of lies were uttered about Peter: that he was a coward, a traitor and much else. The press were truly vicious and he received threats of violence and assassination. Apart from the first few days of the campaign, politics were almost ignored. The tabloids showed their true colours and scurrilous leaflets were issued illegally. Lurid graffiti appeared and a suggestive song was sung by O'Grady from the platform of a horse-drawn cart.

On 7 February I spoke at an election meeting for Peter. It was well attended and full of working people, so I concentrated on what labour had achieved for the working class and on Mrs Thatcher's hypocrisy in quoting from the Prayer of St Francis. Benn, Foot, Skinner and many others spoke at election meetings but their efforts were torpedoed on the eve of the poll by an NEC vote, nineteen to nine, to expel the editorial board of *Militant* newspaper. It was a mad decision and I said so at the meeting, which some of us had wanted postponed. The result of the by-election was a terrible reversal for Labour: Simon Hughes, the Alliance candidate, swept home with 17,017 votes, Peter got 7,698, O'Grady 2,243, and the Conservative, Robert Hughes, 1,631. It was a real own goal and I wrote in *The Times*: 'Bermondsey will doubtless have a salutary effect on all wings of the Labour Party. Right, left and centre must surely see the need for unity in the face of the political enemy.'

From 1981 we had a situation where right-wing MPs were deserting for the SDP, the press was ceaselessly hostile and we were tearing ourselves apart over Militant. It was a recipe for disaster and it was the right-wingers of the NEC and PLP who were setting the pace. Even the Bishops Stortford Accord of 1982, designed to heal the breach before the general election, was undermined by them. At the same time the

SDP was receiving a favourable press. It was obvious that they were considered a good bet to help keep Labour out.

The government had cut living standards, especially for the sick and unemployed, penalized the wives and children of strikers, and used unemployment as a weapon. VAT was kept at 15 per cent. Union power was undermined and workers' rights removed as a result of government legislation. Defence spending had increased, and spending on education decreased. Law and order policy was leading to greater police powers and there was more reliance on the use of arms. The government was increasingly authoritarian while, at the same time, the housing situation was worsening for the mass of ordinary people. It was a mean and vicious government, carrying out mean and vicious policies. In Labour's programme for the 1983 election, the party said it intended to get rid of nuclear weapons, negotiate its way out of the EEC, abolish the House of Lords and work for full employment. It would bring in a Freedom of Information Act. It was a progressive, radical, socialist programme. The press really went to town and every opportunity was taken to attack our policies and make them look ridiculous.

In January 1983, Defence Secretary John Nott was replaced by Michael Heseltine, and Tom King became the Environment Secretary. Step by step Thatcher strengthened her position by getting rid of the wets. In the March budget alcohol, tobacco and petrol taxes went up. Mrs Thatcher was riding high because of the Falklands. Tory ratings in the opinion polls before the general election gave 49 per cent Conservative, 27 per cent Labour and 24 per cent SDP/Liberal Alliance.

The Conservative manifesto pledged more anti-trade union legislation and made a commitment to privatize British Telecom, Rolls Royce, British Airways, British Steel, British Shipbuilders and British Leyland. There was also a pledge to get rid of the GLC which Mrs Thatcher described as a 'wasteful and unnecessary tier'. It was a ridiculous attitude. If the GLC were abolished London would be the only major city in the world without its own council.

As vice-chairman of the Labour Party and spokesman on European affairs I was travelling the country, making speeches, attending the campaign committees preparing for the general election, attending Shadow Cabinet and NEC meetings, and doing my job in Parliament and in my constituency. I was confident that if the Alliance was isolated Labour could win – but I felt that not enough was being done. The press knew that Healey was not in support of Labour's anti-nuclear policy and that this damaged the party. During the election campaign Jim Callaghan openly attacked the party's policy. He said on 25 May, 'Our refusal to give up arms unilaterally has brought better and more realistic proposals from the Soviet Union: Britain and the West should not dismantle their weapons for nothing in return'.

I was furious at this act of sabotage. There had been times during general elections when I had disagreed with policy but remained quiet. That is what Callaghan should have done. Right-wing treachery in the Labour Party over the years has to be seen to be believed. The list of right wingers who have undermined the party is a long one: Brown, Gunter, Marsh, Prentice, Jenkins, Owen, Williams, Rodgers, Marquand, and Taverne, to name just some.

Over a period, the right had created the image of Labour being divided by loony-left councils in London, Sheffield and Liverpool, which were undemocratic and which would undermine democracy and bring in a type of East European state. That meant that every attack on Militant or other left-wingers was a gift to the political enemy. It was the own goals scored by the leadership and the treachery of some of the right wing who could not accept democratic decisions which destroyed us.

Despite all this we in Liverpool went into the general election determined to win. The constituency boundaries had been changed and a number of seats which had been Labour had been wiped out. The task facing us was therefore that much harder. The *Liverpool Echo* made much about leaving the Common Market and getting rid of nuclear weapons. There were banner headlines, 'Heffer says Out of the Common Market', 'Heffer Says End Nuclear Weapons'. In response I put forward a programme for dealing with unemployment in the area. It included a conference of all local authorities, government departments, trade unions and employers' organizations, to determine priorities and to ensure that financial aid would be available, and to develop industry and training on a massive scale. That programme was given much prominence locally. The Heseltine measures had been seen to be merely cosmetic. Labour won all the seats in the city except one, which was held by the Liberals. The SDP candidates, all ex-Labour, were wiped out. Liverpool was even more of a Labour stronghold.

There was a sharp contrast elsewhere and after the General Election we discovered to our dismay that the Tories had increased their majority with 397 seats to Labour's 209 and the Alliance's 23. Clearly the SDP's existence had made a difference. Labour had 49 fewer seats than in any post-war election and its share of votes had fallen to 27.6 per cent. The Alliance received 25.4 per cent. It was a terrible blow.

EIGHTEEN

On and Off the Platform

All the world's a stage,
And all the men and women merely players:
They have their exits and their entrances;
And one man in his time plays many parts,
His acts being seven ages

WILLIAM SHAKESPEARE, *As You Like It*

Mrs Thatcher was back in office, with her government moving sharply to the right. Working people were in for a very bad time. One of the first things she did was to remove Francis Pym as Foreign Secretary and replace him with Sir Geoffrey Howe. Nigel Lawson became Chancellor of the Exchequer and Cecil Parkinson took over the Trade and Industry Departments which were now merged. Mrs Thatcher had her own people in all the key jobs.

Four weeks after the election, Norman Tebbit produced his White Paper on Trade Union Law. It was evident the unions were to be further disciplined and hog-tied. Immunity was to be removed and unions now faced injunctions and liability for damages. The new legislation would substitute contracting in for contracting out of the political levy. Not only was the government determined to destroy the strength of the unions, it also intended to starve the Labour Party of cash.

Within three months of the new government coming into office, the Treasury demanded further cuts in public spending. Local authorities were the main target and a system of ratecapping was to be introduced. Speaking at the Post Office Engineering Union in November 1983, I acknowledged that the election was a serious setback but I believed that Labour had fought the election on the right policies and must not back down. I insisted that an extension of public ownership must be our basic objective.

Following our disastrous showing, Michael Foot resigned as leader and he and prominent trade union leaders touted Neil Kinnock as his successor. Tony Benn had lost his Bristol seat and was therefore unable to stand and Roy Hattersley was being pushed by the right. Finally Kinnock and Hattersley ran as a 'dream ticket' whereby each would support the other whoever was elected leader. I discussed the situation with my friends and it was agreed that Kinnock should not have a free run. Beyond doubt he had moved to the right and would move further. There must be a challenge from the left.

I approached the Tribune group – I was a founder – but it came to nothing. I spoke to the Campaign group and despite the fact that I was not a member it decided to nominate me for leader. I never had any illusions about standing. It was a political decision to put down a marker for the future of left-wing policies. Michael Meacher stood, ostensibly with me, for deputy leader. As it turned out he actually voted for Neil Kinnock, implying it was a Kinnock-Meacher ticket. Over the years I have become used to such things but I am still amazed at his effrontery.

My campaign was helped in the House by Jim Callaghan, the MP for Middleton and by Reg Race outside. I spoke all over the country but was up against a powerful union-backed machine. The election cost money which we had to raise and I called on the NEC to set guidelines for future contests. It still has not done so. I campaigned for an all-out attack on the Thatcher government founded on a partnership of the party and the trade union movement, defence of Clause IV, adherence to policies agreed at Conference, the development of a truly egalitarian society and the extension of democracy within the party using the party's own machinery rather than debates conducted publicly via hostile media.

The result announced at Conference was: Kinnock 71.3 per cent, Hattersley 19.3 per cent, Heffer 6.3 per cent, Shore 3.1 per cent. The press claimed I was humiliated. I was not and did better than I antici-pated. At the first opportunity I spoke from the platform expressing my relief that: 'No one has come to the rostrum and, in any way, been critical of the results of this leadership campaign. The decisions of this party in relation to the leadership have been absolutely clear and decisive. Sour grapes are unnecessary. What we have to do now is to go out with the leadership of the party, fight for the policies of the party, get the people to accept these policies, and in four-and-a-half years' time make certain we have a Labour government under the leadership of Neil Kinnock and Roy Hattersley.'

Kinnock, in his acceptance speech, had talked of fighting for democratic socialism, opposing nuclear arms and upholding the values of the working class. So I offered an olive branch. My reward was a kick in the teeth and a whispering campaign to get me off the Shadow Cabinet and then the NEC.

203

In March 1984, the miners began their great strike which lasted until 1985. The miners had forced the government to retreat in 1981, but Mrs Thatcher bided her time. Nicholas Ridley had devised a plan which was now put into practice. Coal had been stockpiled and some coal-fired power stations had been converted to oil. Ian MacGregor, who had an anti-union record in the US, was made Chairman of the Coal Board. He had implemented massive redundancies in the British steel industry when he was running it. Mrs Thatcher made Peter Walker Energy Secretary – it turned out to be an astute move.

The full power of the police was used against the miners, as was the new anti-trade union legislation. Mrs Thatcher referred to the miners as 'the enemy within'. Dozens of pits were closed, as Arthur Scargill had warned, and the non-striking Nottinghamshire miners became the Tories' heroes. Today, despite their strikebreaking and their founding of the Union of Democratic Mineworkers, they are being rewarded with pit closures in Nottingham.

I knew that the defeat of the miners would be a defeat for the entire working-class movement. The miners *had* to win. That they did not, was, in part, the result of the attitude of the Labour and TUC leaderships. I met Neil Kinnock regularly at NEC and Shadow Cabinet meetings. It was clear that he distrusted Arthur Scargill and would do nothing to help the miners' leadership. I had had arguments with Arthur Scargill over the deputy leadership contest. I considered him intolerant at times and too pro-Soviet. He did not support Solidarity in Poland or the unofficial miners union in Russia. Yet in the great miners' strike we had to put that aside. The miners, Labour's brigade of guards, were in struggle and everyone, in my view, had to work for their victory. No doubt the Labour and TUC leaders thought by distancing themselves from the strike Labour would gain in support – instead, it became further weakened. In 1970–74, when Labour had fought Heath's Industrial Relations Act every inch of the way, it had gained the support of working-class people and won the next election.

The Labour leaders were beginning to be terrified of their own shadows. They seemed blind to the fact that our democratic rights, built up and cherished over the years, were being destroyed, and they failed to fight back. The Thatcherites believed in freedom, but it was freedom to buy and sell; freedom of speech, assembly and political debate were slowly undermined. There had been violence on the miners' picket lines and also at Wapping, Warrington and Grunwick. It was invariably provoked by the police, helped by the new Tory legislation which gave them greater powers than they had ever had before. From May 1979 to January 1988 police strength had increased by 11 per cent. Police pay on average had gone up well above the inflation rate. During the strike the police actually stopped miners going north through the Dartford Tunnel. Those who refused to turn back were considered to have obstructed the police in the execution of their duty, contrary to the Police Act of 1964. But even this was not enough for Thatcher, and the Public Order Act of 1986 was introduced. In 1985, there had been concern at the way in which the Greater Manchester Police had dealt with protesters when Leon Brittan, then Home Secretary, had visited Manchester University. Action had been taken under existing legislation. Brittan had said that the new Act was brought in to 'Bring up to date the age-old balance between fundamental but sometimes competing rights in our society'. It did nothing of the kind. The new Act extended the preventive powers of the police, extended the public order offence which had been introduced in the 1936 Act, and made provision for riot and unlawful assembly. These very wide powers have been used against the students at Westminster Bridge, the Irish Freedom Movement, the Stonehenge hippies and the anti-poll tax demonstrations. They go well beyond anything we have ever seen before.

After the 1983 election when Neil Kinnock became leader, I was re-elected to the Shadow Cabinet. Kinnock offered me Regional Affairs, Overseas Development, and Construction. None of these jobs shadowed a cabinet minister. That was contrary to the rules of the PLP, and I told him so. I refused Regional Policy and Overseas Development but considered Construction so long as the post included Merseyside, which then had a cabinet minister responsible for it. Most of the discussions about the position had taken place on the phone, which I thought very unsatisfactory. Then I read a report by Ian Aitken in the *Guardian* saying that Stan Orme and I were to be put out to grass. I was furious and phoned Kinnock. He said it was nothing to do with him. I did not believe him then and I do not believe him now, but it was at that point that he offered me the Building and Construction position. It was a cunning move on his part. He realized that I was a member of UCATT and therefore had an interest in the subject. Also, my union would have been dissatisfied had I refused. I should have done. I should have refused all jobs and explained to the party what game Kinnock was playing.

Despite the way in which I was appointed I did my job properly in relation to Building and Construction. I took over as a new government bill was going through the House. The minister I faced was Ian Gow (tragically assassinated only a couple of days ago as I write). Despite his Thatcherite right-wing views, he came across as a very pleasant, direct man. He sometimes sounded pleased with himself but he actually had a delicious self-deprecating sense of humour and I liked that. Often in Committee or in the Chamber I would be on the receiving end of his acerbic wit. I really didn't mind.

My assistant at Housing and Construction was John Fraser. He was a very loyal person and only too happy to take the burden when I was busy with NEC commitments. After my appointment, I stated our position: 'Housing has borne the brunt of public spending cuts under the Tories. Less money from the government has caused council rents to more than double. Fewer new council houses are being built than at any time since the twenties. Wrong economic policies, leading to high interest rates, have hit everyone with a mortgage.

'The nation's stock of good homes – that most vital ingredient in any civilized country – is being allowed to rot. Over four million homes in Britain need substantial repairs – yet the Tories have cut back on home improvement grants, and are giving many councils less than half the money they need to keep their housing stock in good repair.

'Rising council rents have forced many council tenants to buy their homes, whether they wanted the responsibility or not. The unlucky ones have found themselves the owners of damp, draughty and unsaleable flats, relics of the bad days of system-built housing.

'Labour stands for a fair deal and a new priority for housing. Those who want to rent should have a good home at a fair price, whether they rent from the council or a private landlord. Those who want to buy should have cheaper conveyancing and lower interest rates.

'Labour governments have done more than any others to help owner-occupiers. We believe that first-time buyers deserve special help, and that the mortgage tax-relief system – which at present helps the better off – should be reformed to give more help to those on lower incomes.

'We do not forget the homeless and the helpless. It is intolerable that in a caring society tens of thousands of people are sleeping rough, and are denied adequate help because of the meanness of this government. It is intolerable, too, that half a million building workers should be on the dole while half a million new homes are needed. Labour believes that they and the building industry should be given the resources to get on with the job.'

Housing did not feature much in the Chamber during my year as spokesman. There were few debates and only occasional questions. The issue should have been raised more often, but efforts to sustain an attack on government policy received little support from the leadership. After the 1984 Party Conference the Shadow Cabinet elections were held and I lost my place. In one sense I was relieved because I had found it a strain to be in almost constant conflict at the Shadow Cabinet meetings.

The left in the Commons no longer had the unity it had displayed in the Wilson and Callaghan years. *Tribune*, which had been a genuine paper of the left, had deteriorated into a mealy-mouthed journal. Under Dick Clements, it had been hard-hitting, never afraid to positively criticize the Labour leadership. Now it was assisting in witch hunting. I had written for *Tribune* long before I entered Parliament and long after. Now I did not write for it and was not asked to. Under Chris Mullin, it had supported me for the leadership but only half-heartedly and belatedly. The only columnist on the paper who has maintained his integrity is Hugh Macpherson.

Tony Benn would never join the Tribune group, even though I regularly asked him to. When he did eventually join he left again within a short time to form the Campaign group with Dennis Skinner, Martin Flannery and others. I believe that the genuine left should have remained in Tribune with me; then the soft left revisionists would not so easily have taken over. Nevertheless the Campaign group issued a very good pamphlet on the Thatcher government after the 1983 election called 'Tory Government Policy – a Threat to Democracy (the Radical Right in Power).' At the end of the pamphlet it pulled no punches: 'Freedom and Democracy, then, belong to socialism. They are the spiritual property of the Labour movement. In our campaigns around specific issues, be they peace, jobs, the defence of the welfare state, or local government, or the trade unions, we must present people with the common thread. Whether it is at Greenham Common, or on a trade union picket line, or in the many other struggles with which the Labour movement is associated, it is the aim and purpose of socialism to defend freedom, and to further democracy We believe it is that message which we need to present in a convincing manner to the public, before this monetarist government runs off with our freedoms, and subverts our democracy.'

I left the Tribune group when it supported the suspension of the Liverpool Labour Party and the expulsions resulting from it. That was enough for me. Afterwards, Harriet Harman and others urged me to stay on as I was a founding member, but I realized that the group was not carrying the torch of socialism but of revisionism. I joined the Campaign group which had supported me in the 1983 leadership election.

In 1983 I was unanimously elected chairman of the Labour Party. The General Secretary, Jim Mortimer, was also on the left. I found him really good, serious and efficient. He had written a number of books on trade unions and his great knowledge of industrial relations was invaluable. I was determined to use my position to good effect but I soon got a taste of things to come.

I attended the Socialist International (SI) conference held in Sheffield. It was, in effect, Neil Kinnock's introduction to the organization. Prior to that conference he had little contact with the SI; he was not a member of the international committee nor can I remember him playing any part in its subcommittees. At the conference there were delegations from Spain, Italy, France, Israel, Greece, Lebanon, the US, Latin America, Africa and Asia. Willi Brandt arrived in a personal jet courtesy of the West German government. A previous SI conference had been attacked by terrorists, so this one took place in conditions of great secrecy in a hotel cut off from the city by squads of police.

It was obvious to me that our policy towards the EEC was being changed surreptitiously. Stuart Holland, who had, at one time, worked in Harold Wilson's office and was very pro-EEC, attended the conference as a front-bench spokesman. Although not a delegate, I discovered he was speaking for the party about Europe on radio and Yorkshire TV. This was done without consultation with the officers of the party, Jim Mortimer, or myself. I made it known that I was unhappy; it was the party which determined international policies, not the leader's office and front benchers on their own.

At the annual Conference a reception is held for members from the SI, people from the various embassies and so on. At the previous Conference some delegates had rightly protested, outside the reception, that the Polish ambassador was present but Solidarity leaders were not. To show *my* solidarity I wore a Solidarity T-shirt on the platform. Some NEC members were annoyed. Later, of course, they all supported Solidarity.

After his general election defeat I kept in touch with Tony Benn; he was on the NEC and we phoned each other regularly. Tony was selected to stand for a parliamentary seat which became vacant in Chesterfield. When he asked me to speak at the opening meeting of his campaign I was delighted. I also canvassed and spoke at the eve-of-poll meeting with Denis Healey and others. Tony won the seat with an increased majority and it was a real slap in the face for the press. There had been an orchestrated campaign against him and, in my chairman's address at Conference, I referred to his election as an example of winning by sticking to socialist principles.

The year 1984 saw the government making cuts in local authority spending and a fight-back by some Labour councils. It was a very busy year for me. I chaired local government conferences, attended many regional conferences and was fraternal delegate to the TUC, the Co-op Congress, and various union conferences. Because of this I sometimes had to be absent from the Commons. I regretted I could not be in two places at once.

It was a privilege and pleasure to chair the 1984 Conference. In my speech as chairman I did my best to give a socialist lead. I said that I was glad we had not panicked after the election and ditched our policies. We were a party with real roots struggling against a form of top-hatted authoritarianism; an Orwellian Big Sisterism where workers were kept in their place. I ended by quoting Shelley:

> Rise like lions after slumber
> In unvanquishable number
> Which in sleep had fallen on you
> Ye are many – they are few.

I sat through every day of the Conference and did not miss one minute. The position of chairman was then an important one. Today the leader is all-powerful and no other power base in the party is tolerated. Power has moved from the NEC to the PLP – in reality, to the leader's office.

The decisions of the 1984 Conference were mixed. On some issues the party retreated but on most there was a reaffirmation of existing policy. The NEC statement on local government called upon authorities 'To work together to resist implementation of cuts in services and jobs, as envisaged by the Conservative government, so that we can place the government rather than local government on the defensive.' It was a very clear, firm policy and Liverpool carried it out to the letter – and at great cost.

During the Conference I had a brush with the owner/publisher of the *Daily Mirror*, Robert Maxwell. It was to have unpleasant repercussions. Maxwell loathes Arthur Scargill and at a TV luncheon he approached me and demanded to know what I intended to do about the miners. I had little idea of what he was on about but strongly resented his interference. He was not a delegate, yet appeared to believe he could bully me. I reacted sharply, told him I was chairman, and it was no business of his. He went away in a huff. It was obvious he had contacts in high party circles and I'm told he dined one evening with Kinnock. Things hotted up. On the last day of Conference the *Mirror* ran a full-page spread headed 'The Fiddler of Blackpool' with a photograph of me in a cloth cap. It was a scurrilous article ostensibly written by Peter Tory and I drew attention to it in my final speech. So did Jim Mortimer who pointed out that I had worked hard to resolve antagonisms in the party and that I had never been devious. He described me as 'a widely read working-class intellectual'. I have to admit that pleased me greatly. Edith Plumb, the Doncaster CLP delegate, gave the vote of thanks: 'To Eric Heffer who has chaired this conference in his own inimitable way. When things have gone astray you have bounced back cheerfully, it is lovely how you have done it and got us through the business.... Thank you Eric, I have enjoyed Conference.' Doris and I received dozens of letters from TV viewers but some lines from Tam Dalyell's wife Kathleen were typical: 'Dear Doris, I feel I must write and tell you how good I thought Eric was as chairman of this year's conference, especially in view of criticisms I heard, but did not see, made in a national newspaper ... his opening address ... set the tone of a serious and humane party that had some idealism and concern about the present ills that beset us. Throughout his good humour did a lot, I thought watching, to prevent divisions.... The wind-up to the conference with Eric quoting from Citrine was masterly. So if you were concerned about any nasty remarks you don't need to be, which is why I thought I'd drop you a line.'

After Conference I wrote a letter of complaint to the *Daily Mirror*:

'Mr Peter Tory's Diary piece of Friday 5 October saying I have been a bungler and that I have not helped the image of the party as this year's chairman of the Labour Party does not seem to be either the view of the overwhelming majority of the delegates, or of other journalists. At the same time as the Peter Tory piece appeared in the *Mirror*, the Conference Notebook in the *Daily Telegraph* said, "Heffer steals the show ... He has surprised them with a showing which has helped the party present itself as more humane and civilized than might otherwise have been the case."

'The article also contains a serious factual error. The petition referred to by Bob Clay in his speech was not voted upon or presented to Conference. I was not approached by a *Mirror* reporter, but by Mr Maxwell during the lunch break. I thought he was complaining about the petition being circulated. I said I had no powers to stop it being circulated amongst the delegates – that was democracy.'

I ended my letter by demanding an apology, and said I would consider taking further action if such an apology was not forthcoming. Mike Molloy, the editor, replied on 17 October 1984:

'I am sorry that the article by Peter Tory has hurt you so much. Peter Tory's opinion, though forcefully expressed, was not his alone. You must have been aware that there were two views about your chairmanship. The *Daily Telegraph* and Bill Whatley illustrate the point.

'Whatever the technicalities, Bob Clay presented the petition to conference and you called for a show of hands, thereby deliberately circumventing the decision not to debate and vote upon the emergency T&GWU resolution reaffirming total support for the miners' action, including defiance of the courts.

'It is not the intention of the *Mirror* to injure. It was our reporter's honest belief that the criticism was justified. It was certainly not his purpose to give "a false and cruel impression".'

In my reply on 23 October, I wrote:

'Bob Clay referred to the petition in his speech. That is all that happened on that question. You are wrong to say I called for a show of hands. I repeat I did not call for a show of hands on the petition, and if you continue to say I did I will have to take further advice on the issue. Mr Mortimer, the General Secretary, made it clear in his truncated letter which you published that I did not call for a show of hands on the petition. How could I? The petition was not before Conference. I asked for a show of hands when Mr Moss Evans on behalf of the T&GWU (after the chairman of the Standing Orders Committee had urgently intervened, during the local government debate, to make a statement) had given his reasons for not going ahead with the Emergency Resolution. I asked that the decision be endorsed by Conference on a show of hands. It was.

'Clearly, whoever gave you the information was confusing that show of hands with the mythical one I was supposed to have taken on the petition. I would therefore like a clear admission on your part that you made a mistake on this. As I said earlier, whether or not I was a good chairman is a matter of opinion, but to suggest I fiddled votes during the proceedings is something quite different, and therefore on that issue a retraction is necessary.'

I wrote again on 2 November:

'To underline what I said in my letter dated 23 October, I enclose a copy of a page of the proceedings at Conference and you will see it was as I said, the T&GWU statement expressing full support for the NUM, and the petition did *not* come before the Conference. I would appreciate an early reply, otherwise I shall be seeking to take further action.'

I received a final reply from Mike Molloy dated 9 November:

'Our enquiries confirm that you permitted Bob Clay MP to report to Conference about the petition which, if put into effect, would have pledged the unconditional support of the Labour Party to the miners, including support for their contempt of court. Moreover you did not disclose to Conference that you had signed the round robin yourself. Nevertheless ... we now accept we were mistaken to believe that the show of hands you called for related directly to the round robin.'

A correction was published in the *Mirror* on 16 November:

'In a report of the recent Labour Party Conference we referred to the fact that Mr Eric Heffer, the then chairman of the Labour Party, had allowed an out-of-order petition pledging unconditional support for the striking miners, including support for their contempt of court, to be reported to and voted upon by Conference by a show of hands.

'We would wish to make it clear that though Mr Bob Clay MP produced such a round robin in the course of his speech, we now acknowledge that the chairman did not ask for a show of hands on it by Conference. We regret any embarrassment our report may have caused.'

I have given this correspondence in full so that the truth will out. If the *Mirror* had not apologized I would have taken it to court. What it had said was libellous in the opinion of barrister friends but I did not rush into court because libel suit costs are, as the Bishop of Birmingham observed in the Lords (17 June 1941), 'nothing to a multimillionaire capitalist ring but are ruinous to private individuals'. I could not risk our house and what little we had by winning the case and perhaps having to pay costs.

No doubt Arthur Scargill and others have borne that in mind when attacks have been made on them in the *Mirror* and other papers. To be goaded to sue – implying if you do not the paper must be right – is a very unfair system and should be changed.

The following year, at the 1985 Conference there were a series of stormy NEC meetings. Arthur Scargill and the miners were under attack from the leadership – as were the Liverpool councillors – for daring to carry out party policy. There had been a poisonous debate on a resolution calling for a future Labour government to review all cases of miners jailed as a result of the dispute, reinstate the sacked miners and reimburse the NUM and all other unions for the monies confiscated as a result of fines, sequestration and receivership. I supported the resolution, but Neil Kinnock urged it be remitted. If the miners did not remit, he made it clear that the leadership would oppose it. The discussion was long and at times bitter. In the end, Kinnock prevailed by one vote. Michael Meacher voted with Kinnock and someone called him a class traitor. The press incorrectly attributed this to me. When asked about it on television I said how could someone be a working-class traitor when they did not come from the working class? That statement could have some significance in view of the court case between Meacher and Alan Watkins of *The Observer* in 1989. (Watkins had written a piece in *The Observer* disputing Meacher's claim to have a working-class background. Meacher sued for libel and lost.)

Neil Kinnock did something most unusual at Conference and decided to wind up for the NEC on the miners. Most NEC members, even those who took his point of view, were reluctant. Ron Todd spoke in support of the resolution which had been seconded by Arthur Scargill. Eric Hammond, EEPTU, attacked the miners' leaders, saying that the miners were 'lions led by donkeys'. In his reply, Ron Todd said that, as an animal lover, he preferred donkeys to 'jackals'. Neil Kinnock's hostility to the miners' leaders was shown not so much in what he said, although at times that was bad enough, but in the tone he used. His face set hard and he spat out his words. He was to adopt the same demeanour when he came to discuss the situation in Liverpool where the council was facing a devastating cash crisis.

In June 1984, Kinnock had visited Liverpool without notifying me as the chairman of the party, or as the senior Labour MP in the city. I heard of his visit on the local radio. I protested strongly to Kinnock's office who said they had been trying to reach me by phone. It was an excuse – they had all my telephone numbers in Liverpool and in London. Kinnock followed this with a letter making the same point. It remained an excuse. It was a further example of the attitude that was becoming the norm in Kinnock's relationship with me, even though I knew more about the Liverpool scene than most people in the party.

Kinnock proceeded to launch a vicious attack on the Liverpool council from the platform of the conference. He gave the impression that it was dominated and run by the Militant Tendency. Certainly Militants were on the council but they were a small minority. I knew that the council had built houses – good houses; that it had built sports centres to keep the youth off the streets. It had kept council rents and the price of school dinners down. It had provided the elderly with telephones. It had effected a long overdue reorganization of education and put a race relations officer in each school. It had created a new park and cleared slums which should have been cleared years before. It made tactical errors but those who try to do positive things sometimes make mistakes.

Kinnock's aim was to split the unity of the councillors and the party in the city. Ironically, in the light of subsequent events in Liverpool, he used the council's decision to issue redundancy notices to its employees as the lynchpin of his assault. 'You start with far-fetched resolutions. They are then pickled into a rigid dogma, a code, and you go through the years sticking to that, outdated, misplaced, irrelevant to the real needs, and you end in the grotesque chaos . . .' his face set with anger as he spat out the words '. . . of a Labour council – a Labour council – hiring taxis to scuttle round a city handing out redundancy notices to its own workers.'

It was too much to bear. I walked off the platform while Kinnock was still speaking, only to hear him say, after the uproar, 'You can't play politics with people's jobs'. He *knew* the council was not doing that. The issuing of redundancy notices was a tactic to put pressure on the government. In June 1984, after meeting Liverpool councillors, Kinnock himself had issued a call to the government for extra funds for the city. That was what the council, the Liverpool MPs, the city Labour Party and

213

the two bishops of Liverpool had been calling for. He knew, as we all knew, that our call would go unheeded.

After my abrupt exit I was chased round the hall by TV, political, and other journalists. I refused to speak and tried to get out of their way as delegates surrounded me and endeavoured to protect me. An old friend, Jerry Bree, brought me a cup of tea but was so emotional that he spilt it over me. I wondered where my wife Doris had gone. As I walked from the platform I had looked for her but her seat was empty. I learned later that she too had walked out when Kinnock made his attack and was surprised, when she looked back, to see me walking off. When I arrived in the outer hall John Hamilton, the council leader, shook me warmly by the hand. I found Doris and we went back to our hotel.

I gave an interview there to Elinor Goodman, the political editor of Channel Four and one of the best, most balanced and meticulous journalists of her kind. Later I gave some more interviews to other networks. I told them I could not sit there and listen to good working people being attacked in such a way by the party leader. I said that Neil had fought the leadership on a left-wing ticket, that I had been a moderate in comparison with some of the things he had said in the past. Bob Parry's response was even more clear and to the point. He said: 'Kinnock showed today that he is the biggest traitor since Ramsay MacDonald. He is the man who kicked Liverpool in the teeth when it was down on the ground.' I say amen to that. I will never forgive Neil Kinnock for what he did to my city and my party.

The right wing were ecstatic about Kinnock's speech. Denis Healey said: 'I think Neil's speech was of historic importance. He has shifted the centre of gravity not just of the Labour Party but of the Labour movement as a whole, decisively. We shall look back on this day as the moment when Labour won the next election.' Hattersley also praised Kinnock, saying it was the best speech he had heard in the twenty-seven years he had been in the party: 'It was historic because it will change the country's perception of the Labour Party.' John Cunningham told some Liverpool delegates, 'Your activities and behaviour demonstrate that you have no place in the party.' Glenda Jackson who, although born on Merseyside, has had little contact with the party there, sent Kinnock a congratulatory telegram. There is no doubt the right recognized that it was again in charge of the party. It would only be a matter of time before the policies were fundamentally changed on such issues as nuclear disarmament. The *Mirror*'s front page read: 'Kinnock the Destroyer.' The *Star*: 'Boy oh Boyo.' The *Daily Mail* crowed 'Only when there is blood on the stage – the blood of his own party – can we be sure that a Labour leader means business.'

In the aftermath of my walk out I was inundated with letters – the overwhelming majority in support of what I had done. A letter from Aberdeen said 'Like a lot of people in the party I feel confused and emotional about the whole business.... I think that most of Kinnock's speech was tremendous, but I feel his criticisms of Liverpool councillors and later the miners were (a) wrong and (b) made in the wrong way and wrong place. I got the feeling that Kinnock was going over our heads to the general public for his justification...'

The Reverend Alan Taylor of St Aiden's, Leeds (who used to live in Walton) wrote: 'I just want you to know that I've always greatly admired you as a man of principle – that is a quality which is one of your many strengths – long may it continue!' A letter from Harlesden, London said 'I'm writing as an ordinary Labour Party member to say having heard what Mr Kinnock said today at Conference, I fully support your action in leaving the platform.' Bridget Harmen wrote that she had spoken in the 1981 Party Conference as a multiple sclerosis sufferer: 'Congratulations may not be the best term to use in view of the emotional strain you must have suffered, as indeed I did, watching on TV. My own feelings come now of deepest anger and impotence to affect issues in the party I have belonged to for over twenty-five years. With best wishes and support for the stand you took yesterday'. Alan Durband, a party member of long standing in Liverpool, wrote: 'I agree entirely with what you say. Neil Kinnock has indeed scored a monumental own goal, much as I wish our case had been put by a more reasonable spokesman than Derek Hatton. To espouse a cause which has been clobbered by everyone requires great political guts and integrity; as a lifelong member of the Labour Party I was beginning to wonder what happened to my youthful socialist ideals, but your consistent support confirms that though the old flame flickers from time to time it has not been entirely extinguished. Congratulations for speaking out.'

W.H. Polter, a joiner from Liverpool, sent this letter: 'I'm writing to say how appalled I am at Mr Kinnock's stance against the Liverpool City Council.... I am not a Labour Party member or a member of any party. However, I have supported the Labour Party all my life and will continue to do so, despite the peculiar twists and turns of its various leaders. I'm just a thick Liverpool joiner but even I can see the wood through the thatch. If a belief in real socialism is sometimes removed from a Labour politician, we are left with David Owen. What a sorry prospect.' What a prospect indeed.

The next day I was back at Conference. David Blunkett, for the NEC, asked Derek Hatton if he would withdraw his motion on the Liverpool crisis in return for a commitment by the NEC to set up an enquiry. I told

Blunkett that Hatton was already walking to the platform (David is blind). Hatton shook David's hand and said, 'In order that unity can happen and we can go out and make sure this government is defeated – yes.' The Conference responded very emotionally to that. Kinnock kept his feelings to himself.

Following Conference John Hamilton, leader of the Liverpool group, sent a telex to Larry Whitty: 'At the meeting of chairmen of City Council Committees this morning, we discussed press reports of a proposed NEC investigation of the District Labour Party. I was asked to inform you of our total opposition to any enquiry. We believe it would be divisive, time consuming and unjustifiable, particularly at a time when we are launching major campaigns against surcharge, and to secure a massive Labour victory in the May elections.' The NEC was made aware of the views of the councillors but it made no difference. It is a sad, sorry story. I fought the leadership every inch of the way and in the process was falsely branded a Militant. I took my position on tolerance, freedom, and socialism as Michael Foot had done in the past – but the NEC was set up like a law court and I felt as if I were seeing Stalinism in action.

The NEC's report on Liverpool, published at the end of February 1986, attested that the District Labour Party had too much control over the city council, and that there was an atmosphere of intimidation at its meetings. It recommended that sixteen people should be charged with breaking the rules. That meant their expulsion. A minority report, signed by Audrey Wise and Margaret Becket, opposed expulsions. The majority report was accepted by nineteen votes to ten.

At the first of the hearings, seven of us walked out of the NEC. That meant there was no longer a quorum and the meeting was adjourned. Kinnock immediately changed the standing orders. In future the committee would not be inquorate after a walk-out. Kinnock became obsessed with the expulsions, and the NEC was involved, for hours on end, as prosecutor, judge and jury. (Subsequently a new committee was set up to consider disciplinary matters and now no one can appeal to the full Party Conference.) The meeting on 21 May, when the process began again, dragged on and on. It was after 1 a.m. that the NEC voted to expel Tony Mulhearn, the Liverpool party president. After Mulhearn had been dealt with, the process speeded up. One by one the Liverpool people were interrogated and judged. Terry Harrison, who had been in the Labour Party long before Kinnock had joined it, was expelled. The whole business made me feel physically sick.

The transformation of the Labour Party into the SDP Mark II really got underway in 1986. The basis was laid in the attacks on Liverpool councillors and the miners. It continues unabated.

In March 1986 the Labour Party/TUC Liaison Committee began work on a document to be presented to the annual conference of the TUC at Brighton. A draft was prepared by the appropriate research department which gave workers full rights in industrial disputes. Kinnock would not accept that. At his insistence another statement was prepared called, 'People at Work – New Rights, New Responsibilities'. It was a complete retreat. In one part it said: 'The new statutory framework will also entail laying down general principles for inclusion in union rule books based on a right for union members to have a secret ballot on decisions relating to strikes and for the method of election of union executives to be based on secret ballots. The aim is to provide effective rights for union members.'

I opposed that strenuously. It was very similar to Tory legislation and that existing in the US. I argued that union members should decide what went in their rule books, not governments. Kinnock spent a lot of time winning over union leaders like Ron Todd who, at first, had opposed the new proposals. At the Home Policy Committee the statement was accepted by seventeen votes to eight and Kinnock suggested that those of us who opposed it were out of touch with rank and file trade unionists. It was a disgraceful statement. My battles on construction sites and on the ships over the years meant I needed no lessons in being in touch with the rank and file. Because of Todd's support the policy was accepted at the TUC Congress on a show of hands. It was one further move away from socialist principles.

It was also in 1986 that the renunciation of unilateral nuclear disarmament commenced. After the 1985 Conference Kinnock raised the issue of defence and the NEC was asked to prepare a new statement. It was put before the NEC in July. I took a stand with Tony Benn against NATO, but we were defeated. At the Party Conference in October a non-nuclear policy was re-affirmed, but Labour was committed to NATO. It was a compromise between the right and the Kinnock supporters but, in reality, it was a move towards ditching unilateral nuclear disarmament. The red rose was adopted in place of the red flag. Reformism had really taken root.

The writing was on the wall for the left. My brother-in-law, David, had warned me after he went to lecture at Glasgow University that there was a determined effort being made by the soft left (LCC) to get me off the NEC. I was their main target and, at the 1986 Conference, I was voted off. In order to minimize its impact, my defeat was leaked to the press beforehand. I learned about it in the newspapers yet I was staying at the Conference hotel. The delegates also knew through the press and TV, so when the NEC election results were announced at Conference

217

my removal was an anti-climax. I spoke to Larry Whitty about the leak but got no satisfactory explanation. In my experience, this was the first time this had happened. No doubt Peter Mandelson, Kinnock's communications supremo, was involved.

In the meantime, Labour councillors from Liverpool and Lambeth were surcharged and disqualified; and more supporters of Militant were expelled from the party. The miners had been defeated and the New Realism had taken over in the Labour Party and the TUC. On all fronts the left was in retreat. There were only four or five NEC members who were prepared to be critical. They were reduced to two, as Ken Livingstone was voted off the NEC after only two years and, with the change of rules, the Young Socialist representative was dropped. Audrey Wise and Joan Maynard also lost their seats. The left on the NEC now consisted of Tony Benn and Dennis Skinner.

Some people thought that when the general election came I would be isolated. I thought my majority might be reduced a little. I was wrong. It went up by 11½ per cent. Today Walton, with a majority of over 23,000, is one of the safest seats in the country. Of the votes, 9,000 went straight from the Tories to Labour. When I returned to the Commons after the general election, I felt my actions had been vindicated by the voters of Liverpool. They had responded positively to a Labour council which had kept to its socialist principles. I was proud of them.

NINETEEN

Stepping Down

Hear a word, a word in season,
For the day is drawing nigh
When the Cause shall call upon us,
Some to live and some to die!
He that dies shall not die lonely,
Many a one has gone before;
He that lives shall bear no burden,
Heavier than the life they bore.

WILLIAM MORRIS, 'Hymns of Labour'

Following the 1987 General Election defeat a 'Socialist Conference' was held at Chesterfield in late October. Those who attended were Labour Party members, the Campaign group of MPs, the Socialist Society, the SWP and other Labour Party and non-party people. It was a large and successful event. I was one of the speakers and issued a statement to all delegates in which I analysed the future of the left: 'The Labour Party has responded to the present situation in a number of ways. There are three broad positions. The right, led by "Solidarity" would move Labour back into a more traditional right-wing stance, not quite repudiating all past socialist beliefs and in fact looking sceptically at some of the new soft left attitudes. They could retain links with right-wing trade union leaders and try to utilize the trade union machine as in the past. The so-called soft left (actually right of centre) has grouped around the Labour Co-ordinating Committee, with the present-day Tribunite group of MPs acting as Neil Kinnock's Praetorian Guard. The genuine left has grouped around the Campaign group of MPs. A few of the left unfortunately are fair-weather friends, as some were in the LCC when they were Tony Benn's supporters. Some could easily and quickly desert their political positions if offered either ministerial office in a Labour government or even front-bench jobs in opposition.'

I called upon the left to organize and to form something like the earlier 1930s Socialist League inside the Labour Party and the TUC.

The Campaign group of MPs should, I felt, become the Parliamentary wing of the new Socialist Group which would be formed in all parts of the country. It should have its own weekly paper filling the role once played by *Tribune* and *Labour Weekly.* The existing Socialist Society could help in publication and education. I believed that the Socialist Group should put forward policies based on Labour's constitution and those put recently by Tony Benn to the NEC which were voted down: 'We must go on the offensive, otherwise the path of revisionism, slide and decline will continue until Britain's politics for years to come follow those of the US with disastrous consequences.' As I write such a movement (Labour Party Socialists) is being formed inside the Labour Party. It has already held a successful conference at Sheffield but only time will tell if it can become a significant force in the Party.

After lengthy discussion the Campaign group decided to enter the contest for leader and deputy leader at the 1988 Party Conference. I supported the move and wanted Tony Benn as the candidate for leader. He was, by far, the strongest candidate available to the left. Many Labour leaders have moved from the left to the right. They become mellow, moderate and revisionist. They make their peace with the system they are supposedly against. Tony had moved in the other direction; if that were a purely opportunist tactic he would have back-pedalled long ago. He has not. Instead he has become increasingly socialist as he has got older. That surely is to be commended. Tony really does believe in democracy. In July 1980 he placed a notice of motion before the NEC which put his democratic view: 'We believe in free and open debate, conducted in an atmosphere of goodwill and in the right of all members to speak and write freely and to seek to persuade others to adopt their views.... We also accept the right of conscience, when members are moved to follow it.' These views are the essence of democratic socialism. They were once advocated by Michael Foot.

Why then did Michael turn his venom on Tony in his book *Loyalists and Loners*? How was it that he was the enemy and previous opponents like Healey and Callaghan were now allies? I believe the reason is that Michael had begun to like office. His socialism was beginning to wither on the stem of ministerial office. It need not be so and Tony Benn has proved that. He spoke out as far as possible in government and protested at the straitjacket of collective responsibility. Others embraced it.

Socialism means a flowering of the human spirit; Tony has consistently supported that view. We are all products of our environment, and he is a product of his. I have not always agreed with him but despite some differences, I have increasingly come to like and admire him. His reaction to events is *always* socialist. His belief in the democratic process may be considered by some to be naive, but it descends from our radical tradition. His fight to free himself from his peerage was in line with Bradlaugh's refusal to take the Oath.

Tony is one of the best debaters in the House. Like Foot, he was once president of the Oxford Union and his case is always well argued. The Tories distrust and dislike him yet they are compelled to listen. Despite the hostility often shown to him, he never gets angry. Nor will he allow himself to become involved in personal attacks. This suggests that, as a leader, he would have kept a cool head. He is always polite and does not bear grudges. Since the retreat of the left under Kinnock and its serious loss of seats on the NEC Tony has suffered many slings and arrows. A lesser man would have caved in. Not he; he believes that socialism will ultimately triumph and continues to work hard for a new and better society. I was convinced that he would have been an inspiring leader and I still am. I was approached to stand with Tony for the deputy leadership. I was reluctant but it was important that he had back-up. A great deal of hostility would be generated by the press and the right and I thought my back was broad enough to take some of the flak. I had urged my friend Audrey Wise to stand. She declined, as did other women comrades. Two years later, Ken Livingstone, in *Tribune*, said that he opposed the contest and was very critical of the group. I cannot remember him opposing the decision at the time. I am sure he voted for Tony and myself to stand.

Our campaign – described by some political pundits as a Last Hurrah – was organized by Jon Lansman, Tony's campaign manager in 1981. I had stated my position on a possible contest in the *Sunday Times* in January when the issue was first discussed. There appeared to be a groundswell for such a contest, I felt, and I did not agree with Neil Kinnock who said that such an election would be 'an unforgivable distraction'. I insisted: 'The idea that Labour Party members should all silently conform is preposterous. Labour is a democratic socialist party, not a Stalinist one.' Anyway the field was clear for a straight fight in the deputy leadership contest because John Prescott, who had said over a period of months that he intended to stand, backed down after pressure from his union (the NUS) and from Kinnock's office. After I had decided to stand, however, he changed his mind and got back into the contest. To this day I am not sure if the leadership had had second thoughts and was afraid that Hattersley might be defeated or seriously damaged in a straight fight. Afterwards Neil Kinnock appeared to welcome Prescott back into the Shadow Cabinet with open arms.

One of the most unkind pieces written about my canditature was by Julia Langdon in *Punch*. She accused me of being jealous of Kinnock and a troublemaker. I was hurt by the piece, especially as it was critical of Doris, but Julia and I remain friends, despite her close connections with the Kinnocks. The decision of the Campaign group to stand Tony and myself was given to the press in March 1988. Immediately there were articles attacking us and cartoons trying to make us look ridiculous. We were depicted as Laurel and Hardy, Hinge and Bracket, Don Quixote and Sancho Panza.

The *Liverpool Echo*, in its usual 'fair and friendly' way, stated in an editorial: 'The present Labour-led city council is still trying to recover from the trail of damage left by those years under Militant. If that is the sort of socialism Mr Heffer and Mr Benn would like to see Labour practise nationally, then these old men of the left really do want the lunatics to take over the asylum.' That was one of the kinder comments. My old friend Alan Watkins got it wrong in the *Observer*, when he wrote about my candidature: 'His fundamental good nature is exploited by the comrades in the Campaign group.' Nobody exploited me. I knew precisely what I was doing.

Tony and I spoke individually or together all over the country. The rally at Liverpool was the biggest. There was great enthusiasm for the campaign and people were turned away from a packed St George's Hall. I said the campaign was about the future of the party. It was good to be in Liverpool because the city council was continuing to carry out Labour policies and in the recent municipal election the party had gained five seats. Labour in Liverpool had fulfilled the promises it had made.

During the campaign Neil Kinnock got himself into a tangle over defence policy. On television he seemed to be backing away from unilateralism. Then at a 'private' lunch (which was reported) at the *Independent* he tried to reverse what he had said. It was a terrible muddle. At a packed meeting in Woolwich I referred to it as 'Valeeta politics' – that is, two steps to the left, two to the right and then you go round and round'. As we now know, Neil Kinnock was ditching his unilateralism and today, under his influence, the party has ditched it too.

Tony and I distributed a nine point manifesto throughout the campaign:

1. We support the restoration of democratic rights to working people through their trade unions, and the liberation of local communities so that the councils they elect can provide a really high standard of essential services.
2. We challenge discrimination and inequality based on sex, class, race, sexuality or faith.
3. We believe that the whole apparatus of the state requires funda-

mental reform if the processes of government and the law are to be more open and more accountable to those they are supposed to serve.

4. We uphold the right of women to control their own lives in the political, economic and personal spheres; we are committed to ensuring that women do have full opportunity to become political and economic decisionmakers throughout society.
5. We want to see proper provision for leisure, for earlier retirement, for lifelong education, for the encouragement of the arts in all their forms, and the establishment of a genuinely fair mass media, free from monopoly private or state control.
6. We demand measures to protect the environment and the animal kingdom from exploitation.
7. We believe that Britain should announce its intention to withdraw from Northern Ireland, and should work with the Irish people, as good friends and neighbours, to help secure reunification and peace.
8. We believe that Britain should be working more actively for peace throughout the world, by diverting arms expenditure to the needs of development; by adopting non-alignment, outside of all military blocs and without foreign bases on our soil; and that Britain should support efforts to secure co-operation across the whole of Europe, free from all restrictions under the Treaty of Rome.
9. We want to encourage closer economic, industrial, social and political links between working people here and those in other countries; we support all those peoples in Africa, Asia, Latin America and elsewhere fighting for freedom against dictatorial and oppressive regimes; we believe in socialism and democracy in all parts of the world, East and West.

We had never expected to win and I was surprised at the excellent response we got. The genuine left in the country rallied to the campaign Groups were set up to support us and they worked hard and well. A unity of purpose had been formed, but when it came to the vote we were well beaten.

Despite the leadership defeat I decided to stand both for the NEC and the Shadow Cabinet. Although I knew I could not win I was very serious about the platform on which I stood and wanted to use the elections to build support for it in the party and trade unions. Others thought I would get back on the NEC. I did not, although I increased my vote over the previous year. In the Shadow Cabinet elections the left did badly. Tony Benn got fifty-six votes to my forty-three.

In March 1988, three Irish people were shot in Gibraltar. The Foreign

Secretary Sir Geoffrey Howe made a statement in the House. As he spoke I became increasingly alarmed. It transpired that those killed were not armed, had not actually planted a bomb, and they were, in effect, executed. I disagree profoundly with the IRA but I do not believe that in opposing it we should adopt its methods. It is counterproductive and aids terrorism rather than defeats it. In the House I was the only member who challenged Howe's statement. I was vilified in the press and it was suggested that I more or less supported the IRA. I received many letters of support, as well as some opposing me and hinting at threats. I was pleased by what Enoch Powell wrote in the *Independent*: 'A massive self-congratulation, intoned by the Foreign Secretary, engulfed the media: it echoed back and forth in Parliament and in the papers. Maybe what happened was perfectly lawful and defensible. Maybe it would have been considered lawful and respectable if officers of the metropolitan police had done precisely the same thing on the streets of London. Maybe; but there is another possibility. The possibility that it was deliberate, cold-blooded premeditated murder.' I was very grateful to Enoch Powell for writing that article. It helped get my position into focus. No one could suggest that *he* was remotely pro IRA.

During this period, I attempted to build support in the Commons for better health and safety regulations at work. Ever since I was an apprentice and knew first hand about the risks of accidents on construction sites, I have felt that those who put profit before the safety of the workers should be dealt with severely. The facts are that, in the last ten years, 1,500 building workers have been killed and deaths and serious injuries have increased by around 65 per cent. In the Health and Safety Executive Report of 1988 'Blackspot Construction', it stated that 90 per cent of the deaths were avoidable and in 70 per cent of cases action by management could have made certain no lives were lost. With self-employment (known as the Lump) there is not the same control as on sites which are union organized and where there is a payroll workforce. Self-employment increased under Thatcher and as a consequence safety has seriously worsened. I have consistently opposed the Lump and tried to introduce Bills to abolish it, without success. In the NEC I also got the Labour Party to agree to develop policies to deal with the Lump for inclusion in our election programme. In the past few years a rank-and-file workers' Construction Safety Campaign has grown. I organized initial meetings in the Commons. The trade unions, UCATT and the T&GWU have also launched a campaign. The average magistrate's fine against an employer whose negligence caused a fatal accident is still less than £500 and the maximum remains £2,000. UCATT wants to see much heavier fines and, in the case of serious negligence, the introduction of custodial sentences. There are little more than a hundred health and safety inspectors to cover all of Britain's construction sites. In the absence of the government doing anything to improve the situation, UCATT has offered to lend the service of its own experienced officials as part-time site inspectors. Of course, a fully unionized workforce is also essential.

In the Commons in 1989, I managed to get 200 MPs from all the opposition parties, and even a few Tories (Labour's front bench declined), to sign an Early Day Motion supporting better health and safety legislation. Eventually, because of constant pressure on the leader of the House, we managed to get an opposition debate. In a good debate, Michael Meacher, on behalf of Labour, pledged full support, but so far, the government has not responded.

In April 1988, my old friend and comrade Harry McShane died. A group of Scottish MPs, including my friend Norman Buchan, put down an Early Day Motion in the House of Commons: 'That this house notes with deep sadness and regret the death in his ninety-seventh year of Harry McShane, one of the main architects of Red Clydeside; recalls that he was born into hardship and was one of nine children from a Gorbals family; notes that through his deep understanding of Marxism he represented a major strand of socialist thinking in Europe; notes and recalls his tireless work on behalf of the unemployed and his leadership of the hunger marches; notes that tyranny from any quarter had a natural and implacable foe in Harry McShane, a man whose socialism was founded upon a deep respect for individual freedom; notes that in 1985 Glasgow District Council recognized that commitment and integrity when it bestowed the freedom of the City of Glasgow on Harry; and accordingly mourns the passing of one of Scotland's most distinguished representatives whose commitment to social justice and the relief of poverty we share.'

· I signed it and also wrote an obituary for the *Guardian*. Harry received fine tributes in the *Glasgow Herald*, the *Scotsman* and other papers. Tom Crainey wrote: 'Red Clydeside never quite passed into history while Harry McShane, one of its prime architects, was alive. Until his death ... his dream of a new social order never dimmed. Many others were to lose faith for one reason or another, but not McShane.'

One of my other great friends, Jerry Dawson, ex-CPer, Labour Party member and ex-Secretary of Merseyside Unity Theatre, also died. I said a few words at his memorial and contrasted Unity's contribution to the Labour and trade union movement with the current feeble efforts of Red Wedge, Billy Bragg and Porky the Poet. Jerry rejected the extremes of 'art for art's sake' and 'art for propaganda'. He believed: 'An historian

225

can turn legitimately to the play for the light it throws on social conditions. A theatre cannot limit itself.' Bertolt Brecht said we must 'transform justice into a passion'. That is precisely what Jerry did.

With the loss of my two old friends, I felt as if two solid pillars had gone. In their own ways they had each contributed to my political and cultural development. I had been considering, since 1987, the possibility of standing down from my parliamentary seat. The idea of being the 'Father of the House' has never appealed to me. I knew I would never be offered a seat in the House of Lords and, even if I had been, I would have refused it. In 1988 I decided it was time to make way for a younger person. Having decided not to stand again for Parliament I did not want to rush and announce it too early. I had no wish to become a 'lame duck' MP. However, the process of re-selection was getting under way in Walton. Some advised me to go through the selection, get re-selected and then tell the party when the election began to look imminent. But that seemed dishonest to me so I told the Walton party that I would not stand again. It had nothing to do with ill-health, although I have since become ill.

Unfortunately, all was not plain sailing. The regional officer of the Labour Party, Peter Kilfoyle, told me he intended to stand. Although unhappy about this, I said little at the time. But, after thinking it over, and coming to the realization that it was unprecedented for a regional officer to stand for a seat, I raised it with the NEC. I am afraid this caused a furore. Peter Kilfoyle's friends in the CLP thought I was interfering with the selection process. This was not so. I simply felt it unfair for a regional officer to use the advantage of that position to get a seat – especially one who had acted on behalf of the NEC to carry out the reorganization and purges of the party membership on Merseyside. The NEC discussed my letter and agreed that the rules would have to be changed so it would not happen again. However, as no rules had been broken, they ruled that this time it was permissible. Kilfoyle was selected, but only just. As someone remarked, 'He has received his sweets.' His selection is a recipe for future conflict. My agent, Laura Kirton, backed Kilfoyle and has turned against the Militant supporters, many of whose ideas she supported in the past. It is all very sad but there was nothing I could do.

In October 1989 I had been the MP for Walton for twenty-five years and the constituency party presented me with a Labour Party emblem made of stained glass. I was very touched and was sorry that some of us fell out later over the selection. At the November CLP meeting I made it clear that I would not be standing again: 'At the last meeting I said I was thinking of retiring as MP at the next general election. That idea was not happily received and I have had immense pressure from all sides of the party to allow myself to go forward again as Labour's candidate and MP. I have given all the representations great consideration and thought and I am grateful that such deep feelings about my retirement have been expressed. However, I have to say, despite all that has been said, I feel it right that I should retire. I am therefore making it clear tonight that I shall not be seeking re-election as Labour's candidate.... There is always a time for everyone to move over and it is wrong for people to cling on when they feel it is time to depart. Politically, I find myself increasingly out of step with the way in which the Labour Party has been going in the last six years.... But despite what has happened in the Labour Party and throughout the European socialist movement – the swing to the right and the abandonment of genuine socialist concepts – I personally want Labour to win the next election. I think it will but it could be a hard fight.

'The victory of Labour, however, will only be a first step and the socialist movement will need to be rebuilt at all levels. As far as I can, and as long as my health will allow, I shall play my part to continue the fight for a socialist Britain which will not be based on the bureaucratic concept of Eastern Europe and Soviet Russia, or the acceptance of capitalist ideas of right-wing social democracy, but on the socialism of Labour's founders as outlined in the party constitution and the earlier party programmes. There is a need for serious socialist education and I will certainly do my part to help such education along, both through practical activity and writing and lecturing.

'Again, let me thank all the comrades who have worked so hard over the years. I really am proud to have served the working class and our people, both as a trade unionist of fifty years membership, as a socialist in the Labour Party, as a councillor and MP.'

The following letter appeared in the *Liverpool Echo*: 'With all the opinion polls and the recent by-election in Mid-Staffs indicating, perhaps, Labour's greatest surge towards political power since 1945, one sad note emerges. I refer to the news that Eric Heffer will not be seeking re-election at the next general election.

'He has been a tireless worker for his constituents and trade unions, and is one of the few politicians of today who does not try to "con" the public with political "double talk". He speaks straight from the heart – genuinely and sincerely. I can recall, many years ago, talking to Bernard Weatherill, the Speaker of the House, who said: "Whether you agree with him or not, Eric is totally honest and totally highly principled." That sums up this great "socialist warhorse" absolutely.

'Most certainly he will be missed by his constituents in particular, and the nation in general. He is one of that rare breed of politicians who can be trusted to tell you the truth and do everything in his power to help with whatever the problem might be.

'Certainly the voters of Walton and the people of Liverpool owe this great man a debt of gratitude for all his efforts in representing the people of Merseyside.' The letter was signed 'Alan Hagan, Warrington'. It made me blush. It is far better to read a letter like this than receive honours or offers of a place in the House of Lords.

Since my announcement, a further crisis has developed in Liverpool. The Socialist Organizer group (based around the paper of the same name) was proscribed because of the argument over the de-selection of Frank Field in Birkenhead. I found this strange because, to the best of my knowledge, it had no base in Birkenhead. It is like the attack on Militant all over again. On 24 July 1990 'Labour Party Socialists' held a press conference at the Commons which I attended. It issued a statement concerning Socialist Organizer: 'There is to be no hearing of the case, and therefore no evidence can be presented, or witnesses cross-examined ... no opportunity will present itself within the Labour Party's structures to challenge these crude assertions ... Lord Gifford QC has stated that it is easier to obtain justice before the British courts than it is to obtain such justice before the NEC.'

On 25 July the NEC – with only Tony Benn and Dennis Skinner against – suspended Socialist Organiser, the Liverpool councillors and the Liverpool Labour Party. Patrick Wintour admitted in an article in the *Guardian* that there are only a handful of Militants who are councillors and reported Tony Jennings – who is referred to as the non-Militant leader of the twenty-nine councillors – as saying: 'The truth is that in Liverpool any time a working-class person stands up to fight, they are immediately called a Militant. But for Neil Kinnock, it's number ten – that's the only issue. Whoever he has to lose, throw out or ditch in the process, he will do it, and willingly.'

In the *Independent*, Jonathan Foster acknowledged 'Mr Kinnock's failure to grasp either the hopelessness of trying to govern Liverpool on a shoestring, or the appeal of the Broad Left. In Everton Park, the achievement is clear – a traditional municipal park created on a site where the council, influenced by Militant between 1983–86, demolished bad housing and built new, traditional houses. "People supported the Labour council" a local woman said. "There was nothing around here before, but now the kids can play, the Orange Lodge can march around banging their drums and the Derry Club don't get upset." About 5,000 houses were built or begun in those three years when Mr Kinnock was becoming irritated by Mr Mulhearn and the garish deputy council leader, Derek Hatton. The banks did well, too. Liverpool borrowed massively to build the park and the houses and interest payments are a huge burden. What would Mr Kinnock have done? Build fewer houses? Have the Orangemen bang their drums disturbingly down Northumberland Terrace? Either way, he would have had to suspend the district party.... In purging the party, Mr Kinnock said that people in Liverpool were "sick and tired of the posturing of people who constantly flout their responsibilities and their obligations". Many Liverpudlians, not all of them poring over *Militant*, agreed, and wondered if he included himself.'

Neil Kinnock has triumphed over the left and is now attempting to expel many good comrades from the party. He has come a long way since I first met him after he was elected as an MP in 1970. In those days, he seemed to be definitely to the left of me. He made little impact in the House. His speeches were not listened to with any great respect and he was obviously concerned about this. I should have realized then that he was personally ambitious. Most MPs are ambitious – but some for their beliefs rather than their careers. There were times when he seemed not to bother with Parliament but he was always extremely active throughout the country, building up his vote for the NEC. I remember meeting him at the Commons when an SWP Right to Work group met MPs following a march. I was in disagreement with their call for a general strike, but Neil supported it. He outshone us all in his leftism. Eventually he was elected to the NEC and voted with the left on just about every issue. He supported the policy and organization changes advanced by Tony Benn and myself. In a foretaste of his subsequent behaviour, however, he did not like the tolerant attitude that Tony and I took towards Militant and agreed with Michael Foot that the editorial committee of the newspaper should be expelled. Foot was later a prominent sponsor of Kinnock's leadership bid and is as much responsible for Kinnock's triumph as anyone. His patronage was vital.

Neil Kinnock built his name not only by speaking to the CLPs, but also by taking the collection at Tribune rallies. He was better than any stand-up comic and had perfect timing. Doris once warned him not to get saddled with this role and suggested he ask Tribune to let him make serious speeches. Coincidentally, he began to make more political speeches from then on. We were very pleased because we felt he was a great asset.

Since 1983 Neil has abandoned his old beliefs: unilateral nuclear disarmament, withdrawal from the EEC, taxing the rich. In practice he has jettisoned public ownership, says nothing about a nuclear-free Europe or ending both the NATO and Warsaw Pacts and has not pledged restoration of the union rights lost under Thatcher. He accepts packaging for the media. Polls seem to dominate his thinking. At times he thrusts out his chin like Mussolini. If Labour wins the next election it will be despite, not because of, Kinnock's supposedly inspirational leadership. Some will say I'm being too harsh and that Neil is really a kind, friendly person. I have not found him so. There is a vindictive trait in him. He does not forgive or forget unless his opponent capitulates entirely. His attitude is somewhat like Stalin's after the death of Lenin. Of course, I do not mean he would imprison his opponents; it is just that, like Stalin, he joined the right to marginalize the left. He then set out to absorb the right by taking over their policies.

Kinnock is the first leader to be elected under the electoral college system and is thus the leader of the *entire* party and not just the PLP. He has greater power than any past Labour leader. When the constitutional changes were made we anticipated greater democratic control for the membership. But the greatest democratic constitution in the world – as the Soviet Constitution once appeared to be – can be manipulated by devious people. It is an old story and arises from the elitist bureaucratic approach from above, rather than socialism from below. Kinnock has proved to be a great cynical manipulator who has used the party's dislike and fear of Thatcher to get revisionist policies accepted. He has gone farther than Gaitskell in revising the party's principles, policies and organ-- ization. He has got away with it because the party elected him in the belief that he was a left-wing leader who would carry out socialist policies. What an illusion that turned out to be.

TWENTY

What Is To Be Done?

I will not cease from mental fight
Nor shall my sword sleep in my hand
Till we have built Jerusalem
In England's green and pleasant land.

WILLIAM BLAKE, 'Jerusalem'

In an article in *The Times*, 12 September 1990, Martin Jacques, Editor
of *Marxism Today* and member of the Executive Committee of the CP,
boasted: 'It is probably no exaggeration to say, odd though it may sound,
that the Communist Party made much of the intellectual running for
Labour's Kinnockite revolution. The Communist Party in the eighties
acted like the Labour revisionists of the fifties, with the difference that
this time, Labour looks set firmly to embrace the social-democratic
message ... [the CP] was the main centre of opposition to the Scargill
strategy in the miners' strike. It has been the main ideological pro-
tagonist against the hard left ... that task is now more or less complete.
The Communist Party can now move on. R.I.P.' The article is extra-
ordinary, but honest, and reveals the role of the CP – or at least its
leadership – over the past years.

An influential figure on the side of the CP leadership has been
Professor Eric Hobsbawm. However, in an article in the *New Statesman*
of 14 September 1990, 'Lost Horizons', he expresses his misgivings
about what has happened and adopts a distinctly uneasy tone. Few
socialist parties, he says, are happy to be reminded of their historic
commitment to a society based on public ownership and planning. The
programme of the Kinnockite Labour Party mentions socialism only
once, and this was inserted, he claims, to appease the survivors of the old
left. With upheaval in the East and retreats in the West, he asks who has
lost. 'The left,' he answers, and adds: 'What it has lost is not reasonable
belief but hope.'

Hobsbawm fails to admit the role that he and his friends played in
destroying that hope. He argues as if the undermining of socialist

231

concepts by the CP and *Marxism Today* had never taken place. Their opposition to Stalinism and the nature of Soviet and Eastern European states is welcome. What is unacceptable is their misrepresentation of socialism itself. Stalinism and socialism are not the same – they are opposites. Hobsbawm writes that in 1989 capitalism regained a sense of historical inevitability and socialism lost both its confidence and its class-consciousness. However, he tries to make up some of the ground that he and his friends have helped lose: 'If socialists lose confidence in themselves, the problems of the uncontrolled development of capitalism will not go away. Others will have to deal with them, because they will have to be dealt with.' Precisely.

In 1983, I was one of the participants in a debate with Professor Hobsbawm in *Marxism Today* about the future of socialism and class politics. Hobsbawm and Bob Rowthorn, in the September and October 1983 issues of the magazine had undoubtedly made serious contributions to a necessary debate about the future of the Labour Party. It was a debate I had wanted *before* the leadership campaign. There were many questions that needed to be asked and answered. Why did the party do so well in Liverpool, and not too badly in Manchester, with known left-wing local leaderships, yet disastrously in other areas? Why were the results in London, the south and south-east worse than in the north? Why did owner-occupiers in new homes vote Labour in Liverpool, but did not in other areas? Why did thousands of trade unionists vote Tory or SDP/Liberal Alliance? Why did women and young people not respond as the party had hoped? What was wrong with our presentation? What effect did the Callaghan and Healey challenge on defence have? Why has the Labour vote consistently gone down since its high point in 1951? To what extent has the working class changed and how much have the capitalist mores of 'I'm all right Jack' taken over, through television and advertising? Has our national cohesion been undermined by the Common Market? What effect did the jingoism of the Falklands war have on the nation as a whole, and the working class in particular?

I argued that Labour is a party based on Clause IV of its constitution and that our debate should be used to strengthen our purpose, not weaken it. One of the excellent precepts taught to the children who attended Socialist Sunday Schools was: 'Remember that all good things of the earth are produced by labour. Whoever enjoys them without working for them is stealing the bread of the workers.' Another was: 'Do not think that those who love their own country must hate and despise other nations, or wish for war, which is a remnant of barbarism.' School was closed with the declaration: 'We desire to be just and loving to all our fellow men and women, to work together as brothers and sisters, to be kind to every living creature and so help to form a new society with justice as its foundation and love its law.' That is the type of socialist society I wish to see.

It is continually being said that socialism is dead. What has particularly encouraged this type of thinking and comment has been the crisis in Eastern Europe where the old bureaucratic system is collapsing and private enterprise is again rearing its head with confidence. To appreciate the need for socialism, it is important to understand that under the state monopolies of Eastern Europe and elsewhere the relationship of the working class is precisely the same as it is under private monopoly: the surplus value goes to the owners of the means of production, and the workers are wage slaves. Capitalism – whether private enterprise or state capitalism – is such that when workers cannot sell their labour power, they become destitute. When in work they are strictly supervised and have no say over the process of production. The means of production, the machines, buildings and raw material are owned by the capitalists. If profit is not made they close the factory. Even if the owners do not organize production they get others to do it for them and continue to receive income. They live at a totally different level from the workers they employ. Those who produce the goods do not receive the total cash made from the goods. Most goes to the owners of the means of production.

The capitalist system is about three hundred years old. It has caused general hardship and exploitation to working people. It is not God's gift to humanity. It is the very reverse. Capitalists develop industries where they can make the most money without regard to the social cost of their actions. Why has unemployment been growing in the developed capitalist countries? The answer is simple. Capitalism creates unemployment. It is endemic to the system. The drive for profit and ever more efficient techniques of production leave a pool of unemployment; school leavers increasingly have no prospects. Unemployment is not sent, it arises from a society organized not by the community but by individual capitalists. There is, however, an alternative to all this where society is run co-operatively with everyone having a say in the way things are done, especially regarding production and the distribution of wealth and goods. As I see it the central problem facing socialists today is how to create a society which will retain democracy, yet bring about fundamental changes. Roy Medvedev, the courageous Russian socialist critic of the Soviet leadership in the past, wrote in his book *On Socialist Democracy*: 'Socialist democracy is simultaneously a goal and a means. Democracy is essential as a value in itself. To be able to express one's thoughts and convictions freely without fear of persecution or repression is a vital aspect of a free socialist way of life. Without freedom to receive and impart information, without freedom of movement of residence, without freedom of creativity in science and the arts, and without many other democratic freedoms, a true socialist society is impossible.'

I am convinced that the mass of the people are deeply concerned about the growth of state bureaucracy. They want the state to protect them from unemployment, from poverty, from the ravages of sickness and they demand legislation to give them greater equality, better safety and health at work, and so on, but they have no wish to become automatons. William Paul, a non-state socialist, wrote before 1914 that 'the extension of state control will bring with it armies of official bureaucrats, who will only be able to maintain their posts by tyranny and limiting the freedom of the workers.' His views contrast sharply with those of Fabians like Beatrice and Sidney Webb who were such unqualified supporters of Stalinist Russia. Early Fabians were obsessed with 'efficiency' and the Webbs were far more interested in what they called 'good' government than in democratic government. Sidney Webb said that the ideal should be 'a discreetly regulated freedom'. In contrast to state socialists, non-state socialists have always seen the state as transitional. The elimination of class, based as it is on the ownership of the means of production, would eliminate the state also. Democratic socialists must get the relationship between the state and the individual right. Working people, over the centuries, have had enough of being collectivized, organized, disciplined; enough of 'careful yet firm guidance' and 'controlled freedom'.

There are those who say Marxism is the reason why freedom does not exist in Eastern European countries. The assumption is that democracy is synonymous with private enterprise. But there are many examples which prove this wrong: Chile groaned for years under a brutal military dictatorship but took its economic ideas from Milton Friedman and the Chicago school of economists. It was a bastion of free enterprise and a military dictatorship at the same time. Italy, under Mussolini, did not destroy free enterprise but integrated it into the corporate state with enthusiastic support from big business. It was the unions which were destroyed, not business cartels. The same was true of Germany under the Nazis. Karl Marx, on the other hand, was a true democrat. In his early days, as editor of the *Neue Rheinische Zeitung*, he wrote: 'Freedom is so much the essence of man that even its opponents realize it.... No man fights freedom; he fights at most the freedom of others. Every kind of freedom has therefore always existed, only at one time as a special privilege, another time as a universal right.'

234

For me a socialist society is one in which individual freedom is allowed to flower. It can only occur when genuine equality of opportunity exists, when racial and religious prejudices are unthinkable, when the extremes of poverty and wealth are removed, when there is a genuine redistribution of wealth, when people work for each other, and when individual greed is not considered a virtue and excused. Such a society would be democratic and pluralistic in every possible way. One-person businesses would be encouraged; the judiciary would not be part of the political set-up; and the media would be free of state control. It would not be a one-party regime, but as democratic in industry as in its politics.

I believe the basis of socialist thinking lies in Christianity. Jesus was regarded both as a heretic and as a subversive who spent his life fighting the establishment. Christians were persecuted by Rome before Christianity became synonymous with Roman power. In Britain, in the middle ages, some priests did not support the establishment; a so-called hedge priest, John Ball, threw in his lot with Wat Tyler during the 1381 Peasants' Revolt. Christianity has, since its inception, had both a progressive and reactionary side but the strands which connect it to socialism go back to the writings of some of the early Christian fathers. St Ambrose said: '... if God's providence never fails to supply the fowls of Heaven, albeit they use no husbandry, and trouble nothing about the prospects of the harvest, the true cause of our want would seem to be avarice. It is for this reason that they have an abundance of suitable victuals, because they have not learnt to claim as their private and peculiar property the fruits of the earth which have been given to them in common for their food. We have lost common property by the claims of private property ... The land was made for all; why do ye rich men claim it as your private property?' St Gregory the Great, who was mainly responsible for the conversion of England to Christianity, said of rich men: 'We must make them clearly understand that the land which yields them income is the common property for all men, and for this reason the fruits of it which are brought forth are for the common welfare.' The formula of the Nicaean Council, which was accepted as final by the Eastern Orthodox and Anglican communions and as infallible by the Roman Catholic Church states: 'We look for a new heaven and a new earth, when there shall have shone the appearing and kingdom of the great God; and then as Daniel saith, the saints of the Most High shall take the Kingdom. And the earth shall be pure, holy, the earth of the living, and not of the dead ... the earth of the gentle and lowly. For blessed, saith the Lord, are the meek, for they shall inherit the earth; and the prophet saith, the feet of the poor and needy shall tread it.'

235

The argument that Christianity is synonymous with capitalism is as false as the argument that capitalism means liberty and freedom. The aim of socialists, like that of the early Christians, is the creation of the Brotherhood of Man and, like Christianity, socialism must convince people that it has a great impersonal objective which will give meaning and dignity to their lives.

Capitalism, despite Eastern Europe and the crisis of Stalinism, is in its long-term death throes. We have been living in a critical situation on a world scale since 1914–18 and yet, at this very moment when serious socialist analysis and action is required, the movement is being deflected into non-socialist channels. Instead of socialist politics we are getting razzamatazz, slick media presentations and TV commercials where leaders are sold like soap powders. It need not be so. Class struggle continues on a global scale. The working class, despite what is said to the contrary in *Marxism Today*, is still with us and, in the last analysis, it is the only force which can effectively change society. If we begin from the premise that the working class is still the engine of socialist change, then it is clear that we have to concentrate on winning its support. This means serious work in the trade union movement as well as in the CLPs. It means developing a programme around which socialists can unite and work for in the trade unions and the Labour Party. All left-wing socialists will have to merge their ideas into the wider stream of socialist thinking and organization. The situation, at this time, is unique. We will have to seek our own way forward without looking too closely for historical guides, although some exist. In the 1930s the Labour Party moved left, but with the rise of fascism it was essential to create a unity of socialist forces inside and outside the Labour Party. Thus, the Socialist League, the ILP and the CP came together in a unity campaign. It is no good relying on workers becoming disillusioned with Labour's swing to the right or the TUC's New Realism – although working-class history suggests that this will happen. It is essential to organize groups nationally around a basic socialist programme. Something like the earlier Socialist League is needed inside the Labour Party and the unions.

Some argue that the time has come to set up a new Socialist Party. This may at some time be necessary but not for as long as the trade unions remain affiliated to the Labour Party and give it its working-class base. The argument for a new party is, to some extent, sterile. It looks for a short cut and there are no short cuts. An organization of socialist Labour Party members should be formed which can bring together CLPs. These are first steps which will develop into giant strides. The programme on which Tony Benn and I fought the leadership contest may have some relevance but it must be recognized that events in

Eastern Europe have transformed the situation. Soviet support for liberation movements has dried up and Africa, Asia, Latin America, and countries such as Cuba, are subject to greater US pressure.

Socialists, however, must continue to support genuine liberation movements. The fact that the US and the Soviet Union worked together in response to Iraq's invasion of Kuwait should not stop us from supporting those fighting for their freedom in Latin America and elsewhere. US policy towards liberation movements in Central and Latin America has not changed and it is our duty, as socialists, to oppose US imperialism no matter how it is disguised. The Brezhnev doctrine may be dead as far as the Soviet Union is concerned, but the Monroe Doctrine has not been discarded by the US.

Socialists must also support those in Eastern Europe who want freedom of expression, a pluralistic society, free institutions, free trade unions, free press, regular elections and the end of one-party rule. At the same time, we who experience the rottenness of capitalist society should give our full support to Eastern European socialists who, in ending Stalinist bureaucracy, do not want unbridled free enterprise instead. Yet, if any of the many nationalities of the Soviet Union want separation and national independence from Soviet rule, we cannot refuse to support them. The Leninist concept on nationalities accepted precisely that but it was distorted and ignored by Stalinism.

In rejecting the EEC as the way forward, socialists must have a clear international position. We cannot go on parroting the same old arguments. The emphasis must be on collaborative European socialist policies for full employment, control of the multinationals, and management of the continent's resources in the interests of the people. Europe must not become the home of unbridled free enterprise but a model for democratic socialism. That should be Labour's objective. In the past, many have advocated a Socialist United States of Europe. This concept has been overlooked or pushed aside, but has a great deal to commend it. One thing is certain – the just society that socialists want cannot be built in isolation. This applies equally to the campaign against nuclear weapons. Socialist policies must create a European nuclear-free zone and end NATO and the Warsaw Pact, but it needs to be stressed that the Rome Treaty itself is an obstacle to the development of a wider European unity. European initiatives independent of the Soviet Union and the United States could and should be taken collectively. In the long run they could save the world from the still-present threat of nuclear destruction. The Council of Europe through its political, economic and social committees does some useful work but, basically, it is a talk shop. I believe its consultative role should be given greater status.

Labour cannot be a little Englander party, but equally, it must concern itself with the interests of the British people. Socialist internationalism accepts growing interdependence between nations, and co-operation with present and future members of the EEC is vital to our survival. The OECD – which embraces the whole of Western Europe, Australia, North America and Japan – must adopt reflationary policies on a planned basis. The institutions of the UN Economic Commission for Europe, which includes East and West, must be supported, and trade negotiated and planned with Scandinavian and Commonwealth countries, especially countries such as India which are now largely excluded from EEC agreements. In their approach to Europe, socialists must be internationalist, not nationalist; socialist and democratic, not protectionist and bureaucratic. That does not mean that Britain has to be straitjacketed by the EEC. To make further European progress we must reassert our parliamentary independence. There is no doubt our future lies in Europe – we are no longer the workshop of the world or the mistress of the seas. We will have to escape America's control. The special relationship talked about by Churchill and Mrs Thatcher is subordination, not equality. Increasingly, we are the US's outpost in Europe, as Israel is in the Middle East.

An essential part of our British revolution will be the need to get rid of US bases, and now that Eastern Europe is freeing itself from Soviet control, the possibilities of a wider Europe are greater. To be successful, however, we shall need a well-organized working-class movement which is not on its knees. It is essential that previous rights of workers should be restored so that, together with their comrades in Europe, they can act collectively to change society. It will also be important for the working class to ally itself with the middle class which today, like the workers, is beginning to feel the full brunt of the crisis of British capitalism. The number of middle-class people who default on their mortgage is increasing. So too is their fear of unemployment.

There is a saying, 'An old tiger does not recover as quickly and readily as a young one'. Britain is an old tiger short of breath and blunt of claw. What we need is a socialist party to unite the working class and the middle-class and give them some teeth. That does not mean embracing Fabianism or the old CP concept of the Popular Front. It means that the Labour movement must be the moving force, but it can only be successful if it draws in its allies. That is not reformism. We have had reformist government. Now we need the democratic socialist revolution.

TWENTY-ONE

The Finest Cause

Named and nameless all live in us;
One and all they lead us yet,
Every pain to count for nothing,
Every sorrow to forget!
Hearken how they cry, 'O happy,
Happy ye that ye were born
In the sad slow night's departing,
In the rising of the morn.
Fair the crown the cause hath for you,
Well to die or well to live
Through the battle, through the tangle,
Peace to gain or peace to give.'

WILLIAM MORRIS, *Hymns of Labour*

I began writing these memoirs after learning that I had an incurable illness. Since their completion, Mrs Thatcher, who appeared to be in an unassailable position as Prime Minister, has been removed – not by the electorate, but by her own party in the Commons. Subsequently she has denied that she will retire from the Commons at the next election. Despite this she will, in my view, settle for a place on the lush, red-leather benches of the Lords, posing as a world stateswoman while, at the same time, becoming a thorn in the flesh of John Major. She is a fanatical capitalist ideologue and still dangerous.

Mrs Thatcher's downfall brought home just how ruthless the Tories can be. To save their party, to ensure political victory, to guarantee continuity of the capitalist system, they were prepared to put the boot in. There is a real bitterness in the Tory Party which will continue to surface and could do great harm to the party in the future.

John Major was a Thatcher protégé and it was thought that he would carry on where she left off. However, it has not quite worked out like that because many Conservatives wanted a *real* change. Major is calm, somewhat shy, and does not hector. He appears, rather, a diffident man, anxious to see the country back on a stable path. He wants to be friends

239

with the European community and clearly does not seek confrontation. He supports Gorbachev as long as Gorbachev is doing what is required by the US, and he accepts the US as the dominant world force. He has said that the National Health Service is important and that under him it will not be further undermined. In a number of other directions, the Tories are slowly but surely retreating towards the centre ground. That shift must not be over-estimated, but it is a beginning. The real difficulty for Major is that he has to get the economy right, to reduce inflation, to ensure that unemployment does not get too high, and to achieve all this before he has to call an election.

The Gulf War has transformed the world scene. It was, as Perez de Cuellar said, a US war, not a UN war. Iraq has been bombed on a massive scale, and untold thousands of Iraqi soldiers and civilians have been killed. As I write, fighting is taking place in the south of the country between supporters of Saddam and Shiite fundamentalists. For eight years, Saddam led his country in a war against Iran. He was backed by cash and arms from the US, Britain and other Western European countries. After the war, he turned on the Kurds and used chemical weapons against his own citizens. Referral of these brutal actions to the UN Security Council was blocked by the US. I am sure Saddam believed he could get away with his occupation of Kuwait after discussions with US officials appeared to give him support. Clearly, he wanted to grab the oil, which was, and is, the main concern of the US and Britain. The war was always about oil. It was certainly not about democracy. Kuwait is run, owned and controlled by one aristocratic family – it dissolved Parliament in 1986. Most Kuwaitis do not have a vote.

The US cared little for the rights of small nations and their protection when it invaded Panama and arrested President Noriega, who was an old friend of the US and once worked for the CIA. It cared little about international law when it invaded a British colonial possession, Grenada, without informing our government, and when it bombed Gaddafi in Libya, killing one of his children. Bush is eager to let the world know that the US is again top dog, that US imperialism is a power to be reckoned with.

The attitude of Labour's front bench to the Gulf War has disgusted me. From the word go, it backed military force. At times, it has been more belligerent than the Tories and Kinnock and Kaufman ensured that efforts to solve the issue peacefully were undermined. At one stage they argued that sanctions should be given more time to work, but nullified this by saying that if war took place they would support it without question. In fact the NEC, with Neil Kinnock's support, opposed the call for a ceasefire moved by Tony Benn and supported by Dennis Skinner, only the day before Bush and Major, for reasons of political expediency, supported one. It then used disciplinary action against Lambeth councillors for daring to oppose the war, and Neil Kinnock either sacked, or forced resignations, from the junior front benchers who spoke out. A real ceasefire, however, did not take place. The Iraqis, who had agreed, under Soviet pressure, to move out of Kuwait, were killed, in fact massacred, in their thousands as they withdrew – a shameful episode which will not be readily forgiven by Iraqi and Arab people. The fighting may be temporarily over, but the peace will be difficult to achieve.

Labour has also introduced a new industrial and economic policy which finally jettisons Labour's socialist concepts, and all the sweet words of Neil Kinnock and Gordon Brown cannot hide that fact. Our economic programme – which drops public ownership and state intervention – and our defence policy indicate that Labour is wedded to the operation of the capitalist system. My prophecy of the SDP Mark 2 has, unfortunately, come true. It is undeniable that socialism has suffered a setback in the face of these events and betrayals. But, contrary to what Mrs Thatcher was so fond of saying, socialism is far from dead.

Looking back over the recent past I remember a brief visit to my home town of Hertford. It was a beautiful day and my rural childhood and youth, my time in the Church, the cubs and scouts, my apprenticeship as a joiner and the beginnings of my political life in the Labour and Communist parties, all flooded back to me. I loved Hertford and it had a great influence on my political formation. The town has a long radical history which stretches back to the English civil war when it was on the side of Parliament. At Ware, near Hertford, the Levellers confronted Cromwell. Dissension was an integral part of Hertford life – witness the number of dissenting Churches and Chapels in the town. I am proud to have played a part in continuing Hertford's great tradition of nonconformism.

But if Hertford was my first love, my passion is for Liverpool, a great city where I was involved in major industrial and political struggle and which sent me to Parliament to keep the flag of socialism flying. Today, the port of Liverpool has declined, unemployment in the city is high, poverty is rife, and areas of the inner city have suffered all the problems of a ghetto. But my respect and love for the people of Liverpool remain as strong as ever and receiving the freedom of their city, as I did earlier this year, was one of the greatest honours of my life.

For me, in these last months, my socialism and Christianity have become even more intertwined. In working for a classless society without poverty for the many on the one hand and riches for the few on the other, I have worked for God's kingdom here on earth.

241

We should always remember the words of Nikolai Ostrovosky and try to live by them: 'Man's dearest possession is life. It is given to him but once, and he must live it so as to feel no torturing regrets for wasted years, never know the burning shame of a mean and petty past; so live that, dying he might say: All my life, all my strength were given in the finest cause in all the world – the fight for the liberation of mankind.'

Index

Matkin, William 69
Matthews, Betty 38
Matthews, George *ix*, 19, 38
Maudling, Reginald 143
Maxwell, Robert 209, 210
May, Stanley 60
Maynard, Joan 172, 198, 218
McAlpine, Sir Alfred 60
McCarthy, Mac 61
McCartney, George 72, 108
McCartney, Paul 107
McCluskie, Sam 123
McCulloch, Bill 80
McDonald, Alexander 144
McGahey, Mick 146
McGarvey, Danny 142
McGinn, Matt 80
McGree, Hetty 96
McGree, Leo 55, 57, 60, 64, 94-7
McLean, John 80
McMillan, Tom 139
McMullen, Peter 32
McShane, Harry 27, 36, 79-80, 114, 225
Meacher, Michael 149, 151, 154, 156, 203, 212, 225
Medvedev, Roy 233
Meir, Golda 126
Mellish, Bob 146, 196-7, 198, 199
Mendelson, John 116, 119, 139
Menon, Krishna 20
Merrick, Tony 140
Mikardo, Ian 30, 74, 114, 116, 118, 119, 124, 133, 139, 141, 156, 159, 169, 171
Miliband, Ralph 72
Miller, Ralph 69
Molloy, Mike 210, 211
Moonman, Eric 198
Moore, Patrick 158
Moores, John 102
Morgan, Kevin 19
Morgan Giles, Charles 143
Morrell, Frances 151, 154, 158
Morris, William 65, 68, 111, 239
Morrison, Herbert 22, 30, 93
Mortimer, Jim 182, 207, 208, 209, 211

Mortis, Dr 13
Morton, A.L. 22
Mosley, Oswald 16, 17
Mulhearn, Tony 69, 216, 228
Mullin, Chris 207
Murphy, Arthur 56
Murphy, Lawrence 56
Murray, Bob 28
Murray, David *ix*, 28
Murray, Doris *see* Heffer, Doris née Murray
Murray, Ken 28, 44
Murray, Herbert 44-5
Mussolini, Benito 16, 82, 230, 234

Nagy, Imre 83
Nairn, Tom 165
Nash, Liz *ix*, 62, 193
Nasser, Gamal Abdel 85, 126
Neary, Paddy 90, 100, 101
Nenni, Pietro 81
Nettleton, John 46
Newman, Cardinal 6
Nicholls, Bernard 10
Nicol, Muriel 158
Noel, Fr Conrad 15, 40
Noonan, Robert *see* Tressell, Robert
Noriega, Manuel 240
Norris, Gareth 122
Nott, John 200

O'Casey, Sean 77
O'Connor, T.P. 71
O'Grady, John 196, 199
O'Smotherley, Jimmy 8
O'Toole, Alan 46
Ogden, Eric 112
Orbach, Maurice 126
Orlova, R. 83
Orme, Stan 114, 118, 133, 139, 141, 166, 205
Orwell, George 22, 66, 112, 196
Ostrovsky, Nikolai 242
Owen, David 187, 188, 201, 215

Paisley, Ian 71
Palme Dutt, R. 18, 20